Smoked

· ·

A True Story About The Kids Next Door

HarperCollins*Publishers*

Photographs follow page 146.

FIRST EDITION

Designed by Barbara DuPree Knowles

LIBRARY OF CONGRESS CATALOGING-IN-PUBLICATION DATA
Bing, Léon, 1950–
    Smoked : a true story about the kids next door / Léon
Bing. — 1st ed.
        p.   cm.
    ISBN 0-06-016920-6
    1. Murder—California—Pasadena—Case studies.
    2. Teenagers—California—Pasadena. I. Title.
    HV6534.P37   1993
    364.1′0979493—dc20   92-54745

93 94 95 96 CC/RRD 10 9 8 7 6 5 4 3 2 1

To
Eric Ashworth
Larry DuBois
Stuart Timmons
and
as always, my mother, Estelle Lang.

acknowledgments

My thanks to my editor, Craig Nelson; demanding, brilliant, and always, maddeningly, right. Thanks to the ever-patient Lauren Marino, too. And my thanks to Mark Hayden.

My thanks to Edward Hibbert, the wild man.

My thanks to everyone connected with courtroom F of the Pasadena Courthouse: Judge J. Michael Byrne, Michael Tofoya, Lauret Henry, and "Freddie" Fredericks—they made my job much easier.

My thanks to my daughter, Lisa Bing, for her help during the trial.

My deep appreciation to Sandie Wells.

My thanks to the kids from South Pas who were so generous with their time and episodes of their lives.

My thanks to Woofie and Dexter Bing, still the best dog, the best cat, in the world.

And finally, my thanks to Dave Adkins.

All of the individuals portrayed in this book are actual people. However, in order to protect the privacy of certain individuals (particularly underaged children who were not participants in the trial of David Adkins and Vinnie Hebrock), the names and identifying characteristics of those individuals have been changed or omitted.

Murder is the last thing anyone thinks of when they talk about Pasadena. The Rose Bowl, that most romantic of all bowl games, might come to mind, or the pre-game New Year's Day Rose Parade, with its elaborate floral floats and white-gowned, teenaged Queen. You might think of privilege, perhaps, and of unspoken, restrictive covenants, of right-wing politics.

The Pasadena of legend is standoffish and rigidly independent; at one time it was the bastion of rich white Gentiles. It is within the enclaves of old Pasadena money that you see masterworks, preserved like primordial flies in amber, of the American Craftsman movement: the Gamble House and the Blacker estate, created by Charles and Henry Greene, or the Millard House, designed in 1923 by Frank Lloyd Wright.

But something else has begun to creep in now, too.

As you drive the road that winds steeply up above the lavish grounds of the Annandale Country Club, you can see older estates of great wealth mixing with the newly constructed Post-Modern conceits of upscale, middle-income suburbanites. The peach-colored exteriors and bleached-wood trim of these recent additions seem out of place and vaguely unwelcome in this silent, tree-shrouded setting.

The house at the end of Fairlawn Way is located at the fork of a cul-de-sac where a pair of squat stone columns gives onto a long driveway flanked by a double avenue of cedars. The first thing you see, up that driveway, is the garage and the guest apartment above it where the murders took place.

The main house, a sprawling fifties ranch-style, forms an L-shape around the swimming pool and patio behind the garage. The entire property has been meticulously landscaped: pots of geraniums in bud, saplings rooted in ten-gallon containers waiting to be planted, a gigantic and ancient prickly pear at the lip of a hill next to a shoulder-high wooden fence. The fence provides some degree of privacy to the occupants of the home; without it, anyone standing on the hill would be able to look directly down into the main house.

But it is the garage with its upstairs guesthouse that captures the eye and holds it; not only because it is the thing you see at the end of the drive. You find yourself staring, caught up in your own dark imaginings, because of what you know went on behind the bank of shuttered windows that overlook that well-swept driveway, those young and thriving trees.

. . . .

The call came in shortly after midnight. Probably Heather with some request or other, he thinks, and allows himself to drift back into sleep, knowing that his wife will handle it. He is dimly aware of her voice asking questions. Then the lamp at the side of the bed goes on and he can feel himself being shaken.

"Get up, Darrell! There's something wrong—Peggy just called, she's hysterical. Something's wrong up at Kathy's!"

Now his wife is dialing the phone, waiting for the other end to pick up, dialing again when no one answers. Her breath has begun to come in hiccupping little gulps.

"Nobody's answering at the guesthouse!"

"Try the main house."

She yanks open the nightstand drawer, pulls out her phone book and flips pages. Finding the number she wants, she punches in another call. No answer.

prologue

He is already dressed. Now she begins to throw on her clothes . . .

As the car noses up the long driveway at Fairlawn Way, Darrell Goodwin can see lights blazing in both the guesthouse over the garage and in the main house on the other side of the swimming pool. But in spite of all those lighted windows, there is an eerie hush about the place. There is no sign of activity. There are no people around.

Goodwin feels the icy tug of fear. He glances over at his wife. She is motionless; both hands grip her upper arms.

Wordlessly he backs the car out of the driveway and heads for the Pasadena police station.

It is just before two o'clock in the morning, March 22, 1991.

Goodwin gives the officer on duty what information he has, then, unable to wait helplessly at the station where time has begun to take on a surreal quality, he drives back to Fairlawn Way. He parks in the driveway and he and Mimi Goodwin sit, waiting for the police to arrive.

The driver of the black and white gets out of the car and walks around to speak briefly to Goodwin. Then the Goodwins are told to stay where they are, that the officers will investigate the property. The Goodwins watch in silence as the two men take out their flashlights and begin to climb the flight of outside stairs leading to the guesthouse.

In a short time one of the officers reappears at the balcony of the deck that fronts the guesthouse. He hesitates for a moment and then beckons for Darrell Goodwin to come up.

The three dead girls found inside the guesthouse of the estate on Fairlawn Way had all been killed by single shotgun blasts to the head. Darrell Goodwin made the identifications, at the scene, of his daughter, eighteen-year-old Heather Goodwin; her best friend, Kathy Macaulay, also eighteen, who lived there; and Danae Palermo, seventeen years old and a friend of both Kathy and Heather.

prologue

At some time in the early morning hours of March 22, 1991, the phone in the guesthouse rang. It was answered by Detective Michael Korpal of the assault and homicide bureau, who'd been with the Pasadena police for fifteen years. The person on the other end identified herself as eighteen-year-old Peggy Shurtleff; she was the girl who had called the Goodwin house earlier to tell Heather's parents that "something is wrong up at Kathy's." She now told Korpal that a friend of hers, a sixteen-year-old boy named Cayle Fiedler, had come to her house shortly before midnight to tell her about the murders.

She gave Korpal two other names: David Adkins, Kathy Macaulay's sixteen-year-old boyfriend; and Dave's buddy, seventeen-year-old Burton Vincent ("Vinnie") Hebrock.

An all-points bulletin for the three boys was issued. The story made the front page of the *Los Angeles Times* and was carried in newspapers around the country. Television news shows opened with the latest bulletins on "The Annandale Murders." Journalists and camera crews swarmed outside the grounds of South Pasadena High School, collaring any kid who was willing to talk. The frenzy would continue well into early April, refueled by both legitimate and rumored details. People were more than interested: they were nailed. This wasn't about teenaged gangsters in inner cities blowing each other away in the course of a drive-by shooting. This was about the kids next door.

....

Cayle Fiedler checked in with the police on the afternoon of March 22. He told them he was with his mother in Washington State and would be turning himself in to the Pasadena police the next day. He said he had witnessed the murders and that they had been committed by the other two boys after a day-long party up at the guesthouse. He named David Adkins and Vinnie Hebrock as the killers, and he said

prologue

they had fled the state in Kathy Macaulay's mother's 1986 Mercedes-Benz. He also told the police that Dave and Vinnie had the murder weapon, a 12-gauge, pump-action Mossberg shotgun, with them.

Shortly past 9:00 P.M. on March 22, 1991, Dave Adkins and Vinnie Hebrock were arrested at a Greyhound bus station in Salem, Oregon. The dark red Mercedes was parked in an alley just behind the station. The 12-gauge Mossberg and a bag of Peters Brand shotgun shells were picked up in a wooded area near Grants Pass, Oregon, two days later.

. . . .

"I heard that Heather was lighting a cigarette and got shot in the head. Kathy was at the stereo, changing the station, and when she heard the shotgun go off, she turned around, threw up when she saw Heather, and then they shot her. She fell up against the stereo. Danae was on Kathy's bed, asleep, passed out—whatever—and they shot her. And that was that. And then Cayle woke up."

The person speaking is eighteen-year-old Denise Ellroy. She and I are seated at my kitchen table and she has been talking about how "the inside story I got was pretty much straight from the source." The source, it has been strongly implied, is Cayle Fiedler, a close friend of Denise, and the alleged witness to the murders, on March 21, 1991, of Kathy Macaulay, Heather Goodwin, and Danae Palermo.

Kathy Macaulay first met Dave Adkins in the summer of 1988 at Andy Simon's three-day party. She was fifteen years old and had just completed her freshman year at South Pasadena High School; he was thirteen, about to begin eighth grade at middle school. She was small, with traces of puppy fat still clinging to her frame, and pretty, with light brown, curling hair and a quick, eager smile. He was tall for thirteen; working out had broadened his shoulders and chest. His face, with its rain-gray eyes and sullen, sensual mouth, was framed by a thick tousle of dark blond hair.

They were both flirts. Kathy went about it rather feverishly; as an ego boost, she played the coquette with almost every boy she brushed against. Dave knew, early on, the value of a cherishing glance; it was as useful a tool as his good looks or his ability to street fight. His lazy smile and warm interest in what another person has to say were the first things that struck me when we met, in jail, a month after the murders.

Kathy came from a background of privilege: her mother was a clinical pathologist, her stepfather a physician. Dave and his fifteen-year-old brother Dan had been raised by a single parent, their mother Pam, who usually kept two jobs going—both waitressing and baby-sitting—in order to make ends meet. Lack of funds never seemed to bother Dave Adkins. It was as if he had always known that people would provide him with whatever he needed. Girls especially. And, because South Pasadena is a city devoted to the protection of its image as a stronghold of fading American virtues, money—or the lack of it—is not a consuming subject. There persists in South Pasadena, and in Pasadena itself, the sense that it is perhaps ill-bred to question (even privately) the state of one's neighbor's financial affairs. There also exists in both cities, as all over the country, the urge to look the other way. If it appears, no matter how marginally, that someone is keeping up, then that must indeed be the case. Later, after the murders, a few people did venture opinions when Dave Adkins and Vinnie Hebrock were called "poor boys in a rich man's town." But money (or the lack of it) was not considered by the opinion makers a viable reason for homicide.

When Dave Adkins and Kathy Macaulay met, they provided, each for the other, a completion; Kathy was popular at school but what she wanted most was to be perceived as mellow, while Dave was in solid with some of the coolest kids in South Pas. They were older, these kids, and they were Dan Adkins's friends, but they treated Dave with respect. Kids his own age bored him; most of them still acted like babies. With Dan's crowd, Dave felt as if he were among equals: he could drink as hard and smoke as much as any of them. He was cool. In later conversations he would say, "I was one of them, and more."

The night of the party, Dave Adkins snuck out of the garage he has converted into a makeshift bedroom. The house his mom rented is on a nice enough street in South Pasadena, and she's got it fixed up with brightly patterned material pinned over the worn spots on the furniture, plants everywhere, and the old Indian rugs she's had for as long as Dave can remember. It's an okay house, but it's smaller than just about any other house on the block. Dan and Dave share the single bedroom while Pam sleeps on the living-room couch. The garage gives Dave some privacy, and it looks good, with piles of pillows, a couple of Grateful Dead posters, and part of his Teddy bear collection. There's even a red light bulb for the ceiling fixture, and that looks radical when Dave turns it on: everything bathed in an intense, rosy glow. Sometimes he sneaks a few sticks of his mother's incense out of the house; the sandalwood scent hides the smell of pot.

Carrying his skateboard under one arm, Dave moves swiftly down the driveway. He keeps a weather eye on the house, hoping that his mom won't spot him and start asking questions. Pam Adkins has always disapproved of Dan's friends, and now that Dave has begun to hang seriously with them, things are worse than ever. Dave loves his mother, and he knows all too well that everything she does is for him and his brother, but she can be a real pain. Pam rags too much, and not only about stuff like homework and curfews.

Once he makes it past the end of the driveway, Dave gets on the board and rolls the few blocks to Andy Simon's house. Andy told everybody at school that his folks are going to be out of town all weekend. So this party has to be fully happening.

The Simon house is quiet as Dave sprints up the front steps; for a minute he figures he's got the wrong night. Then the door swings open and he moves inside. People are sitting around watching MTV; a couple of girls are cooking up something in the kitchen. Dave peers into one of the bedrooms—kids are spread out all over the bed, getting high on weed, drinking beer, messing around. Dave grabs a beer and sits down at one end of the couch in front of the TV screen. There's a cute girl sitting by herself in the middle of the couch. She looks familiar, he's seen her around at other parties and at school football games. She keeps sneaking glances at him, too. Then she reaches out and her fingers graze the tattoo about the bicep of his right arm. Blue letters spelling out his first name.

"Oh—*you're* Dave." Her voice is light, chirpy.

"Yeah. In case I forget my name." He likes the way that

sounds. It's what he always says when anyone mentions the tattoo.

"I'm Kathy. I've heard a lot about you."

"I heard you were pretty cool, too." She smiles and looks at him for a long moment. Gnarly, he thinks to himself.

Next thing, she's bringing him beers from the kitchen and lighting his cigarettes. He figures she's maybe a little bit sorry for him because he's so much younger than the other kids, but then she says something that surprises him.

"Oh, God—that guy who just came in? He's real possessive of me, and I don't want to be with him. Can I say I'm here with you?"

The guy is already on top of them, leaning down to grab Kathy's wrist. She jerks away, tells him she's here with her boyfriend.

"Oh, yeah? Who's that?" He looks to be at least seventeen.

"Me." The word just pops out of Dave's mouth.

The guy looks down at Dave and the corners of his mouth lift in a lazy little grin. Dave doesn't say a word. He gets slowly to his feet and, placing the fingertips of his right hand against the guy's chest, he exerts just enough pressure to back the guy up a step. And if there is any thought of taking it further, nobody makes a move in that direction. The guy simply backs off.

Kathy stands up and, taking Dave's hand, leads him to an empty room at the back of the house. And as they move through the swirl and eddy of the party, she's telling him how impressed she is with his courage. Once inside the room, she closes the door and takes a bong out of her bag. Next she pulls out a plastic baggie of weed, fills the bowl of the pipe, and fires up, inhaling deeply. Then she passes the pipe to Dave. Embarrassed, he admits he doesn't know how to use a bong. Kathy instructs him patiently and they sit cross-legged on the bed, smoking and talking.

Kathy tells Dave about her real father, a Marine officer stationed in Thailand, about her brother, a student at Stanford, and her sister, who is studying law.

Dave tells Kathy what little he knows about a father he barely remembers, a man who left when Dave was three years old. He tells her about a time when he was a little kid, five years old, maybe, visiting his aunt in Oregon and seeing a man at a McDonald's who looked like his father, with the same tattoo of a monkey, and how he, Dave, felt ashamed when he began to cry, right there at the table, because he missed his dad so much. He even finds himself telling her about J.D., his mother's boyfriend, the closest thing he had to a father. Dave tells her how much he loved J.D., who showed him how to ride a motorcycle—a Harley WideGlide—and how to work on the engine. He talks about how J.D. would take him fishing and camping and how J.D. taught him and Dan how to shoot. And then he tells Kathy about the night, up in the mountains, when J.D. got killed. He was out riding with a bunch of his biker buddies when some guy in a Ford Bronco swerved into him. Nearly a year has passed since J.D.'s death, and Dave knows for sure now that nothing will ever be the same for him, his brother, or their mom.

He can't believe he's talking about this stuff, these feelings, with some girl he just met, but Kathy is leaning forward, listening as if she needs to know everything there is to know about Dave Adkins. Listening for real, not just faking it like so many girls do when they want to impress you.

When Dave asks Kathy about her folks, she shrugs slightly, and tells him they're okay, you know, they're cool. Then she changes the subject, telling him about the crowd of girls she used to run with, the cheerleader crowd, the people who were headed for schools like UCLA and Yale. The snobs who partied only with the cutest football players. They dropped Kathy at the beginning of the ninth grade when she began to gain weight. And that hurt. But then she got picked up by Heather—the girl who is now Kathy's best friend—and her crowd.

Dave knows Heather Goodwin. By reputation, anyway. A rich kid, like Kathy. Heather's father is some kind of big-deal lawyer, and they live in San Marino, but Heather's cool, with her black leather clothes and that ring in her nose. She's a tough little chick, a stoner who knows how to kick ass if somebody gets in her way. Even guys.

As they talk, people keep coming to the door, kidding them about being on the bed. Kathy glances at Dave and an amused look passes between them. They haven't even kissed yet. And then Kathy shuts the door again and they do kiss. And it's intense. For Dave, it's better than any kiss he's ever had before. They smoke some more, kiss some more, and suddenly it's four in the morning. Time for Dave to skate on home.

He's still asleep early the next morning when his mom calls out for him to come on in the house. Some girl named Kathy is on the phone.

"Can you meet me at the Roundtable in about half an hour?"

Sure, he tells her.

"Great. What'll you be wearing?"

"Huh?"

"You know, what color shirt and stuff. 'Cause if my mom won't drive me to meet you, I'll have a taxi pick you up and bring you to my house."

....

The Roundtable is a pizza joint on Fair Oaks Avenue in South Pasadena. Formica tables for four, a counter where you get your slices and soft drinks, that's about it. This is where the cool kids from South Pas congregate: the partiers, the stoners, the snobs.

South Pasadena High School consists of lush green

lawns and a spread of gray and white buildings of indeterminate architecture. It is located in a neighborhood of carefully maintained Craftsman bungalows and Queen Anne houses only blocks away from the bustling business section of South Pasadena, a town whose residents enjoy the inevitable comparisons to scenes from other small towns iconized in the paintings of Norman Rockwell. South Pasadena is only minutes away from Pasadena proper, but the differences between the two cities are profound.

Pasadena is a place of gated and walled estates. Cal Tech, the Norton Simon Museum, and the Huntington Library, with its permanent collection of Gainsboroughs and Romneys, its first folios and Gutenbergs, are all located in Pasadena. More Nobel laureates live in Pasadena than in any other American city. South Pasadena is more . . . cozy is as good a word as any. The Fair Oaks Pharmacy still maintains a working, marble-countered soda fountain, and goods are displayed in gleaming mahogany cases. The Rialto Theater (the only movie house in South Pas) looks very much as it did when it first went up back in the early thirties. The decor is faintly Babylonian; the curtain that sweeps back to reveal the screen is crimson velvet; there is a balcony you get to by climbing one side or the other of an impressive double staircase.

Families tend to settle in for generations in South Pasadena. There are approximately 1,200 students at the high school, and in more than a few instances, there are kids studying here whose parents—one or both—were members of the student body twenty-five years ago. Most of the people who graduate from South Pas go on to college; it has the third lowest dropout rate in L.A. County. It has something else, too, according to many of its students: a serious drug and alcohol problem. And it is that single aspect, more than any other—income, background, or goals—that seems to bind most of the kids from South Pasadena together in a humid climate of intimacy.

Today, sitting with a bunch of kids at the Roundtable, there has been some conversation about the rumors making the rounds at school. A couple of girls are spreading a story that has them up at Kathy Macaulay's house when the shooting began. They're telling people they escaped death by climbing out the bathroom window. Other kids, quite a few, are saying they were on the phone to Kathy—or Heather—at the moment of death. They're saying they heard shots and terrible screams, that they heard cries of "No! No! What are you doing? Please! *No!*" And then the blasts of the shotgun, and then an awful silence. The kids at the Roundtable today view such stories with contempt.

All of them saw the side of the Phys Ed building, though, where someone wrote a message to the three dead girls just after the murders. The message consisted of the words: "IN LOVING MEMORY OF," printed gang-style, and under that the three names, "Katherine, Danae, Heather." Whoever wrote it signed with the name "Bird 1."

Gang nicknames and slang are popular with both Pasadena and South Pasadena kids; many of them have formed into small wannabe groups with names like South Side Gang and Palmetto Boyz. They use gang hand signals patterned after those identified with the Crips and Bloods— L.A.'s legendary and lethal African-American gangs—and they dress in a similar fashion: low-slung jeans, baggy shorts, and baseball caps. The similarities seem to end there, however. North Pasadena, or Altadena, which is the territory of real Crips and Bloods, who live and wage a deadly war in the projects there, is as remote to the upper-middle-class families of Pasadena and South Pasadena as another galaxy.

Some kids, quite a few, think Cayle Fiedler wrote the farewell message on the side of the gym. "Bird" was his street name, and there was a rumor going around that he was affiliated with one of the gangs. But Cayle had dropped out of South Pas, and he lived in Alhambra, a nearby suburb, as did Danae Palermo. So, even though it is a dramatic image—the eyewitness to the murders sneaking onto the school grounds before he leaves town—it is simply not realistic.

These kids would rather talk about drugs, anyway. They have mentioned, more than once, getting high on "koolies" and "dippers" (joints laced with PCP, an animal tranquilizer); they talk about the times they have been fried on acid. They tell me Cayle Fiedler sold dope once in a while, and that Dave and Vinnie did, too. Weed in half-pounds and pounds, and sometimes coke, in grams. The kids also say that Kathy and Heather were real stoners, that Heather "really let it grab hold of her life."

"We always used to party together. Lots of beer, lots of weed. Kathy would always pick me up at my house, and it would be like you'd have *no* say-so. She was in control and you'd party till she was ready to stop." Dennis is fifteen years old, but looks a couple of years older. He's short, with smooth, compact muscles and shaggy, white-blond hair. A cyclist's cap rides low on his forehead and he is wearing wire-rimmed, clip-on dark glasses. He looks like a cute, tough surfer. "We had a lotta gnarly times—me and her and Heather. Went up to some waterfall once, the three of us, with a big ol' bottle of tequila. They were always down to party and have a good time."

The boy sitting next to Dennis—he will give only his nickname, Bail—nudges Dennis and mutters something to him. Dennis nods his head. "Yeah, he's right. Kathy always knew how to turn into the innocent type for your folks. You know, so they wouldn't, like, get all worried when you got in her car with her."

Nicole, one of the girls at the table, pipes up: "Kathy was pretty cool, though." Nicole, in fact, resembles the pictures I have seen in the papers, and on television, of Kathy Macaulay. Her hair has been lightened to a tinselly blond, and it is not so much combed as carefully raked; her eyes are accented with a grayish-blue shadow.

Amy, the girl sitting next to her, nods her head. "Yeah. She had a lotta money but she didn't, like, flaunt it, or act ..." She shrugs eloquently. Amy's hair is buzzed off at the sides, and she is wearing a Butthole Surfers T-shirt.

I ask about Dave Adkins.

"Dave and his brother Dan are the two biggest hoods in South Pasadena. *They're* trouble—Dave was always cool, though. He didn't ever act like a dick." The boy who says this is speaking for the first time. He's tall, with dark hair and solemn, watchful eyes. There is, at the edges of his voice, a small catch, an echo of a stammer.

And Vinnie? Was he a dick?

Shrugs all around. "That guy Vinnie was just a real loner. He's been around since, like, the sixth grade or something, when he moved here from Florida. But nobody really liked him. Nobody really knew much about him. He dropped out of school way early. I think Kathy and Dave just felt kinda sorry for him, or something, so they let him tag along." Bail provides this information.

Months later I would learn, from Dave Adkins, the real reason for his relationship with Vinnie Hebrock. Pity had nothing to do with it.

The afternoon is wearing thin; Nicole and her friend, Amy, get ready to leave. Amy has a baby-sitting job, Nicole works the dinner shift at a nearby restaurant. They gather up their stuff and move toward the door. But Amy stops and turns back to look at me. "You know, I can deal with these murders, I have to. But three people my age, who just as well could've *been* me. . . ." She shakes her head in a slow, uncomprehending movement.

Nicole has turned back to face our table, too. Now she shifts her bag from one shoulder to the other. "The worst thing to me, more than anything else, is how their parents must feel. My own mom was all, 'Oh, honey—I'm so *sorry.*' " Her tone has lifted in unconscious imitation of her mother's voice.

Amy nods her head. "Yeah. For my mom it's the fact that it really *could* have been me, 'cause I used to go up to Kathy's all the time. I hung out with those people, I partied with them. And that really brings things home."

They waggle their fingers at the three boys and they're gone. Nobody says anything for a couple of long beats. Then the dark-haired kid speaks softly:

"You know what? I keep on wondering if at the moment it happened, if killing another person was, like, the most incredible high. Like, *whoa!*"

Dennis looks at him for a second or two, his face expressionless. Then he lifts the brim of the cyclist's cap and rubs the skin of his forehead hard with the heel of his left hand. "It's so much of a shock, 'cause Dave Adkins is no way the kind of person to go out, and come back later, and pull the trigger three times. No way." Another beat of silence. And another. "But he did do it. And I don't know what to say about that."

*T*he taxi driver deposits Dave at Kathy's parents' home. Kathy pays the fare, then she takes Dave on a fast tour of the house. He gathers impressions of gleaming wood, sparkling glass doors, and rich upholstery. A grand piano in the living room, large paintings against smoothly papered walls. A vast, wood-burning fireplace. In Kathy's room there are antique quilts and flowered sheets on the bed, stuffed animals arrayed on bookshelves and an elaborate stereo setup with cassettes strewn everywhere.

When Dave asks Kathy where her mom is, she tells him she's gone for the day. He asks if they can smoke some weed and she leads him out to a large balcony overlooking the hills. As they fire up the joint that Kathy takes out of her pocket, Dave is thinking how cool this girl is, how cool this whole situation is. The day slips into evening as they sit smoking and talking. Her life. His life. They discover they know the same people, like the same music. The oldies—Led Zeppelin. The Eagles. The Dead. Kathy listens to the Cure, and some of the Metal bands, too: Metallica, Iron Maiden. Dave likes Guns N' Roses. And the Beatles.

As they talk, both kids begin to relax with each other. Kathy tells Dave more about her family; she seems to glow when she mentions her father. Her mother divorced him over ten years ago, Kathy says, and got married again soon afterward. She refers to her stepfather as "the Lame." Her real dad is an officer in the Marines, she tells Dave again, with pride; she just wishes he weren't stationed so far away. It would be so cool to be able to see him any time she wanted. Kathy is dismissive of her stepfather, but when she begins to talk about her mother, anger bubbles to the surface. Her mom's too busy with her work (and the Lame) to pay attention to Kathy. Most of the time her mom doesn't even bother to rag on her, that's how far off she is, in her own world. Dave shakes his head slowly, grinning a little; that's just about *all* his mom does—rag on him. Kathy's lucky.

Kathy looks up at him for a long, long moment before she speaks again, and when she does, the anger has gone out of her voice. She tells Dave it's not about being lucky when you feel invisible most of the time. It's about crying alone because nobody cares enough about you to see you.

It's dark when Kathy suggests they go back to the party. She leaves a note for her mother: "Spending the night with Heather," and the two kids head back down the hill on Kathy's motor scooter. Dave drives. As they pull up in front of Andy's house, Heather's mom is dropping her off. Kathy waves to Mrs. Goodwin, then Dave and the two girls go into the house. The party is still going full tilt. Jason Cheever, Dave's best friend since grammar school, is there. Denise Ellroy is there and Amy Faulkner. So is Danae Palermo.

At 1:00 A.M. Dave calls his mother to tell her he'll be sleeping at Jason's house. No way, she tells him, and delivers a 3:00 A.M. curfew. At 2:45, Dave tells Kathy he's got to bail on home; he doesn't want to blow it with his mom. Kathy has a plan: "Stay till five of three and you can borrow the motor scooter."

When Dave gets back to Andy's the next morning, all of the same people are still there and everybody is crashed or asleep. But Kathy is out front waiting for him. They spend the rest of the day together, smoking weed, talking nonstop. It's as if it's more important to get to know each other than it is to make out. For the first time Dave feels like he might be getting into a real relationship with a girl.

When Kathy goes out of town with her folks a few days later, Dave can't help feeling like she let him down.

....

Kelly French has joined her friend, Denise, and me at my house. Kelly is sixteen and she has the pale, haunted look of a Symbolist painting. She is a dropout from both South Pasadena High and Continuation classes, but she is studying to take the GED equivalency exam. The murders have shaken her badly. She can no longer sleep without a light on in her room, and the windows are now covered day and night to make sure that no one can look in and see her. She stays home most of the time, afraid to leave the house; afraid that something will happen to her, will happen to her mother.

The night after the murders, after Kelly had been interviewed on television, somebody left a terrifying message on the answering machine in her room. The speaker, some unknown boy, whispered, "You're dead, Kelly." She never found out who it was, but she still has bad dreams about a faceless kid stalking her to kill her. She misses Kathy; her wallet is stuffed with snapshots of the two of them together, and with friends. Dave Adkins and Cayle Fiedler are among them. Kelly fans the pictures on the tabletop, then she begins to move them around, placing one on top of another as if she were playing a bizarre game of solitaire. When she speaks again, her voice is nearly a whisper.

"You know, I called Kathy's house a couple of times by mistake, 'cause I was so used to dialing her number. And her answering machine was still on. It was so strange, so sad."

Denise reaches out and the tips of her fingers brush the back of Kelly's hand.

"Kathy was a wonderful person."

Kelly nods her head. "She was great. Everybody liked her—the girls, the boys, everybody. The boys really liked her, too." Then, defensively, as if I were about to ask an embarrassing question, "And, yeah ... she *was* sleeping around with some people."

I mentioned that one of the boys I talked to had said that Kathy had gotten angry with him when he didn't want to continue a sexual relationship with her. He had said that she was too aggressive for him, that it was always *her* show.

Denise speaks up quickly. "Kathy was never pushy. She was just naturally"—she hesitates, wanting to find the precise word—"friendly." Kelly's laugh rings out; it is the first time she has shown any emotion other than grief.

Denise goes on. "She was, 'This is what I'd like to do, and if you can come along, if you can do it too—fine.' "

Kelly's voice slides in now. "But Kathy was never a bitch." She takes a beat. "Now, Heather—Heather was *scary*."

....

When Kathy Macaulay went out of town for two weeks, she left Dave Adkins with a strange sense of loss. But it's summertime, and the parties are happening, and he's a little bit pissed off, and in a couple of days he starts going around with another girl, Jamie. And cheating on her with Melanie Pinkney, a thirteen-year-old throwback to the Peace-Love generation of the sixties. Melanie and Dave have been friends since the sixth grade, but neither she nor Jamie know about each other, or about Kathy, who's checking in with daily postcards to Dave. Her constant message (framed by hand-drawn hearts and x's) is that she can't wait to get home and be with him. Dave's interpretation is that she will be ready to make love when she returns, and to that end he wants to get rid of both Jamie and Melanie.

Dave is with Melanie at his house when Vinnie calls to invite him to come on over; Dave's best friend, Jason Cheever, is there. With Melanie in tow, Dave walks over to Vinnie's place. Vinnie Hebrock is nearly a year older than Dave Adkins, but he is shorter by eight inches. Possessed of a permanent, myopic squint, he is the product of a family background that is perhaps most readily described as Snopeslike. Youngest of eight children born to Burt and Faye Hebrock, Vinnie would, in later conversations, call himself "the peewee out of the bunch." After his parents divorced, his father took him to live in the small town of Lockhart, Florida, some thirty miles west of Daytona. Vinnie was eight years old at that time, and he would live there, with his father and grandmother (until she died), for the next five years, unschooled and undisciplined.

There is an unsubstantiated story that during the time Vinnie lived with his father, he was used as an accomplice in a series of home burglaries. It is said that Burt Hebrock would stake out houses and then, when the owners were away, he would push his small son into the house through a pet door and the child would open the front door from the inside to let his father in. There could not have been a great deal of profit from these break-ins, if the story is true: Burt Hebrock worked most of the time as a tractor mechanic.

When Burt dropped dead on the job, Vinnie was sent to live with his mother and older sister, Tiki, in a small apartment over an automotive body shop located in a blue-collar area of South Pasadena. Faye enrolled the boy in school, but he was unable to read or write. He dropped out of classes a couple of months later, and by the next year he was on probation for a minor drug charge. His only friends, in the summer of 1988, were Dave Adkins and, to a lesser degree, Dave's best friend, Jason Cheever. Jason tolerated Vinnie, but that was about as far as their relationship went. Vinnie was too gross, too desperate for acceptance. He didn't even qualify as court jester: his jokes were too sick, his attempts at wit too dull. There was a certain tough-guy posture that was off-putting as well. Too many stories about street fights in which Vinnie kicked ass; too many accounts of shootouts that featured

---

Vinnie swaggering away from the bleeding body of someone who had "dissed him."

The thing was, nobody from South Pas had ever seen Vinnie in action. He was all talk. About girls, too. Whenever the conversation got around to girlfriends and sex, Vinnie would make vague mention of an unnamed steady who lived out of town. But nobody ever saw him with a date; nobody could even imagine such a possibility. Vinnie's effect on girls was always the same: they wanted to get away from him as quickly as possible. Even the girls who *only* liked outlaws drew the line at Vinnie. Outlaws had to be cute, like Dave. Or Jason. Vinnie Hebrock was just too raunchy.

But Dave liked Vinnie, so Vinnie got to hang around. Whenever anyone would question Dave about the friendship, or make a crack about Vinnie, Dave would always say the same thing: "Vinnie's okay—he's cool."

But there were limits to Dave's goodwill and patience. One evening, in the garage at the Adkins house and in front of Jason and another boy, Vinnie started to talk shit; he began to ramble about how much tougher he was than any of these South Pas chumps, Dave included. He posed and strutted, speaking, as usual, in the accent and rhythms of a black gangbanger.

"You ain't nothin', Adkins. I can *kick* your ass." Hands jabbing the air, thumbs up at right angles, index fingers pointing.

"C'mon, Vinnie. Chill." Dave's voice remains at a conversational pitch. He turns his attention back to the other two guys.

But Vinnie gets right up in Dave's face. "I can kick your ass any time I want to, homeboy."

Dave glances at Jason Cheever for a split second, then he uncoils in a single, fluid move and knocks Vinnie to the floor. Coldcocks him flat.

And goes back to the conversation without a missed beat.

Vinnie shook his head a couple of times, to clear it, got back up, and reached out to take the lit joint Dave handed him. The incident wasn't mentioned again that evening, but word got around, and the mystery surrounding Dave and Vinnie's friendship deepened.

Jason Cheever is eighteen now, two years after the murders, and in his senior year at South Pasadena High. His parents divorced when he was in grammar school and he and his older brother Jake live with their father. There is a warm relationship between both parents, however; they are bonded by their love for their sons. Dave Adkins was welcome (despite his reputation for fighting) at the Cheever home from the time he and Jason became classmates in grammar school. Vinnie Hebrock was another story. Jason remembers clearly what his mother said the first time she and Vinnie met: "If you continue to see him, you're going to end up killing someone. Or getting killed. Or going to jail. This kid is trouble." And now, two years after the murders, Jason says he knew his mom was right; the same message lurked at the back of his own mind. He ignored it because of Dave. Vinnie had become a part of the package; he was the medicine you took if you were going to hang around with Dave Adkins. What nobody could figure out was why one of the most popular kids would take up with one of the most disliked.

Or if they did know, they weren't telling.

. . . .

Dave Adkins met Vinnie Hebrock in the spring of 1987 while they were crossing the street. Dave was with a kid from his class, Gary Holland, and they had just been kicked out of the auto parts store owned by Gary's dad. Mr. Holland got pissed off when the boys came in to ask for a few bucks. They'd spent all their money on burgers and fries at HiLife Burgers, a popular after-school hangout, and Gary's dad did some yelling about irresponsibility before he told them to beat it, he had work to do. Both boys knew the real reason behind his anger: he didn't like his son spending so much time with Dave Adkins.

As they crossed the street in front of the body shop, Dave noticed another kid as he stepped off the curb on the other side. He was short, this kid, and he kept his head down as he walked, as if he were looking for a ten-dollar bill lying on the pavement. But when he came abreast of Dave and Gary, he looked up.

"What's up?"

For a second Dave thought the kid was talking to him. But then Gary said what's up back and the kid turned around and walked back across the street with them. Gary made fast introductions and the kid—his name was Vinnie—invited them to come upstairs to the apartment he shared with his mother and sister. Pointing to a squat brick building that housed a general auto body shop on the ground floor, Vinnie grinned crookedly.

"I got some rad fuckin' weed upstairs. C'mon up—we'll smoke a bowl. Nobody's home but me."

As soon as they walked into the small, dim apartment, Vinnie fired up a resin-encrusted bong. Then he handed it to Gary, brought out a shoebox filled with weed, and began to pick out the seeds and stems, tossing them on the floor, squinting to see as he searched for more. Dave and Gary exchanged glances; the soiled carpet was covered with debris—Dave could feel all kinds of grit beneath the soles of his sneakers. He could see a layer of grime over everything in the room: tabletops, the arms and backs of chairs, the TV screen. Even a pile of old magazines in the corner was furred with oily dust. Dave suppressed a smile, thinking what his mother would have to say if she ever got a look at this place.

Suddenly Vinnie set down the shoebox with a thump, got to his feet, and walked swiftly out of the room. When he came back, a pair of eyeglasses was resting unevenly on the bridge of his nose. One of the stems was missing and a piece of string had been attached to the temple of the frame, stretching back to wind around Vinnie's ear. Dave would have laughed out loud at anyone else wearing such a lame contraption but, somehow, on Vinnie, it was okay. Dave liked Vinnie, liked talking to him. The little dude sounded like he knew what was up for real. When Dave mentioned that he was in the sixth grade, Vinnie laughed and said he had dropped out of school. Said there were better ways to spend time than sitting in some classroom.

Dave looked at Gary again and this time he nodded his head in silent approval. This guy, Vinnie? Way cool.

It didn't take long for Dave Adkins and Vinnie Hebrock to become buddies. Dave started walking over to the Hebrock apartment after school, or Vinnie would meet him at the HiLife or the Roundtable. Sometimes Vinnie would go over to Dave's place, but Dan didn't like him and said so, often. Surprisingly, Pam thought Vinnie was okay; he had gone out of his way to show some manners when they met. It would be a while before she changed her mind about him.

When Dave and Vinnie were alone, the two things they talked about most were drugs and crime. Vinnie was an expert in both categories; he knew how to score drugs and where to sell them. He said he had done everything: coke, speed, 'shrooms (hallucinogenic psilocybin mushrooms), and, of course, acid and weed. And there was always a pretty good stash of weed and, sometimes, acid, hidden at his place. Whenever they got together, the two boys got stoned. That was when Vinnie would talk about breaking into houses, or stealing cars. He could pry open a locked door and hot-wire an engine in seconds, he told Dave. He knew the exact moment to pounce and snatch a purse or a briefcase that might hold cash. He said he knew where to get rid of big stuff, like TV sets and computers. Even knew someone who would buy CD's and videotapes, no questions asked. Easy money.

Dave drank it all in. None of his other friends were interested in pulling off crimes; not Jason, not Gary, not anybody. Vinnie Hebrock was the first person to plug into Dave Adkins's fantasies and go them one better. Vinnie might not know how to act with other people, but when it was just him and Dave alone, he had more going for him than anyone else around.

. . . .

In the summer of 1988, Vinnie Hebrock, his mother, and his sister are still living in the apartment over the auto body shop. But now Vinnie's sister, Tiki, has a husband and baby in residence, too. The dingy little rooms have been further crowded by the addition of a clutter of items scored at swap meets and garage sales: sofa beds, reclining chairs covered in various leatherlike materials, chipped Formica-topped tables, novelty lamps. Scattered about in random piles are other found objects: TV sets and radios, motorized toys and gadgets, all in different stages of disrepair. Vinnie has taken to sleeping behind a makeshift screen at one end of the iron balcony that fronts the side of the building. From nine in the morning to six at night the shrill whines and burrs of metal on metal funnel up from the work area two stories below.

Faye Hebrock is rarely at home during the day. She works, as a waitress and counterperson, at a gourmet delicatessen in the business section of Pasadena. When she comes home at night, she barricades herself in her bedroom with a television set.

As Dave and Melanie Pinkney walk the few blocks from his house to the Hebrock apartment, he is only marginally aware of Melanie's running commentary about a party he missed the night before. No way is he interested in the party; he was with Vinnie last night.

"Hey, dude—we gonna do this, or what?"

Vinnie's voice sounds thin, forced. He has just taken a

deep hit on the joint he's holding between his thumb and forefinger.

"Fuckin-A we're gonna do it." Dave reaches across the littered card table and takes the joint. He pulls a hit, holds it down, releases it slowly.

The two boys are in the living room of the Hebrock apartment. Faye Hebrock is back in her bedroom; the hum of televised voices filters through the walls. Tiki is out somewhere.

"Dale . . . ?"

Vinnie looks up from the joint he is rolling. They have begun to call each other by the names of a pair of cartoon characters. Dave is "Chip."

"You sure nobody's gonna be home when we get in?"

"Fuck, man—I already told you a million times: they both go to work. I checked the place out and I seen 'em."

Dave gets to his feet.

"Let's hit it."

The telephone sounds just as Dave opens the front door. Vinnie picks up before the second ring.

"Yeah." He listens for a second, looks at Dave.

"Nuh-uh. I ain't seen him all night." Listens some more, nods his head. "Right." Barks out a short laugh. "Right. Yeah, see ya, bro'."

"Who was that?"

"Jason." He looks sharply at Dave. "Did you wanna talk to him?"

"Nah."

The target apartment is located on a side street a few blocks from the Hebrock place; it takes only minutes for the two boys to walk there.

"How do you know they got money in there?"

"Man"—Vinnie's voice sounds aggrieved—"I *told* you, I checked it out, okay?" And, after a few beats, "There's jewelry and shit, too. We're just gonna grab the stuff we can shove in our pockets and get the fuck out.

"It's that one, there." Vinnie has paused in front of a two-storied apartment house built around a courtyard. "C'mon."

Vinnie leads the way to an alley between the target building and the one next to it. Padding a couple of steps behind, Dave is aware of a thin, acrid odor. He's noticed it before; it's what Vinnie smells like when he gets nervous.

"I wanna make sure nobody's home, then I'm gonna pop the screen." Vinnie is whispering hoarsely.

"Shhhh." Dave's nervous, too.

Vinnie looks right, looks left, then, standing on tiptoe, he peers into a darkened window on the ground floor.

"Fuck!" He darts away from the window, pressing himself against the wall, yanking Dave's arm to pull him back as well.

"They're in there. Fuckers."

"You sure?"

Vinnie is already walking away, down the alley toward the street.

"Hell, yeah, I'm sure." He turns around, trotting backwards so he can look at Dave.

"C'mon. I got another idea."

"But what about...?" Dave gestures vaguely in the direction of the courtyard building.

"Don't worry about it. We'll come back another time."

They're moving at a brisk clip, headed toward Fair Oaks Avenue. It's close to midnight now; people are leaving coffeehouses and bars. The two boys saunter past a group of men standing in front of a small, European-style café. One of the men separates himself from the others and walks quickly past Dave and Vinnie. He does not notice either of them and he is not aware of them as they follow him past the curve of the intersection to a darkened parking lot behind a bank. He doesn't know his assailants are behind him until they are upon him.

"The money. Give it!" Vinnie is standing close to the guy's left ear, far enough behind him so the victim can't see his face. Dave has grabbed the guy's right wrist and is twisting it halfway up his back. But this guy is young and strong and he begins to struggle. He breaks free from Dave's grip and turns, swinging wildly. Dave drops him with a single punch to the jaw. Vinnie goes to his knees next to the guy, tugging the wallet out of the hip pocket of his jeans. And he's just gotten back on his feet when the guy comes up off the ground swinging again.

Dave squares off to hit him, but this time it's Vinnie who makes the moves. He beats the guy back down with a series of short, brutal jabs to the face. Then he scoops up the wallet from the ground, holding it carefully with the tips of his fingers, and pulls out three or four twenty-dollar bills and a couple of singles. He stuffs the money in his pocket and tosses the wallet so that it lands on the unconscious man's chest.

"C'mon, Chip. Let's book."

Nobody says anything for a couple of blocks. Then Dave turns to look at Vinnie.

"Man, you sure gave that guy a beating."

Vinnie shrugs carelessly. He reaches into his pocket and hands Dave his split of the cash. After another few seconds of silence he begins to speak.

"Fucker brought it on himself. If those other two faggots hadn't've been home we wouldn't've had to jack this one."

"How come you held his wallet like that?"

"Fingerprints, man. Always gotta watch out for fingerprints."

After their trial for murder, Dave would say, "Vinnie was the perfect crime partner. He knew the criminal way real good."

....

The first person Dave Adkins sees as he walks into the Hebrock apartment with Melanie Pinkney is Heather Goodwin. Kathy Macaulay is standing next to her. Kathy, never able to hide her emotions, grins widely at Dave, then she spots Melanie and looks away fast, nonplussed. And before Dave can speak or make any kind of move, Heather's all over him.

"Who the fuck's this other chick? You're supposed to be with Kathy!" Heather gestures wildly at Kathy and Melanie in turn.

Jason Cheever looks questioningly at Dave. Dave shrugs. Kathy places her hand on Heather's right arm; she just got back in town, and if she's hurt by the sight of Dave with another girl, she's not ready for a scene.

"No, no, no. It's okay, Heather . . ."

"It's not okay!" Heather jerks her arm away from Kathy's touch. Vinnie and Jason walk quickly into the kitchen, away from the action. They recognize all the storm signals; if this continues, Heather will get physical. And neither of them wants to be caught at the epicenter of one of her tantrums.

Now Heather turns her fury on Melanie; her voice is filled with raw energy.

"You're not one of us! What are you doing thinking you can get along with Dave? Stay the fuck away from him—he doesn't want you in his life. You're bad for him!"

When Dave doesn't speak out, Melanie does. "You should only know how good for him I am!"

A year after the murders, Melanie will say that Heather was shrieking with "such fierce malice, I was dumbfounded."

But Heather is not about to give in. "Yeah? Well, you got *no* business with Dave Adkins! He's with Kathy!"

"I'm with no one, dude. Chill out." But Heather is beyond hearing Dave's voice; she is lost in her anger. Heather, with her fresh tattoos and her black leather pants and boy's undershirt. With her hands clenched into fists. Barely five feet tall, she weighs no more than ninety pounds. Strawberry blond hair buzzed on one side, defiantly chopped on top to straggle in ragged strands over her face. The hair masks finely chiseled features, deeply intelligent eyes. The single word most often used, by adults, to describe Heather Goodwin's looks is "elfin." It is a word she detests.

"If she doesn't leave, I'm gonna kick her ass!" Heather's face is contorted with rage. Melanie, the Peace and Love girl, turns quickly and walks out of the apartment and down the stairs leading to the street. Dave shrugs, hell with it.

"Later." And he follows Melanie out into the street. Heather pounds down the stairs after them.

"You're not going anywhere!"

Melanie turns and faces her.

"Hey, you told me to leave, and I'm leaving." Then she turns again and starts to walk away. Heather's left hand reaches out, grabbing Melanie's arm to whirl her around; her right fist slams into Melanie's jaw. Melanie stands her ground, but she will not fight back. To do so would be against everything she believes.

Now Dave is screaming at Heather, pulling her away from Melanie.

"Fuck! What's happening? This is bullshit, Heather—what the fuck, why're you tripping?" He is holding both her arms, keeping them down at her sides, and suddenly she goes limp.

She stares at him intently for a long moment, and when she speaks again, she isn't yelling any more.

"Oh, man, don't you fuckin' get it? It's 'cause Kathy likes you so much."

Dave Adkins ignores the shift of something deep inside. As if a key had suddenly gone minor, sounding a muted warning he is too young and too careless to hear.

Kelly French continues her recollection. "When I first met Heather, I was, like, keeping away. Every time we went out together, we'd be with Kathy, 'cause she was Kathy's friend. So we would go out and party together, but, like I said, I was keeping away until she started talking to me. 'Cause you didn't just, like, walk up to Heather Goodwin and, like, 'Hey, what's up, be my friend.' "

Denise Ellroy cuts in. Denise, only a year and a half older than Kelly, is more mature. She has already assumed a rather brusque, even-eyed vision of the way things are; if she was ever prone to dreaminess, the murders have stripped that part of her away. Now, when she talks about Heather, she looks at me, and at Kelly, with a cool, hard gaze. "Heather'd beat a *guy* up. I mean, she had her moments when she could be really nice. But then there'd be the times—I don't know if it was three weeks of PMS or what, but—there'd be times when it was just"—her voice takes on a rapid-fire delivery— " 'Don't touch me, don't look at me. You look at me sideways and I will kill you!' "

I ask about Heather's home life. Kelly answers, describing the house in San Marino, one of the wealthiest enclaves in Pasadena. She talks about how tidily kept the rooms were, how everything was always precisely set in its allotted space: the television screen tilted to an exact angle, the remote control placed just so next to it, the phone cord coiled in perfect spirals. She tells me about the fresh flowers massed in vases in every room, and about Mimi Goodwin's paintings, about her small studio at the back of the house.

Then she begins to talk about Heather's room, and what emerges is a strikingly different image from anything else in that house. The stolen street signs, the Iron Maiden and black light posters on the walls, the huge Confederate banner. She tells me about the clutter of rolling papers and bud, the bongs and pipes, the cigarette butts clogging the ashtrays. About Heather's box of tattoo equipment, the different shades of ink and the needles. And about the tattoos Heather etched into her own skin: the bracelet of stars, moons, and crosses on her wrist, the nickname "Tinker" (for Tinkerbell, because Heather was so tiny) scripted on the inside of one finger, and the "stoner's dot" next to it. All of the kids at the core of the group had a stoner's dot; it was supposed to be a mark of identification and protection in case any of them was arrested and jailed. The dot would tell other prisoners that the wearer was okay, that he or she wouldn't snitch.

Kelly goes on to say how "nice and friendly" Mimi Goodwin was to all of Heather's friends, how she was always available to drive the kids to each other's houses for sleepovers and parties. She tells me how Saturday nights were considered to be Heather's parents' "private time." But, she adds quickly, "they didn't, you know, ignore her. They let her borrow the car when she wanted to, and stuff. Even after she dropped out of school in the tenth grade—I mean, her folks *wanted* her to go back and graduate and go to college, but they weren't ragging on her all that much. She was pretty happy at home, I guess. But her . . ." Kelly hesitates, searching for the word she wants.

Denise supplies it. "Her image." She turns to Kelly. "Right? Her image?"

Kelly nods her head. She is only a little surprised that Denise knew what she was going to say next. And I'm reminded that these kids have known each other since grammar school. All of them.

SMOKED

. . . .

Dave and Kathy are together again after that afternoon at the Hebrock apartment. Usually they meet at Jason Cheever's house. It's not a good idea for Dave to take Kathy to his place. The first time she met his mom he could tell, even though Pam was polite enough, that she couldn't stand Kathy Macaulay. She just kind of froze up the minute she saw her. Even Kathy felt it, because she mentioned it to Kelly French the next day. Kelly says that Kathy was hurt, and a little bit angry, at the rebuff, " 'cause Kathy was always real polite with people's parents. My mom liked Kathy a lot for a really long time, 'cause Kathy showed up at school, and went to classes and stuff, and my mom thought that would be a good influence on me. But then she found an empty tequila bottle Kathy left in my room. After that she was pretty much ragging on me not to see so much of Kathy anymore. But Dave's mom didn't even have *that* kind of reason not to like Kathy. She just took one look and that was, like, *it*—over with. Dave was way pissed off about it. He hated the way his mom never gave Kathy a chance."

. . . .

Heather is pushing hard for Dave to "ask Kathy out," to ask her to go steady. But Dave is more interested in making out. He's used to getting laid, he tells Heather, and he's sick of messing around without a proper payoff from Kathy.

Al Binder was the person who came closest to being Heather Goodwin's soulmate in the summer of 1988. Two years older than she, he was a known rebel given to twin Mohawks, often dyed into alarming colors (his hair was a bright poison green the day they met—and clicked—at the Roundtable). He wore torn Levi's with thick leather belts, chains, often two or three at a time, Harley-Davidson flattop boots, and a scuffed leather jacket (spray-painted with anarchistic slogans) over his bare chest.

Al and his older sister were born in Argentina, of an American mother and Argentinean father. When Al was eight years old his parents divorced and he and his sister were brought, by their mother, to live in South Pasadena. The boy was so angered by the breakup of the family that he refused to speak English for two years. He even refused to learn anything in that language.

By the time he was in his mid-teens, he was a full-fledged punker, living (on and off) at home, drinking and using drugs, falling asleep in the back booths of fast-food joints on Hollywood Boulevard.

In the summer of '88 Al was spending as little time as possible in South Pasadena. He hated the place, considered it to be the most prosaic of cities. But he had been going to Continuation classes so that he could make up enough credits to get into tenth grade at South Pasadena High in the fall. Heather Goodwin was enrolled in San Marino High School, near her parents' home, but she was trying to get a transfer to South Pas, where she felt she could get along more easily. She had had too many fights with the kids in San Marino, she told Al that first day.

One of the kids at the Roundtable invited Al to a party to be held that night. While the kid was telling everybody how bitchin' the party was going to be because his folks were out of town, Heather looked up at Al Binder and smiled shyly. "You really should come."

Al Binder broke one of his own rules that night: he went to a party in South Pasadena. He and Heather sat drinking—Colt .45 for him; she stuck with wine coolers. They smoked joint after joint and talked while the party roiled around them. Kathy Macaulay was there with her friend Peggy Shurtleff. Kelly French and another girl from South Pas, Andrea Tynan, were with some kids from Alhambra. Dave Adkins came by with Jason Cheever and Vinnie Hebrock. Girls from local private schools arrived in groups. Kids got drunk and went outside to get sick. Kids got stoned and turned the music up higher; portable CD players tangled with MTV. People had to yell to be heard.

Heather and Al sat head to head, talking through everything, not noticing anything but each other.

As always with Heather, the initial subject was music. The kind of music a person liked told her what she needed to know about them. Al named his favorite bands: Dead Kennedys, the Adicts, the Germs, the Dickies. Suicidal Tendencies. Heather nodded her head approvingly and pulled her shirt away from one shoulder to show him a tattoo that duplicated the Cure's logo.

This was all small talk to Al. The kind of music you like is only the music you like, he told her. Look at all the jerks who listen to really good stuff. He wants Heather to talk about herself.

Heather shrugs; it's not much of a gesture. What did he want to know?

How come she gets in so many fights in San Marino?

The reply is fast in coming. Heather hates San Marino, hates the kids there. They're just like their parents, snobs with lame ideas about how you should live, dress, think. Anyone different gets picked on and put down. If you don't wear fuckin' Stussys or Laura Ashleys, you get looked at funny. It was like, you can get wasted on beer and acid and speed, you can throw up all over the place, you can do anything you feel like, but you have to look right doing it. It's just too fuckin' hypocritical for Heather. All that "If you don't conform, you're fucked" shit.

"People used to think they could fuck with me, see. I was always the smallest one in my class, and I guess I've always been what they consider weird, so . . . a lotta bullshit. Only now"—she makes a fist with her right hand and holds it up in front of her face—"if anyone tries to pull any shit on me, they get this." She smiles briefly, sweetly. "I'm a pretty good fighter."

"Oh, yeah?" Al reaches out, grabbing her fist. Then he drops a kiss on the knuckles. Heather actually blushes.

"What do your parents think about your transferring?"

"I don't know." She pauses, thinking. "My mom really tries to understand me, you know? But we're pretty much talking two different languages most of the time. I love her, and all, and I know she loves me. It's hard, though, 'cause she'd like me to be more ... you know, 'normal,' and for me, this is normal. But, shit, at least she's there for me."

She looks away, eyes scanning the action at the other end of the room. Kathy Macaulay is sitting in some guy's lap; her arms are entwined around his neck and she's screaming something into his ear. The guy's laughing, but he looks uncomfortable.

Heather looks at Al again. "You wanna hear something pitiful? Me and Kathy Macaulay have known each other since like the third grade, and she's been coming to my house for sleepovers practically every week since we met. And in all that time I don't think my father has ever said one word to her. Not one word." She smiles again. This time the expression isn't sweet. "Of course, he doesn't talk to *me,* either. He just hangs out in this room he has and smokes cigars and reads and—I don't know, thinks deep thoughts, I guess. I used to think him and my mom made up for all that silence on Saturday nights, when they were alone. But, I don't know ..." She pauses for a beat, looking away from Al. Then her eyes snap back to meet his again. "Hey, fuck it. Let's get wasted."

The party rages on through the night. More drinks. More dope. At some point Heather got a razor out of one of the medicine cabinets in a back bedroom and carved the symbol of anarchy into Al's upper arm. Ⓐ

SMOKED

Morning found them walking in Garfield Park with Kathy Macaulay. Four years later Al Binder would say, of that first night, "It happened. I was in love." But he was too shy even to kiss Heather Goodwin for two weeks.

They would make an interesting couple, these two. The small, angry girl with her fierce need to be understood, and the shy, Mohawked young man who had refused to speak English for two years.

....

When Kathy asks Heather if she and Al will double-date with her and Dave, Heather is delighted. Al says it's okay with him, he likes Dave Adkins. Al has one condition, though: they have to go to Pasadena. Any place in South Pas is out.

The E-Bar is located in a picturesque alley near Colorado Boulevard, Pasadena's largest artery, and it is reminiscent of one of those fifties coffeehouses where Beat poets would read Ginsberg and Ferlinghetti aloud. A selection of various coffees, cappuccinos, and fancy desserts are offered at the bar; the inside walls serve as a gallery for local artists. The exhibit changes every month, and the paintings are for sale.

Al has brought Heather here several times in the past week or so. They sit for hours, nursing Double Mochas and watching the ongoing chess games. When the urge to get high strikes, they take a break in the parking lot next to the alley. The lot ends at the railroad tracks that intersect Pasadena; when the trains roll, the thunder of their engines fills the air.

The E-Bar has become a favorite retreat for Al and Heather; being here with Kathy Macaulay and Dave Adkins is another story. The place is just too mellow for them, Dave especially. When he begins to get restless, Kathy takes over. She has noticed a guy at one of the end tables, he's one of her brother's college buddies. Kathy walks over to him and, after a brief conversation, she comes back and tells the others to meet her in the parking lot in five minutes.

When Kathy returns, she's lugging a couple of two-gallon jugs of cheap wine. The four kids stay there, in the parking lot, and proceed to get drunk. At one point Kathy takes a large gulp of the wine, presses her lips over Dave's, and releases it into his mouth. He swallows and they kiss deeply. Then, giggling, Kathy whispers something into Heather's ear. Heather giggles, too, and gestures for Dave to move a few steps to the side with her.

"Kathy wants to fuck you."

"Cool."

The group takes a taxi back to Kathy's house. As they close the front door, a woman's voice floats down the hall.

"Katherine? Who's that with you?"

"It's just Heather, Mom."

"Okay. Good night, then."

The four kids move swiftly back to Kathy's room at the other end of the house. Al flops down on one of the twin beds and passes out. Heather tries to rouse him, but he's through for the night. He doesn't even stir when Dave leans over him to deliver a hard punch. Heather gives up. She gets to her feet and goes to stand at the window, looking out at the dark shapes of the trees that crowd the house, smoking cigarette after cigarette as Kathy and Dave get into the other bed and make love for the first time.

. . . .

"Heather was real petite, just tiny, but she acted really tough, and she had a reputation built on that image. And yet, like most teenagers, she was truly insecure inside. She just needed that tough facade. And Kathy needed it, too—she seemed to feed off Heather's complete recklessness. Kathy needed to be close with someone other people were afraid of."

Melanie Pinkney says that she "feels like a spin-off from

SMOKED

South Pasadena, ready to move on to a higher plain." She's not sure what that plain might be, she just knows it isn't to be found in the city where she has spent all of her life. Melanie is seventeen now, and the impression you get when you first look at her is that she is impossibly beautiful. Thick, dark hair tumbles about her face; her complexion is a deep, glowing olive; she has large, gray eyes starred with bristles of lashes; her mouth is full and sensual. As you talk with Melanie, you begin to see something behind her eyes, something beyond the intelligence: this is a girl carrying around a sadness so profound that it is corrosive. She seems to have spent most of her life disliking her existence.

Melanie lives with her parents and younger sister in a moderately sized wood and stone house only a couple of blocks away from the house where Dave Adkins lived. Most of the homes in this solid, middle-class neighborhood look pretty much the same: California bungalows built within a few feet of one another during the first ten years of this century.

"A lot of people were afraid of Dave too, 'cause he could really fight, but I don't think that was the reason Kathy was with him. Kathy Macaulay—and every other girl who ever got involved with Dave Adkins—looked on him as a real prize. I knew he wasn't any prize, I grew up with him. I'd seen the trouble, I'd ridden the roller coaster of never knowing where he'd be, but I was emotionally attached. Always. I just knew he wasn't a prize, and none of the others seemed to get that."

Melanie and I are seated in a booth at a small hamburger joint near Pasadena City College. Melanie is in her first year there, majoring in English and International Business.

She goes on. "Dave was so cute. And he was so reckless." Past tense, I notice, as if Dave Adkins no longer existed. "We all know girls are always attracted to bad boys. But Dave had something else, too: he was charming, and he retained that charm under *any* pressure." She takes a beat, thinking about it, smiling slightly. "He still does." The smile evaporates. "But any girl who ever got involved with Dave, at any level, paid for it emotionally. Because Dave acts, *always,* on pure whim."

She polishes off the last of her french fries. "There's a quote that fits Dave, something about 'the most intelligent choice not being the most commonly taken.' Dave just slipped naturally into the wrong choices." Her lips curve into another smile; this one is rueful, self-deprecating. "Me, too. There was a time when I could always be counted on to make the wrong choices."

She is looking straight at me, her eyes unflinching, her tone unapologetic. "When you get used to fucking up, you keep fucking up. Because it's what you know. It's security." She leans forward, as if she could make a stronger point by moving closer to me. "Because that's your turf—fucking up. That's your terrain. And you're not comfortable anywhere else."

Melanie relaxes against the booth again. Her eyes move past me, toward the entrance of the restaurant, then she looks back at me. "Dave Adkins never took a step back to think. Never. He just *did.* Dave only thinks of ramifications when they come. While he's doing something—whatever it might be—*that's* his focus."

She looks down at her hands, which are folded on the table; she has well-shaped, short, unpolished nails. No rings; a man's watch on her left wrist. She looks up at me again and smiles. "When I was Dave's girlfriend, on and off in the seventh and eighth grade, he'd be very protective of me. He looked out for me. But for himself, like when we'd talk seriously, and I'd tell him he had to straighten out . . ." The thought remains unarticulated. She shakes her head in a slow movement and then her shoulders give a little hitch.

"But there was only one of me among his friends, and lots of them. And their influence was stronger." Melanie Pinkney is wrong about one thing: Dave Adkins did have many friends, and a few of them may have exerted some influence over him, but there was only one person near Dave whose voice carried any true resonance. That was Vinnie Hebrock.

....

By the end of the summer of 1988, Dave and Vinnie were heavily involved in criminal pursuits. They were breaking into houses, stealing cars (Dave perfected his driving skills on stolen cars), snatching purses. They were dealing drugs. There were times when, having been spotted by the police in the course of a robbery, they had to make a run for it. And it was at these moments that Vinnie proved how well versed he was in "the criminal way." He knew every rabbit hole and cranny in South Pasadena. He knew where to dive behind a bush or a rock, where to roll, stunt-man-style, down a culvert. Vinnie proved to Dave, over and over, that he knew how to fool the cops.

Later, after the escape, the two boys would go back to the tiny apartment over the body shop where they would smoke weed and laugh about their exploits. Dave Adkins had found, in Vinnie Hebrock, not only a coconspirator but a teacher. And, if the other kids perceived Vinnie as a social misfit, a wimp, that was okay too. Dave, the golden boy, had found a perverse and private hero.

*I*n the fall of 1988, Dave Adkins entered the eighth grade at South Pasadena Junior High. Kathy Macaulay moved up to tenth grade at the high school. Heather Goodwin was accepted at South Pas, but she dropped out in the first few weeks of the first quarter. Danae Palermo was in the ninth grade, but she would be dropping out of South Pas during the year.

Dave and Kathy are seeing each other almost every day, making love whenever they can. Dave is seeing Melanie, too, but Kathy is unaware of it. When Dave is with Kathy, she often suggests a trip to the mall. They prowl the aisles and, whenever one or the other spots something that would look good on Dave, Kathy buys it for him, using her mother's credit card.

In the meantime, Dave was having disciplinary problems at school. Sandie Wells was his English teacher at the time, and although she does not remember Dave during that September of 1988 (she wouldn't get to know him until April 1989), she knew about both Dave and Dan Adkins. She would say, four years later, "The Adkins brothers had reputations, and those reputations preceded them. They were troublemakers, and troublemakers and Special Ed students were often mainstreamed to me. The Adkins brothers fell into both categories."

In the fall of 1988, Dave Adkins was cutting classes and getting into fights. There was a rumor going around—which was never proven—that he was selling pot. He was, in fact, according to a later conversation, rolling "three big ol' joints every morning: one to smoke on the way to school, one for lunchtime, one for the afternoon."

Then he and Vinnie were picked up for breaking into a house near the junior high and stealing a television set. (He'd tell Sandie Wells, months later, that the authorities let them off with a warning.) Soon after that he got into a fight with another kid at the Roundtable. The kid said something Dave didn't like and Dave punched him out, breaking the boy's glasses. Charges were pressed by the kid's father and Dave was convicted of assault and sent to Mira Loma detention camp in Lancaster for a term of ninety-nine days. During that time Kathy Macaulay bombarded him with letters, telling him how much she loved and missed him, how she would be waiting for him when he got out.

. . . .

Kathy Macaulay is not the first girl to see Dave when he is released (a week early for good behavior) from Mira Loma; Andrea Tynan is. She is a friend and classmate of Kathy's, and she is considered by the guys to be a good buddy. The Adkins brothers, Jason Cheever, and Cayle Fiedler are among her close friends, so on the evening of Dave's release, Dan takes him to Andrea's place. Like so many of the kids in South Pasadena, Andrea has turned the family garage into something like a studio apartment. Tonight she's there with some guy nobody knows, but she greets Dave warmly, taking the lit joint from between her own lips and sticking it into his mouth.

Andrea Tynan has the kind of looks that make you think of a rather vicious doll; her face is full-cheeked, her eyes are round and blue, her mouth is round and pink. When the lips part, they reveal small, even teeth. Any other resemblance to a toy ends with Andrea's physical appearance. She is quick to fight and has a well-earned reputation for toughness.

Dave takes a deep hit on the joint, then another. As he holds in the smoke, his eyes move appreciatively around the garage. Motorhead is surging out of the twin speakers mounted in the rafters. Loud, angry music.

Ultimately the conversation gets around to Kathy. Dave says he's been trying to call her, that he keeps getting her answering machine. He hasn't left any messages, he says; he wants to surprise her.

Andrea and Jason exchange glances; Dave catches the look.

"What." It's not a question; it's a demand for information.

Andrea sighs dramatically. "Dude, you gotta be realistic about her."

Anger flares briefly in Dave's eyes. "Hey, Andrea, if you're gonna tell me a shitload of bad news about Kathy, I don't want to hear it."

"Dave—she's been totally cheating on you." Andrea's tone is flat, matter-of-fact.

Dave struggles to keep the hurt from showing. "Oh, yeah? Who with?"

The Motorhead tape ends. Somebody replaces it with a Metallica album and cranks up the volume. Now everybody in the room has to yell to be heard.

"It's not just one guy, dude! It's a whole bunch of guys."

"You're fucking lying, Andrea."

Now it's her turn to pin him with a single look. Then she turns and walks away, moving to the other side of the room to slide down next to the guy who's here with her. Dave watches as she slips into the curve of the guy's arm, then he walks outside.

"Hey, bro' . . . you okay?" Dan has followed with a freshly opened can of beer. He offers the can to his brother.

Dave takes a long pull on the beer before he answers. "Yeah, I guess so." He hands the can back to Dan and, for an instant, considers telling him how he really feels. How his heart is cracked—not just in half, but fucking shattered. Crushed.

"Dave . . . ?" Dan's voice is full of concern.

"Listen, I don't want you to say anything to Mom about this. You know how she feels about Kathy, she fuckin' hates her, and if she thinks I got cheated on, she's gonna be all 'I told you so' and 'she's a slut' and shit."

"I won't say anything, bro'. But a lotta people are talking."

"I don't give a fuck what people are saying. Just don't you say anything to Mom. Lemme talk to Kathy first. I want to see if she's gonna lie to me or not."

Dave doesn't see Kathy until Monday, after school, at HiLife Burgers. She's sitting with Danae Palermo, and when he walks in with Jason Cheever and takes a seat in the booth behind her, she doesn't notice him. Danae does, though, and she leans over to whisper to Kathy.

"There's Dave."

"Yeah, right." No way does Kathy believe her. She doesn't even turn around to look.

Dave gets up and places both hands over Kathy's eyes. "Guess who?"

She names three or four different guys. The people around them have gone very quiet; Jason has gotten to his feet too, and he and Danae exchange a long look. Dave catches it and lowers his hands to his sides.

"It's Dave." His voice has dropped to a whisper; his expression is unreadable.

"Yeah, right." In exactly the same tone she used the first time.

Dave sits down now, in the booth behind Kathy. A long moment goes by. Then Kathy raises up slightly and looks over the back of the booth; she sees the tattoo on the back of Dave's biceps, she sees the unruly mass of his hair. And she leaps to her feet, scattering napkins and plastic knives and forks. Almost every kid in the place is watching now.

"Oh, God—it really *is* you! I can't believe this, dude. I've got some stuff I bought for you in my bag!"

She reaches into her shoulder bag, brings out a leather bracelet and a bottle of Drakkar Noir cologne, and if Dave has doubts about who those things were really bought for, he keeps them to himself.

"You gotten high yet? Come on up and you can check out my new house." Kathy is talking faster than usual.

Danae has been looking out of the window; now she turns and tells Kathy that their ride is here. Kathy tugs at Dave's hand.

"Come on, dude. Danae's boyfriend'll drive us home."

Dave looks over at Jason. Jason shrugs. Whatever Dave wants to do is okay with him.

When Dave scrambles into the backseat of the car next to Kathy, she picks up her notebook to make room for him. The name "George" is scrawled, several times, on the denim cover. Dave says nothing.

Kathy's folks' new home, on Fairlawn Way in Pasadena, is even more impressive than the old one. The pool area is much bigger; there's a Jacuzzi and a place for barbecues. The main house looks huge and the view is unbelievable: Annandale Country Club spreads out at the foot of the hillside. There's even a guesthouse, over the garage.

Kathy and Dave, Danae and her guy, go up there. It's still a mess from the recent move: packing cases, some of them still unopened, are stacked against the walls, odd pieces of furniture that might not make it into the main house have been set down haphazardly by the movers. But you can tell, right away, that when this place is fixed up, it's going to look like a real apartment. There's the one big room, with a balcony all the way around, there's a kitchen with a microwave set in over the electric stove, and a tiled bathroom. Bitchin', Dave thinks.

"Cool, huh? I told my mom I want to live up here. It'll be just like living in a treehouse—and I can play the stereo without her ragging on me." Kathy hands Dave a lit joint.

"Yeah."

He takes a hit, passes the joint back to her. He can feel the strain between them, and he doesn't know how to reach across it. He looks around for Danae and what's-his-face. They're in a corner of the room, sitting behind one of the packing cases. The guy whispers something and Danae laughs softly.

Dave reaches out to pull Kathy close, but when he tries to kiss her, she ducks away.

"What the fuck, Kathy..." He makes the move again. And again, she pulls away from him. She shakes her head in a brisk gesture.

"I can't do this." And she walks outside, to the balcony overlooking the driveway. Dave follows her and notices, without thinking about it, that Kathy's mother is home now. Her red Mercedes is in the driveway.

"Kathy . . ."

She continues to look straight ahead, at the view.

"Kathy."

"What?"

"Did you cheat on me while I was away?"

"No! No way!" But she answered too fast, and she's still not looking at him. And Kathy has always been one to look you straight in the eye.

"Then why won't you kiss me?"

"I just feel, you know, weird about it." Now she turns to face him. "You know?"

"No, I don't know. Weird how?" What he's thinking is that this is such bullshit.

"Well . . . 'cause you've been away so long." Kathy looks out at the view again. "Just weird, okay?"

When Dave gets home, he calls Jason.

"She lied to me, dude. What do I do now?"

"Tomorrow, tell her you know. If she denies it, dump her. If she tells you the truth, that could be a step forward in mending things between you guys."

But at school, the next day, Kathy keeps on denying she ever cheated on Dave. She insists that people are just telling lies about her. When Dave asks about George, whose name is written all over her notebook, she begins to cry.

"Okay, that's twice you lied to me, Kathy. Don't let there be a third time." He takes a beat and looks at her intently. "Did you cheat on me?"

"No!"

"Okay, Kathy. Later days. We're not going out anymore."

. . . .

Denise Ellroy and Kelly French reserve their fondest tones for the times they mention Kathy Macaulay and Dave Adkins. Kelly, in particular, seems eager to convince me of Dave's consistent niceness to her. "He was never mean one minute and then back to being nice, the way he was with Kathy."

When I ask for an example of that behavior, Kelly describes episodes between Dave and Kathy when he would rear and plunge from light to dark moods. At school or at a party, Dave could be kissing Kathy, holding her hand or fiddling with her hair, and in an instant, without warning, be yelling at her, calling her "a fuckin' bitch." Kathy took the ride with him; she would match Dave, insult for insult, shouting and posturing. At times it seemed like a well-rehearsed act, and it usually ended with both participants settling back into a cuddle. But it wasn't an act. Kathy's feelings were always hurt.

SMOKED

When I ask about Dave's attitude at school, Denise defends him instantly, talking about his lack of application, blaming the drugs and how stoned he always got. She repeats, often, her belief that Dave Adkins only needed to straighten out his life and figure out what it was he wanted. That basically he was a good person who made some bad choices.

When they talk about Cayle Fiedler, both girls mention his smarts first. Denise calls him "a *very* intelligent child," laughing at herself for referring to Cayle as a child. She adds another observation about Cayle: he's a good friend. Dave Adkins is a flirt, but Cayle knows how to be a friend. Neither girl places a negative spin on Dave's flirtatiousness; they're comfortable with it, the same way they're comfortable with Cayle's intelligence.

Neither Denise nor Kelly knows much about Vinnie. Neither girl likes him and Denise dismisses him as a wanna-be tough guy. They know him only as Dave Adkins's tagalong, a perpetual outsider with none of the right moves. As they talk about him, one thing becomes clear: no matter who pulled the trigger of that shotgun, the blame must lie with Vinnie Hebrock.

Finally, I ask about Danae Palermo. Denise answers quickly: "Danae dropped out of school in the tenth grade, I think it was. Then she went to live with her grandmother in Alhambra and nobody saw her much after that. I heard she kept a bong in the refrigerator, and smoked opium on a wire right out in the living room, and her grandmother never caught on. But I don't believe that. I think people just like to talk shit. 'Cause I know for a fact she was taking some classes at Glendale Community College."

She pauses for a moment and looks at me again. "I think Danae was trying to get her life together, you know? But . . . the night of the shooting? She was just *there*. Like in really bad luck—she happened to be there, at Kathy's, that day."

Denise pulls in a deep breath. She holds it in for a beat, then she lets it out again in an extended sigh. "Danae was like a drive-by shooting: some people just have the bad luck to be there."

Denise looks at Kelly again; she is clearly protective of the younger girl and seems to be worried about her. "You know, it's just the thought of all these people who are so close to you, and these people who you graduate high school with, who you went to school with, who you *are* going to school with, who you hung with . . ." Her voice falters for an instant, then regains strength again. "I mean, when you're younger, your parents say, 'You should choose your friends wisely,' or they say, 'I don't like that person, I don't think that person's the right kind of company for you to be hanging out with.' My mom would say stuff like that to me, and I'd be, like, 'Oh, *please!* Gimme a break—what can happen? Nothing's happened so far, has it?' And then . . . you hear about *this* happening. And it's time to look around, and go, 'Whoa! This could happen to anyone. It's happening to me.' "

We talk for a moment about the healing process that must take over now. For everyone who was close.

"Yeah, but . . . the memories." Kelly's eyes are on the snapshots on the table in front of her. "Like the color purple, and Venice Beach, 'cause that's where we used to go all the time, and tan Ford Broncos, 'cause that's the kind of car Kathy had . . ."

"And songs. Things that stir your memories. Like that Jimi Hendrix song? 'Purple Haze.' And 'Dream On.' And 'Me and Bobby McGee.' " Denise's voice is soft, almost dreamy.

"I'm just scared to death all the time." Kelly has gathered up the pictures. Now she slides them back inside her wallet. "Sometimes I dream that Heather is living with me. I don't know why it's Heather, I was so much closer to Kathy. But then I wake up, and I'm alone in my bedroom, and it's night, and there's that big window. And it's scary." She actually shudders. "My house is real scary at night."

Denise laughs. It's a loud and nervous sound and there is no trace of humor in it.

"Hey, Kel . . . all houses are scary at night right now."

Kelly doesn't seem to hear her; she goes on with her thought. "You know what I think about all the time? I think, what was Kathy thinking after she saw Heather get killed? Did she think she was next? Was she thinking about all of us in those few seconds just before it happened? That's what me and my friends all say—what was Kathy thinking about just before it happened to her?"

*T*he Monday after Dave and Kathy broke up, he met Missy Gillette at HiLife Burgers. He had seen her around at parties, and at games, but she was older than Dave; in fact, she and Kathy were only one semester apart at school. But where Kathy is small and round and cuddly, Missy is tall and slim, with a mane of taffy-colored hair. And where Kathy is warm and eager to please, Missy is aloof, sure of herself. Jason Cheever had taken her out a few times while Dave was away at camp, and now he wanted Dave to meet her.

"Didn't you used to go out with Kathy Macaulay?" She's putting on lipstick; now she looks at him over the top of the mirror. She's so confident, so aware of her good looks.

As is Dave. He knows exactly what his impact is. "Yeah, but we're broke up." He reaches out, brushing a stray hair away from her face.

She gives it a couple of beats while she finishes with the lipstick and snaps the compact's tiny lock. Then, without even looking at him, "Okay, you can walk me home."

Two weeks later they're going out. During that time Melanie calls Dave constantly and he puts her off with vague stories about helping his mother, and working to make up his grade point average. Kathy never calls at all. To seal his relationship with Missy, Dave gets a tattoo—D.A./M.G. and a heart—on his chest. He has to be careful around the house, covering up whenever Pam is around. His mother hates tattoos. Dave thinks, privately, that they remind her of his father.

Missy Gillette is great to go out with, but she's competitive with Dave. If he drives fast, she drives faster. If he gets drunk, she falls down. It's as if the unspoken rule between them is "You can jump? I can fly." And Missy knows how to push Dave's buttons in ways Kathy never dreamed of.

"So-and-so grabbed my ass outside of Gym today. He keeps coming on to me." Or, "So-and-so left a really gross message on my machine last night." Dave knows Missy wants him to prove he'll do anything for her. He knows that what she wants is for him to beat the hell out of any guy who looks at her, to show her—and everyone else—just how much he really cares. But he's not about to mess up his probation; he's not going back to camp. Not even for Missy Gillette.

Still, she finds ways of getting Dave in trouble. Like the time she got him to take her mom's new Nissan Z to go to the store. Missy told him she knew how to work a stick shift, that she'd do the driving, take all the responsibility. Then, when they were on the way, it became clear, pretty fast, that Missy had never driven any kind of stick. She was stripping gears right and left, putting the car all over the road. So Dave had to take the wheel. And it was all so cool, driving that car with a girl like Missy sitting next to him. They must have lost track of the time, because when they got back to Missy's house, her mother was already there. And when she saw them coming back in her car, she went nuts.

Missy simply blamed Dave for everything. She told her mother that he talked her into taking the car.

Then there's the time with his mother.

It's Saturday afternoon and Dave has just arrived at Missy's house when the telephone rings. It's for him, Missy says, holding out the receiver.

Pam's voice, on the other end, is almost tearful. There's a leak under the kitchen sink, that same pipe Dave fixed before. Can he come home for a little while, just long enough to take care of it again? It will save the expense of calling in a plumber. Dave says sure, he'll be right there. When he hangs up the receiver and looks at Missy, she's wearing the expression that tells him there's trouble brewing.

"What's the matter, Missy? You know I gotta do this for my mom."

"Where's Dan? Why can't *he* do something once in a while?"

" 'Cause he's a total fuckup, that's why. What're you making such a big deal for, anyway? I only have to walk eight fucking houses away. I'll be back in fifteen minutes."

Nothing from Missy; she turns away from him. Dave comes up behind her and puts both arms around her waist. Usually, whenever he does that, she turns to face him in a warm embrace. This time she keeps her back to him.

"Hey, no kiss? No goodbye?" His voice is soft, wheedling.

She pulls away from the circle of his arms. Then she turns to face him.

"Why don't you just go kiss your mother, asshole."

He doesn't say a word. He walks out of the house, slamming the front door as he goes. He strides toward the street. There's a massive eucalyptus tree on the Gillette property; Dave walks straight at it, moving at high speed, pulling back his right arm as he goes, turning his hand into a fist. Then, with all the strength he's got, he hits the tree trunk, hits it so hard he can feel the tiny snap of a bone in his hand. Pain shotguns up his arm, but he barely pauses. He cradles his right hand in his left as he travels the half-block to his house; the hand has begun to swell badly and blood is oozing out from under every nail.

He concocts a story about getting the hand slammed in a car door, then he works on the leaking pipe with his left hand, using the right only when he must. Pam insists on taking him to the nearest emergency room, where he is fitted with a semi-cast.

Dave and Missy make up, as they always do. The following weekend they go to Disneyland with another couple. But, when the guy asks what happened to Dave's hand, Missy pipes up.

"Oh, he hit something that couldn't hit back."

But still, the lure is too great. Going out with Missy Gillette is like dating a movie star. As Dave would say, in a later conversation, "I kept on going out with her because all my friends kept saying how great looking she was, how she was just so cool and beautiful. And the sex was great. But, man, she *was* such a bitch."

Missy was more demanding, more of a "bitch," perhaps, than Dave was prepared for. During the initial months of their relationship, according to Jason Cheever, Missy wanted Dave with her all the time. "Pretty much twenty-four/seven, and when he'd decided to go someplace with me, she didn't like it."*

According to Jason, Dave Adkins was completely manipulated by Missy Gillette; he became her creature. They fought often—and bitterly—about Dave's relationships with Jason and Vinnie. She didn't like Jason because she knew he was highly critical of her. She loathed Vinnie on general principles. His unattractiveness and crudeness repelled her. The deeper truth was that Missy Gillette resented anyone who got too close to Dave Adkins. She required constant, undistracted attention. Jason remembers questioning Dave, putting him on the spot about Missy and her demands:

"Hey, Dave—why do you let her pull this shit on you?"

And he remembers that Dave had no answer to give.

Missy was relentless. She would call the Cheever house with urgent inquiries about Dave's whereabouts. "Is Dave there? Is he with Jason? Is Vinnie with them? Where did they go?" Anyone who answered the phone would be grilled. It reached the point where Dave begged Jason and his brother,

*Jason means twenty-four hours a day, seven days a week.

Jake, not to say he was there when Missy would call, tracking him.

He was not at the Cheever house as often as Missy imagined. The time he put in at detention camp had not diminished Dave's attraction for rambling with Vinnie. The two of them were still going out at night, joyriding, breaking into apartments and houses. Perfecting the criminal way.

There was another crowd, boys and girls, all of them eighth graders, with whom Jason—and Dave to a lesser degree—were involved. These were the outsiders, the outlaws who weren't jocks or socialites, the ones who wore black and listened to Heavy Metal and Death Rock. Some of the kids in this crowd (who called themselves "the Family")* were into games. One of the games was "Chicken," and it was about rubbing your arms, and the back of your hands, with a pencil eraser until you drew blood. The more scabs you were able to show, the less of a chicken you were. The kids in the Family had known each other since elementary school, and most of them had begun some kind of sexual activity as far back as the fourth grade. A couple of the girls even posed for topless photographs; one girl smiled into the camera while she held a can of Diet Coke between her budding breasts.

Jason Cheever described the group: "We had a whole little family thing going back in the eighth grade. There were even some kids who would call me 'Daddy,' call my girlfriend Karen 'Mommy.' Dave was looked on as my brother—like an 'uncle.' Kathy and Heather, Andrea and Peggy too, were a subclique to the Family clique; they were friends with all of us. But they weren't part of the group that really relied on each other for that family feeling. We really were like a little family, we backed each other up. Like, I relied on Dave's brute force and strength. And he counted on my smarts."

Melanie Pinkney was very much a member of the Family.

*Not a reference to the Charles Manson Family.

Her memories, however, are a little darker than Jason's. She particularly remembers his girlfriend during that period: Karen. "For someone who had the position of 'Mommy,' Karen was always into her power trip. She was real smart, but she was too twisted. She just manipulated people all the time, dictating behavior in the group according to her whims. She could really hurt some feelings if someone didn't act the way she wanted them to. Like, if she was angry at someone, she'd expect you to have the same attitude. And if you didn't, she'd go off on *you,* she'd hit every vulnerability, make you feel like nothing. Karen thrived on that kind of stuff; the worse she could make you feel, the better it was for her."

Melanie feels that she and Jason had similar roles in Dave Adkins's life. "He talked to Jason, and he talked to me. About so many parts of his life. We were romantically involved in an on-again, off-again pattern—sometimes I'd be his girlfriend—but mostly we'd talk. I was, like, a mentor."

When Melanie talks about those times, back at the tail end of the eighties, her voice goes softer than usual and the expression on her face becomes sadder. She seems to be nostalgic for a time in her life that provided as much unrest as happiness.

She goes on: "But Dave was so committed to Missy Gillette. He never was with me when he was with her. And yet, she was so threatened by our friendship. Whenever he'd come to me—just to talk—she'd be all 'I'm gonna kick Melanie's ass.' She told the world she was gonna kick my ass. And she never did. Missy Gillette was all talk."

To illustrate the point, Melanie tells me about an incident that happened at school.

"Missy walked up to me in front of Spanish class and started bitching me out: 'Stay the fuck away from Dave. He doesn't give a shit about you. He thinks you're nothing.' "

Melanie tells me what her reply to this was:

"If Dave has to go to that level, tell you that kinda shit to make you feel good, that's fine with me. But know he's doing it because of your pitiful insecurities. It's charity work."

At this point Melanie remembers that "Missy looked like smoke was gonna come pouring out of her ears." Classes had just let out and kids sneaked covert looks as they walked past the two girls; this is a small school, everybody knows what's going on with everybody else. And Dave Adkins, the bad boy stud, is always an exciting subject.

"I'm gonna kick your ass, Pinkney!"

"Fine. Kick my ass."

"Next time. Next time you fuck up."

"What's the matter with this time, bitch? I'm right here."
Until this moment, Melanie had been amused; now she's beginning to get angry, and she doesn't want to. She knows that when you lose your temper, you lose the fight.

"If I hear one more thing about you and Dave, I'm gonna kick your ass!"

Missy is feverish now, her voice has notched up into an even shriller register. Her eyes dart away from Melanie's cool, even gaze. Beneath the flower-child veneer, Melanie Pinkney is much more the street fighter than Missy Gillette, and both girls know it. When Melanie speaks again, her voice is back to low, conversational tones.

"Why wait? Come on—do what you need to do."

Missy looks once at Melanie, looks away quickly.

"Next time . . ." She's muttering now. Melanie laughs softly as she walks away from Missy. She's thinking the win was almost too easy.

"I was always considered a threat by Dave Adkins's girlfriends, and they acted accordingly: instant prejudice." Melanie smiles now. "Dave probably liked it, being prized. It made him harder to get. He likes to play you, once he's got you. He likes to see how much he can get from any one girl—financially, emotionally, physically."

The inevitable question is, why bother with Dave Adkins? What could be the payoff? Now Melanie really laughs—a deep, full-throated chuckle. *"Payoff?* Nothing." She shakes her head, still laughing. Then her expression sobers again.

"When Dave was with you, he was with you and he'd pay attention to you. And then he'd be gone. He'd come back, sometimes, and grace your life with his presence, and you'd feel all cool—'cause he was *the prize."* Her tone is freighted with sarcasm, but there's something there, some unvoiced remnant of feeling that tells you somewhere, somehow, Melanie still considers Dave Adkins to be a prize. "And then, like I said, he'd be gone again. But while he was there, I guess that was the payoff. His *being* there, for that minute."

She takes a beat or two, smiling, remembering. "It wasn't quite like that with me, 'cause he respected me. Because I was smart. One thing you have to say for him—Dave Adkins recognizes smarts."

In view of the events that would later come into Dave Adkins's life, Melanie's observation would seem less than acute.

Hey, dude—let's go out tonight. Let's do something."

Kathy's voice on the phone sounded pretty good. Dave had run into her last night at a party he went to with Jason and another kid in their class, Eric Bonworthy. He hadn't seen Kathy in a few weeks, not even around school, and she looked great. A little thinner, maybe, and her hair was now a luminous blond. Her nails looked too long to be real, and she had them painted a light purple shade, but they were sexy looking. She was dressed entirely in black. She flirted with Dave all evening, told him she'd call him the next day. And now, here she was. They make arrangements for her to pick him up at Jason's house.

"You wanna do a line of speed?" It's the first thing she says as he gets in the car.

"Okay." Speed is one of the few highs Dave hasn't experienced. But he remembers how patient, how nice she was that first night when she showed him how to use the bong.

Kathy rummages in her bag, comes up with a small brown glass bottle with a tiny spoon attached to the cap. She flicks the bottle a couple of times with one finger, then she scoops out a spoonful of white powder and holds it up to Dave's nostril.

"Okay. Go."

He sniffs, hesitantly; a trace of the powder tickles its way up into the nasal passage. Dave knows he's doing this wrong and he's afraid of Kathy's contempt.

"C'mon, man." Impatience in her voice, that's all. "Hold

the other side shut and suck it straight in, like coke. It's a bitchin' high."

This time the speed goes straight up; burning, icy. Almost immediately another mound is held up to his other nostril. He takes it in smoothly this time, but he can already taste the pungent, bitter taste at the back of his throat. He can feel the beginning of the rush. And he knows he's not going to like the way he feels; this stuff is *too* gnarly, *too* wired.

"Let's smoke a joint." He has begun to sell grass with Vinnie and he has some with him.

"Cool." She reaches into her purse for her lighter. Dave pulls a tightly wrapped joint from the pocket of his T-shirt.

They stop at a liquor store and Kathy buys a quart of Southern Comfort, then they drive up to Fairlawn Way. Kathy has moved most of her things into the guesthouse and is pretty much living there now, going back to her room in the main house only when her brother is home from Stanford. On those occasions the guesthouse is his.

There are still a few unpacked crates stashed against one wall, but now a king-size mattress has been brought in and made up with a red blanket and colorful sheets. Part of Kathy's flag collection is up on the wall; one of the flags is an old Confederate banner, a gift from Heather. Posters have been tacked up everywhere: the Dead, Aerosmith, stylized drawings of marijuana plants. The fancy stereo has been set up in a cabinet underneath the bookshelves that line one side of the room next to a rice-paper shoji screen. As usual, cassettes and CD's are scattered everywhere.

Kathy puts on one of Dave's favorite tapes: the Beatles' "Abbey Road" and they make themselves comfortable on a pile of brightly colored pillows. They drink Southern Comfort, smoke joints, and finally, they begin to kiss.

Afterwards, in the car, Kathy turns on the ignition and lets the motor idle. Then she turns to look steadily at Dave.

"Any time you want me, just let me know."

"Whatever."

He's thinking that's kind of a slutty thing to say.

. . . .

Dave and Kathy see each other for about a week, but it's all about sex. No long walks, no holding hands. Just sex—up at the guesthouse, or in the garage at Dave's place when Pam is at work. There have been a few screaming matches between Dave and his mother about Kathy Macaulay. When Dave asks why Pam hates Kathy, Pam denies it, saying only that Kathy is too spoiled, that she has too much freedom, that she's a bad influence. Privately, Dave wonders if his mother isn't a little bit jealous of Kathy; she has everything that Pam had to do without while she was growing up: money, a great house, a chance at college. And now she has Dave Adkins too.

. . . .

Sandie Wells remembers, very clearly, the day Dave Adkins came back into her classroom after his release from Mira Loma in April of 1989. As she recalls now, she was "somewhat taken aback because I knew he had a hot temper and got in fights. The vice principal of the school told me Dave was on probation, that if the kid even 'breathed wrong, he was out.' "

Sandie Wells has the kind of blond, rigidly bred good looks usually associated with high-income conservative cities like Pasadena. She was widowed ten years ago; there were no children. She keeps horses and dogs. And she is a tireless, impassioned teacher, unflagging in her devotion to her students.

"I remember he was wearing jeans and a jeans jacket with the collar turned up when he walked into the classroom. And I immediately blew it by calling him 'Dan.' He said, very quietly, 'I'm Dave.' "

We are sitting in my living room; Sandie turns and looks out at the courtyard for a long moment. These recollections are clearly painful for her. "I remember how polite he was, constantly saying, 'yes ma'am and no ma'am.' It was ... I don't know, *too* polite. I would have preferred that he simply call me Mrs. Wells.

"What began my involvement with him—other than as a student in my classroom—was when I noticed bruises and, as I recall, cuts, on his arms. Sufficient bruising for me to take him aside and ask him about them. He said he'd gotten them in a fight with his brother. And he said that there were problems at home—with Dan. But there was nothing that could be done about it. And I said, 'There's always something to be done.'

"I spoke to a distant relative of the Adkinses, someone I happened to know, hoping Dave might be able to stay with them." Sandie hesitates, thinking. "That didn't pan out." When I ask why not, she shakes her head in a brisk movement; that particular subject is closed.

She goes on. "A couple of days later, I did something I had never done before: I gave Dave Adkins my telephone number. Because by then I knew that he and his older brother Dan were fighting all the time, and Dave usually lost."

The next major event that took place with Dave Adkins came about during a class outing in which three hundred eighth graders from South Pasadena Middle School were taken to South Pasadena High School for high school orientation. One of the teachers accompanying the group suspected a kid of having a bottle of liquor on him. The teacher and a couple of counselors made a move toward the kid and he bolted. So they grabbed Dave, who was sitting next to him. The way things turned out, Dave was clean. It was a case of wrong place, wrong time.

That next day, however, one of the counselors told Sandie Wells that an eighth-grade girl had told him that Dave Adkins was doing cocaine. Sandie stated flatly that she didn't believe it. But she had doubts. That afternoon, after class, she took Dave aside. He denied everything. This is like that deal with the bottle of liquor, he told her: he got grabbed and accused and he was totally clean. Same thing now, with cocaine. He looked urgently at Mrs. Wells, pleading for her to believe him. Sandie returned the look, taking her time, making up her mind.

"Okay, Dave. I don't believe in rumors. So here's the deal: I'm going to trust you until you give me reason not to. But do not bullshit me."

Now, in my living room, Sandie still remembers the flare of surprise in Dave's eyes. And, remembering, she smiles. "I do *not* speak to students that way, as a rule. Never." Then, after a long beat, "That's when Dave began to trust me. Because I spoke to him in his own language. He told me that months later."

When Dave found out that Sandie Wells kept horses, he asked if he could come out to the ranch where she boarded them and learn to ride. Sandie told him if it was okay with his mom, it would be okay with her. But, she stressed, he had to get his mother's permission.

Sandie ended up going over to the Adkins house to meet Pam Adkins. "We just chatted. About Dave, about school—just general conversation. But Pam was clearly nervous. And that made me nervous, too. But she thought it would be good for Dave to learn how to ride."

Early the next Saturday morning Sandie picked Dave up at his house. He was quiet in the car as they drove the Ventura Freeway into the San Fernando Valley and, Sandie remembers, he asked permission to turn the radio to a classical rock station. Then he turned his head to look out the window at the passing landscape.

Once they were mounted and moving along the trails that lead to the foothills, Dave began to talk. He told Sandie about the fight that got him sent to Mira Loma and the time he did there. He told her about J.D., the man he and Dan had come to look on as a father. Then he began to talk about Kathy Macaulay. He told Sandie that Kathy was his first real love, and he spoke frankly about their sexual attraction for each other.

Now, talking about that first ride, Sandie laughs softly. "I was glad we were on horseback, because I didn't have to face him when he—this *child,* this eighth grader—talked so openly about his sex life." Her expression turns serious. "Of course, I wasn't so embarrassed that I didn't give him a real lecture about the importance of practicing safe sex."

Later, during the drive back to South Pasadena, Dave turned away from the window to look at Sandie.

"Why do you care about me?"

Sandie remembers she had to think about it. At the time, it didn't occur to her that this boy made her wonder about the son she might have had if her husband had wanted children.

I ask about the three dead girls. Kathy, Heather, Danae. And about Vinnie Hebrock.

"I didn't know Heather at all. And Danae wasn't in my English class. I do seem to remember her from study hall. My impression is of a lively girl, very beautiful. I don't know if Danae was a good student or an indifferent one, but my impression was that she was bright.

"I had Kathy Macaulay in eighth-grade English in 1986. And I remember her as being a very sweet girl. Not a particularly gifted student. Not that she wasn't bright; she simply didn't apply herself. And she seemed like a child who was going through the throes of something in her teen years. We didn't get close, but I liked her, and she seemed to like me. She seemed like a gentle girl."

Sandie takes a moment, thinking about this young girl, a member of Sandie's English class, a girl who was to be murdered by another of Sandie's students, a boy to whom the teacher did get close. "I heard, from other people, how very unhappy Kathy was. That she had very low self-esteem, and that she wasn't happy at home. I don't know why. As I said, we never got close."

Vinnie Hebrock was placed in Sandie Wells's English

class and in her homeroom for a brief period in 1987, a year before Dave Adkins came to her. She remembers Vinnie as a quiet boy who sat by himself at the back of the room. After ten days he was sent to Special Ed, where it was determined that he was at a pre-primer level in reading. In fact, Sandie recalls, the teacher would send Vinnie out into the hall with a teacher's aide to read. To spare him embarrassment.

One incident stands out in Sandie's memory. "I was in the Teachers' Lounge, and suddenly someone burst in and said that a fight had broken out by the students' lockers. I ran outside to break it up."

The fight was between Vinnie Hebrock and one of the seventh-grade girls. Vinnie's shirt was torn, hanging in a flap off one shoulder, but he wasn't striking out at the girl. Not yet. He was swearing at her. Terrible words in frightening combinations; phrases no child should know. Vinnie wasn't crying; his rage had taken him past that point. He had been caught in the floodtide of his words and it was sweeping him along. The girl was clearly terrified. She was simply standing there with most of the fight gone out of her, staring at Vinnie, unable to move away from him, even though he was about to hit her.

Sandie Wells stepped in between them. She ordered Vinnie to back off, but she had to say it twice before he seemed to hear her. She could see him refocus then, standing quite still, staring at her for a moment, placing her in his mind. She moved a couple of steps closer to him, ready to take him aside, for a talk. But Vinnie whirled and ran.

The teacher turned to the seventh-grade girl. Through a torrent of sobs the girl told Sandie what had happened. The girl had called another seventh-grade girl an alcoholic. Vinnie, who had been standing nearby, heard her say it and it set off a chain reaction. He had defended the other girl's honor in the only way available to him.

Shortly after that episode Vinnie Hebrock dropped out of school for good.

SMOKED

It was a different story with Dave Adkins the following year. While he was in the eighth grade, Sandie Wells was able to work with him until his grade average came up to a C overall. And she helped him to make up the required 180 citizenship points required for graduation by letting him do yard work for her, and recommending him to other families for painting and chores. He did all the work and received, for the only time, an A in citizenship. Dave Adkins would be allowed to graduate with his class.

....

If Kathy Macaulay has her mind set on anything, it's going to Dave's eighth-grade graduation exercises. She teases and pesters him about it constantly, and even though it would be okay with him if Kathy attended, the one thing Dave knows for sure is that it's going to make trouble. Missy Gillette is back in his life again. She called him one night at about ten o'clock, as if nothing had happened, and they talked until twelve-thirty. So now they're going out again, and Missy has no idea that Dave is seeing Kathy, too, on the sly. If she finds out, there'll be hell to pay. But Kathy won't let go of it, and finally, Dave caves in.

Missy is the first person he spots in the audience. She and Pam have scored seats in the third row of the packed auditorium. Observing his mother and Missy chatting together like girlfriends, Dave can't help wondering why Pam is so mellow about this girl and so bitchy about Kathy. And sitting there on the stage, watching them together, unobserved, the answer comes to him: Missy Gillette and his mother are the same kind of people. Both of them claim to love him more than anyone else, but they're possessive and jealous, and both are nags, ready to get on his case about anything, everything.

Dave scans the rest of the audience. There, seated front and center in the balcony, is Kathy; Andrea is sitting next to her. He begins to twist the ring Sandie Wells gave him as a graduation present—silver, in the shape of a bear claw. Okay, he reassures himself, if nobody sees anybody else, everything'll be cool.

He hasn't counted on Kathy Macaulay's obsessive enthusiasm for him.

When the principal calls out Dave Adkins's name, Kathy's war whoop rings through the auditorium. *"Owwwwww! Dave!"* Andrea begins a series of shrill whistles. And everybody downstairs turns to look up at the two girls in the balcony. Missy's face closes angrily. Pam frowns and flushes a bright red. In a later conversation, Dave will say, "Right there, I knew I was busted."

After the ceremony, Dave slips out the back of the auditorium. He manages to dodge Kathy and Andrea, but there's no way he can avoid his mother and Missy.

Missy is yelling before he reaches her and Pam.

"What's that slut doing here? Did you invite her to your graduation just to make me look bad?"

"Yeah, right, Missy. Like I can control who comes to the fuckin' graduation." It's a lame thing to say, and the way he's saying it sounds weak, he can hear himself. He glances at his mother. Pam looks hurt and angry, too. Like this whole thing is his fault. Yeah, right.

"You're so full of shit, Dave."

"Hey, Missy—whatever."

It's the only thing he can think to say. Because it's the single attitude that always works. With Missy, with Kathy, with any girl he knows. It works with his mother, too. When he turns cold, they back off. But this time Missy isn't buying it; she delivers a venomous look at Dave, then she turns and strides away.

Pam stands looking at Dave for a beat, then she turns to walk away too. Dave calls out after her.

"You think I'm full of it too?"

His mother faces him again; anger and disappointment is clear on her face.

"David, I think you're doing what you always do. Getting your own way without much thought about anyone else's feelings."

And then she's gone, too, walking fast to catch up with Missy.

"Your mom's way pissed at you, huh?"

Jason Cheever has come up behind Dave. Jason's parents and his older brother are standing a few feet away, with a small group of friends and relatives. His mother looks over and waves at Dave. He waves back, then he looks at Jason.

"Yeah, she's all 'you don't care about anybody but yourself.' But Missy is such a bitch, dude. My mom wouldn't ever be ragging on me that way if she was here alone."

"C'mon, Dave. Your mom fuckin' hates Kathy."

Dave smiles in spite of herself. "Yeah, you're right."

And now Kathy and Andrea are bearing down on them. Kathy is carrying her camera, fiddling with the lens as she walks, and Dave can see how high she is, just totally wasted. Andrea too.

Dave and Jason pose together for a couple of snapshots, then Kathy hands the camera to Andrea and slides in between the two boys. Then she and Dave pose alone, his arm around her waist, her face tilted up to smile at him. Finally, Dave and Jason pose with three other boys in the graduating class, all of them smiling out from under a rose-blooming trellis, all of them wearing their white shirts and thin, dark ties.

When the picture taking is done, Jason goes to join his family again, and Kathy grins archly at Dave.

"Hey, this is your big graduation night, duder. We gotta go do something."

"Yeah? What?"

"Well, we can start off by going up to my place and getting fucked up."

Dave thinks about how his mom and Missy stomped off after ragging on him, and he shrugs. What the fuck.

The eighth-grade graduation dance is the next evening. Originally, Dave had intended to take a pass; he told Sandie Wells that the kids in the eighth grade—excepting Jason Cheever—were just too square. But Sandie convinced him it was a celebration he shouldn't miss, and suggested he take one of the girls in his class as his date. He invited Chris O'Donnell. She'd been flirting with him all year, and she's as cute as any girl around South Pas. Chris will be the perfect prom date.

School policy is clear: no limos at any dance. But Dave and Jason and another kid—Bradley Wong—have chipped in to rent one of those big white stretch jobs. Jason is going stag to the dance, but Chris and Brad's date are clearly impressed as the limo slides up in front of their houses. The driver, a young black guy, makes a big deal out of opening the door and helping the ladies, as he calls them, into the car. He tucks the long skirts of their formals inside and comments on how beautiful they look. And he calls the guys "sir." His name is Andre, he tells them, and he asks what kind of music they'd like to hear.

Dave and Jason exchange glances. Dave's thinking this is how a rock star must get treated.

The illusion is shattered when they roll up to the school gym. Mr. Trachtman, one of the teachers, is at the door, and when he sees the limo he hurries over to the passenger side, cupping his hands to see who's inside. But the tinted windows stop him cold, and that really pisses him off.

"Who's in there? Who is that?"

The kids are laughing like crazy in the backseat; they can see Trachtman clearly, and he's nearly foaming at the mouth. He can't see them at all. He storms around to the driver's window and raps sharply.

"Open up in there!"

The dark gray glass slides down.

"What's up with you, man?" Andre's voice is soft, filled with controlled anger.

"These students know the rules. No limos at any school function. Now, I want you to drive away from here. Right now."

"Man ..." Andre shakes his head in a slow back and forth movement.

Now other kids, all of them wearing some version of dress clothes, are coming up to the car, calling out greetings to the five kids inside. Andre gets out from behind the wheel and stands, waiting, looking down at the teacher. Trachtman, intimidated, waves his hand in a small, angry gesture of dismissal.

"All right. We'll let them go in this time."

He chooses to ignore a loud snicker from someone back in the crowd.

After a couple of dances Dave signals to Jason.

"Hey, dude, let's go get some hoosh. We need to be fuckin' wasted for all this."

"I'm out, dude. We smoked the last of it earlier."

"Kathy said she was gonna be over at Andrea's. You *know* they're gonna have some herb."

Kathy and Andrea are standing in the driveway, in front of the garage, when the limo pulls up to the curb. And both girls walk slowly toward the car until Dave rolls down the window and leans out, waving at them. Then Kathy begins to run; she has a loopy, slightly awkward gait. It's the way a kid runs. Andrea maintains the more sedate pace; it's important for Andrea to seem unimpressed.

Kathy drops a fast kiss on Dave's mouth, nods to Jason, and clambers into the backseat. She bounces up and down a couple of times, her hands caressing the leather upholstery. She pushes buttons until she finds the sound control, then she raises the volume of the loudspeaker. Public Enemy moves up a notch.

"This is totally cool. Where you guys going?"

Dave and Jason exchange a fast look.

"Oh, I get it. Prom night. What'd you do, go stag?"

Dave takes a beat before he answers. He looks away from Kathy's insistent gaze.

"Nuh-uh."

"No? Well, fuck you, Adkins." She opens the door again, but she doesn't get out of the car.

"C'mon, Kathy. Don't act like a fuckin' bitch."

She doesn't say anything. But she keeps her head turned away from him, pretending to look out the window. Her eyes are bright with tears. Jason gets out of the car to make small talk with Andrea. The driver pushes the control that activates the window separating him from the passengers.

"C'mon, Kathy . . . I really thought you'd want to see this fuckin' limo." Then, when that doesn't seem to be working, "I really wanted to see you in it."

"Who's your date for the dance?" Her tone is softer now, but she's still angry, still hurt.

"Just some girl from my class. Mrs. Wells made me ask her."

"Who is it?"

"Chris O'Donnell."

"Then why can't you take me back to the dance, too? We could go up to my house first so I can change. I've never even been in a fuckin' limo before." Her voice is sexy-pouty now. "You wanna get high?"

"Yeah . . ."

Kathy pulls a tightly wrapped joint from the pocket of her T-shirt, palming it quickly.

"C'mon. Let's go inside and talk for a minute. I got an idea."

. . . .

Chris is disappointed at being taken home by eleven o'clock, but Dave spins a tale about limo expenses and curfew. Brad Wong and his date have made arrangements to go out with another couple, so now it's just Dave and Jason and three more hours to go with Andre and the car.

They drive up to Kathy's house. She's waiting at the foot of the driveway with Heather. Next, Andre swings over to Altadena to pick up his girlfriend.

"Okay, where y'all want to go now?"

The four kids look at each other. Then, in unison, *"Holly-weird!"*

The stretch limo pulls onto the Hollywood Freeway. Kathy fires up a joint and hands it around; Dave passes it over the divider to Andre.

The next two hours go quickly. Andre sends his girlfriend into a liquor store to pick up a couple of bottles of cheap champagne, and then he just drives around, tape after tape of rap music blasting out of the speakers.

For Dave Adkins, this is the perfect culmination of his junior high school years. He's ready to move on.

....

Dave and Sandie Wells spoke often during the summer of 1989. And when Pam Adkins went out of town on a baby-sitting job, she asked Sandie if Dave could stay with her. During the weekend Dave told Sandie about his drug dealing. He said that he and Vinnie did most of their buying in downtown L.A., in a predominantly black area. He told her Kathy Macaulay had provided his initial bankroll—three hundred dollars. When Sandie commented on the dangers of that part of town—the gangs, the drive-by shootings—Dave countered by saying that was where the action was, it was where he and Vinnie had to go to get drugs at a reasonable price.

Without any knowledge of Dave and Vinnie's crime sprees, Sandie knew somehow that what Dave really liked was the element of peril. For Dave Adkins, the danger was part of the draw.

Dave seemed intent upon giving Sandie as many details as possible about his dealing. He told her that after he and Vinnie scored, they would go back to South Pasadena, either to Dave's garage or to the Hebrock apartment, where they would divvy up the pot into eighth- and quarter-pound packages which they would then sell. They kept half of the bulk amount for their own use.

He showed Sandie the "stoner's dot" tattoo on the inside of his finger, and when she tried to dissuade him from further drug involvement, he told her he wasn't involved; he was a "dealer," not a "pusher." He stated, rather proudly, Sandie recalls, that he only sold to people who "*asked* for it."

It struck Sandie that Dave seemed to be at his happiest—elated, almost—whenever he talked about Vinnie Hebrock. When Kathy, or Missy, or his mother was discussed, his voice dipped to a lower pitch and the words came more slowly, as if talking about them exhausted him.

The only other person Dave enjoyed talking about was Jason Cheever.

. . . .

"At South Pas we were considered 'the bad kids.' We didn't cooperate with the rules, we got bad grades, we ditched school, we smoked cigarettes, we smoked pot, we drank, we beat up on each other. We were always getting into trouble, and I guess we were looked down on. But we didn't do harm; we mostly did that to ourselves."

Jason Cheever is talking about himself and Dave Adkins in the sixth and seventh grades. They met initially in elementary school, where Dave was "the rough kid" who got kicked out for fighting. When they met up again in the sixth grade, Dave was still rough, but by that time, so was Jason, and they began to hang out. "Twenty-four/seven" is the way Jason puts it.

We are in the dining room of the Cheever house, a Craftsman bungalow of considerable charm. The gleaming cherrywood table was handcrafted by Jason's father, an architect. Jason's older brother, Jake, is sitting with us. Tall and muscular, Jake is on the football team at Cal State Riverside, where he is in his sophomore year. Jason isn't as tall as his brother, and he is more slender, but there is a resemblance between them. Both boys have strong, confident voices, and they each engage whoever they talk to with the unaffected, steady gaze of someone who is at ease with the truth.

Jason goes on: "You know, it was Dave's brother, Dan, who was considered a total hood, but Dave was more misunderstood. Just totally, by everyone. I mean, he came off like a badass, but we all did. We all had the attitude of, 'If you mess with us, we'll fuck you up.' You know, we walked around with our attitudes, acting real hard. Bumming around. Acting like gangsters. It was just, like"—he moves his shoulders in a slight, shrugging movement that seems almost apologetic—"our thing. Things have turned around for me now, though, since all of this happened." He glances over at Jake and grins. "Even though I'm still considered a fighter at school. My friends, too."

Jake breaks in. "Maybe things are a little bit different now, but mostly there's the perception of the tough kids, or the wanna-be gangbangers—which Jason used to be. And then there's a certain group of kids who are the partiers and the fighters. And they're kinda cool, and everyone looks up to them. And that's the football players. 'Cause if you play football at South Pas—which both Jason and I did—everyone looks at you differently. You're a jock, so you're cool. You're a jock and you party and you're cool. You're accepted."

The image of Kathy Macaulay being dropped by the cheerleader crowd in the ninth grade when she began to put on weight comes to mind. And stunted little Vinnie Hebrock, with his nearsighted squint and bad-guy attitude. And Heather Goodwin, with her homegrown tattoos and outrageously dyed 'hawks.

As if to bear out the thought, Jason speaks again. "It's

about how you look, and what kinda clothes you wear. It's all about physical, all about reputation."

Jake talks briefly about how it was when his family moved to South Pasadena from Pasadena when he was in junior high school. He remembers the feelings of apartness, of being tolerated by kids who had known each other "from day one," and whose parents, in most cases, had gone to the same school their kids were attending.

"We were still outsiders. It's like you're popular, but you're not. The whole thing's so"—he hesitates, wanting to find the right word—"so *generational*. And everybody's just so vain of that. Which is funny, in a way, because we had the *most* drug abusers in the Class of Ninety. And nobody in South Pasadena wants to take a look at that."

Jason leans back in his chair, stretching widely. "South Pas is just so baked on, you know what I mean? It's like getting a fake tan, and hair extensions, and fake nails, and fake eyelashes." He sits forward again, drumming softly on the table with both index fingers. "You know what it's like here? It's like a Ray Bradbury story, where everything is supposed to be just perfect, 'cause that's how it looks. Only it's not."

Jake nods his head in solemn agreement. "Yeah, and there's an incredible degree of naïveté here. You can tell people in South Pas anything—*anything*. And if you lie convincingly enough, they'll believe it."

Now it's Jason's turn to nod. "Here's the perfect example: so many of the girls in South Pas really like Cayle Fiedler. They think he's the perfect guy friend, just this 'neat person.'" His voice assumes a sour edge of sarcasm on the last two words. "Okay? Well, I know Cayle, and he's a very bad kid. He came to a party here once and he was all fucking around and being real loud, with his fucked-up jeans and skinhead attitude. Just acting like a real thrasher. Anyway, he got in an argument with some kid, and the kid wanted to fight him.

And Cayle was all 'Yeah! Bring him on!', and he opened his jacket and showed me a gun. A little thirty-eight, right there." Jason pauses, thinking back to that moment, thinking, perhaps, how close all of them were to the shocking event that would shred the fabric of their lives. "Cayle was known for carrying guns sometimes, and stuff like that. He told me, if I wanted, that he could get me a nine millimeter."

But what about the parents? Couldn't they see through a kid like that?

Both brothers laugh. Jake speaks first.

"With the grown-ups it's all about good manners. As long as you're polite, that's all it takes."

"Yeah, and Cayle was real good at that. He'd be all 'How are you today, Mrs. So-and-so?' and 'Can I help you with that?' You know." Jason smiles; it's a grim little slice of expression. "I guess we were all pretty good at laying on the act."

Jake breaks in. "Not Vinnie. He never fooled anybody. The first time our mom met him, she said he reminded her of the devil. And I never liked him from day one."

I ask why. Jake is ready with his reply.

"It had to do with his attitude. His presence. The way he'd talk to you. He wanted to be tough—he'd brag about having shot this guy or that guy. He'd brag about ripping off some guy he went to buy pot from, and then pulling out a gun and shooting him.

"And he bragged about stealing a gun from Andy Simon. And a bunch of acid."

And yet, Jason hung out with Vinnie Hebrock.

Jason grimaces. "Yeah, I did. I hung with him. And I don't know why . . ." He takes a couple of beats, thinking about it. "Probably because I wanted to be *so* badass." Then, as if I had asked, "Dave too, probably. Although I honestly think Dave felt sorry for Vinnie more than anyone else. Nobody else could stand him. Not Heather, not Kathy, for sure not Missy."

Recalling that Jason had introduced Dave to Missy Gillette, I ask him about her. He takes a moment before he speaks.

"Missy was really spoiled. By her mom, and just about everybody else too, I guess. She was gorgeous, and she knew it, and image meant everything. When she was going out with Dave, she just complained and nagged all the time—she wanted Dave to be more than he was. Not just grades and stuff, either; she wanted him to have a whole different image." He thinks for a beat or two. "More like Depeche Mode, maybe, than the Dead, you know? She was pretty dominating with him."

And Kathy? Wasn't she kind of dominating too?

"Kathy was pretty much Dave's lifeline. He basically lived with Kathy: she supported him; he ate because of her, he had clean clothes because of her."

Jason goes silent for a time, remembering, wanting to get it right. "Dave really liked Kathy a lot. And, if he could have, he would have been just with her. But he also liked Missy a lot. And, if he could have, he would have been just with her. See?"

He nods his head in a fast up and down motion, like someone who is sure they have delivered the correct answer to a riddle. "But I think he liked both of them the same—for different reasons—and he couldn't pick one or the other. I think Dave was looking for Kathy's attitude and Missy's looks stuck into one."

Jason glances over at his brother; Jake has been listening intently. From outside the kitchen door one of a pair of family dogs sets up a racket of barking. Jake murmurs an apology and gets up from the table. Jason goes on talking.

"I remember once I tried to interest Dave in a really nice girl, the friend of a girl I was going out with. Pretty, not demanding at all—just a really nice girl. So they went out a couple of times and Missy just *hated* her. So Dave gave up. He went back to Missy, and then he went back to Kathy, and the whole thing started up again."

I ask about Dave's mother, Pam. Where was she during all of this? How much input into Dave's life did she provide? Jason laughs out loud. Then, embarrassed, he stops abruptly and gives me a serious look.

"Are you kidding? Dave's mom was usually asleep on the couch. And we'd all be back in the garage, getting stoned."

Sometimes. Dave was seeing Vinnie Hebrock as often as he was with either Kathy or Missy. Jason Cheever would hang with them on occasion, but when it was time for a ramble, Dave and Vinnie would go out alone. If they didn't actually commit any crimes, they would stalk the streets, checking out places that seemed ripe for a break-in. Vinnie talked constantly about scoring a police scanner, a device that looked like a walkie-talkie, with a number pad and an antenna. Vinnie told Dave if you had one of those babies hanging off your belt, you could plug right into the police lines. You could be *doing* the crime and you'd know if and when the cops were going to show up.

Vinnie swore they'd have one before long—he was onto a lead. In the meantime, there was dope to deal and purses to get snatched. Summer of '89 was going to be bitchin'.

. . . .

Coming back home the afternoon after the graduation dance, Dave is surprised to see Missy's car parked in front of the house. He's surprised again when she throws her arms around him and begins a rambling apology for walking out on him after the ceremony. Ignoring the angry look his mother throws at him, Dave returns Missy's hug, knowing she has provided him with the perfect out.

"Come on down to my house later. My mom's away." Missy's whisper tickles his ear.

Pam Adkins turns and walks quickly out of the room.

. . . .

"What's that red mark on your chest?"

They've just eased themselves into the hot tub on the patio at Missy's house. Missy leans forward to poke at the reddened patch of skin. Dave pushes her hand to one side; she knows what the mark is, she's given enough of them: it's a hickey.

"Kathy Macaulay gave it to you, didn't she?"

Nothing from Dave.

"*Didn't* she?"

"So what? You fuckin' bailed on me. . . ."

"Does that mean you have to go fuck her? It just gives me the creeps that you go from me to her, it's like you put us in the same category." She slides away from him, edging toward the other side of the tub. Dave knows all her moves; in another minute she'll be out of there, ordering him to get dressed and go on home.

"Chill out, Missy. I got the fuckin' hickey at the dance."

"Oh, yeah? Who gave it to you?"

"Who do you think?"

"Chris O'Donnell did *that?*"

He doesn't say anything. He sinks down in the steaming water, looking up at Missy with a teasing, unblinking stare. She looks away, looks back; her lips twitch into a thin smile.

"Why, that little slut."

. . . .

That fall, Dave Adkins enters South Pasadena High as a freshman. He hasn't called Kathy Macaulay since the night of the eighth-grade graduation dance and now, at school, they tend to avoid each other. It's another story between Kathy and Missy Gillette. There is open warfare between them and any time they pass each other, in the halls or at the cafeteria, hissed insults are exchanged.

"Bitch!"

"Slut!"

Everyone at school knows about the feud. As usual, Dave keeps out of it.

A month into the school year, Dave and Missy get into one of their fights. She tells him a boy in her class reached around the back of her desk, grabbed both her breasts, and squeezed hard. There are tears in Missy's eyes as she tells the story, and her voice comes in breathless little spurts as she talks about the physical pain, the emotional humiliation. Dave feels the burn of frustration as it begins to build.

"Who did it, Missy?"

Her eyes slide away from his face. "Oh . . . just some guy."

"Tell me his name, Missy."

"Why? What're you gonna do?" She's getting nervous.

"I'm gonna kick his ass for him, that's what I'm gonna do."

"Oh, no. Don't do that . . . " The way she's looking at him now, it's like she's flirting with him. The tears have vanished.

Frustration turns to anger. "Missy, what the fuck do you tell me this kinda shit for?"

"I told you because I thought you cared what happens to me! I guess I got that wrong."

"You know I care, but you tell me like you *want* me to do something, and then you tell me not to, and when I don't, you look at me like I'm an asshole."

"Yeah? Well, maybe that's all you are."

And she turns, walking away from him, leaving him to stare after her.

Dave hangs around the house that night. He knows the odds against Missy calling him are high, but he doesn't feel like going out. He fires up a joint, leans back against the stack of pillows in the garage, and listens to music. Fuck Missy Gillette. Fuck 'em all.

. . . .

"Dave put up with a lot of nonsense from Missy. We talked about it one night and he admitted that she was always at him, always yelling at him. I remember that was the first time we discussed the similarities between Missy and Dave's mother."

Sandie Wells has some vivid memories of Dave's relationship with Missy Gillette. She was a frequent visitor, with Dave, at Sandie's house, and more than once they argued in front of the teacher. Missy was, according to Sandie, physically aggressive. Hitting Dave. Scratching him. Biting. "He either put up with it, or he walked out of range."

Sandie was not teaching in the fall of 1989, she was pursuing a career in real estate; but just before the end of the year, she was called into a conference at South Pasadena High with Pam Adkins and the vice principal. The meeting was to discuss Dave's absences and his tardies. The two women were told he was literally failing every class and the vice principal stated, quite clearly, that if Dave didn't shape up, he would be sent to Continuation. Or, worse, to the probation officer, who would probably send the kid back to detention camp. The Job Corps was also mentioned as another possible solution. But, Sandie recalls, Pam Adkins didn't like that suggestion. "Too many criminals."

"When I talked to Dave about all of this, he didn't seem very interested. I might as well have been talking about a third person." The concern is still evident on Sandie Wells's face as she talks about it now, almost four years later. "Dave did tell me, however, that he was hanging out with a bunch of seniors, friends of Missy's. He told me they were his buddies, told me they were 'looking out for him, not letting him get high.' It was obvious to me that these older kids were using Dave to score drugs for them, and he was using [drugs], too.

I tried to convince him that he was being taken advantage of. Deaf ears."

When Pam was out of town on one of her baby-sitting jobs, Dave stayed with Sandy. One afternoon he and Missy Gillette got into an explosive fight while they were talking on the telephone. The argument was about a series of lies Dave had gotten caught in, and the conversation ended with Missy slamming down the receiver on her end.

"The instant Missy hung up on Dave, he burst into tears. He was just sobbing, begging me to drive him back to South Pas immediately. Well, that's a thirty-five-minute drive from my house, and I told him, no, I wouldn't take him back to South Pas. I suggested that we talk about the fight, and maybe we could figure something out together. Dave's tears escalated into near hysteria at that one. Finally, I got him calmed down enough to talk to me. He said, 'Just give me five minutes to go outside and smoke a cigarette, then I'll come back in and we can talk.'"

The telephone rang while Dave was outside and when Sandie picked up, Missy was on the other end. Sandie told her to hold on, she'd go get Dave.

He was gone.

Sandie got in her car and went looking; she didn't want to call the police on the kid. He was on probation, after all, and this could get him sent back to camp.

When she couldn't find Dave anywhere around her neighborhood, Sandie went back to the house, to wait. For Dave to show up. For Dave to call.

It was Missy Gillette who called, two and a half hours later. Dave is at her house, she says, he walked the whole way. Missy tells Sandie Wells it's okay with her mom if Dave spends the night. But Sandie must pick him up in the morning and take him to school.

The following morning, when Sandie picks Dave up at Missy's house, she tells him he's about to miss one more day of school. They're going back to her house for a *long* talk. Dave becomes agitated; it's very important that he go to school today, he *can't* miss classes today. Sandie ends up taking both Dave and Missy to school. As Dave gets out of the car, Sandie tells him that she'll be back at three-fifteen, to pick him up.

Three-fifteen. No Dave. Sandie waits until three-thirty, then she goes inside, to the school office. She is told that neither Dave Adkins nor Missy Gillette showed up for classes today.

Sandie is determined to find Dave. She drives first to the Roundtable. Nobody there has seen Dave for at least a day. She gets the same story at HiLife Burgers. There is no answer to her insistent ringing of the Gillette doorbell. Finally, she drives over to the Adkins house.

She can hear the pounding of the bass as soon as she gets out of her car. The front door is half-open. Sandie steps inside.

Dave is lying on the living-room floor; he's clearly stoned. Missy is stretched out on the couch. The air is blue with smoke and heavy with the smell of pot.

At that moment, Sandie Wells gives up.

"I've had it, Dave. You can stay here till your mom gets back."

Dave doesn't even bother to look at her.

"Whatever."

When Pam Adkins calls a few days later, apologizing profusely for her son's behavior, Sandie has only one word for her.

"Whatever."

Isn't this your third tardy today?"

Dave is at the locker he shares with Jason Cheever when he hears Kathy Macaulay's voice behind him. He's been running late all morning and his mood is foul. He and Missy had a blowup about him talking to Melanie last night. Now, hearing Kathy's voice, he doesn't even turn to look at her.

"Yeah. So?"

She moves in closer until she's standing next to him.

"Well, that means you have to go to Saturday school. I'll be there too."

"So what?" He still hasn't looked directly at her. If only he could act more like this with Missy.

"What's wrong with you?" Kathy's voice is filled with concern. Now he turns to look at her.

"I been having a lotta problems lately."

"Tell 'em to me."

He shuts the locker door and spins the lock.

"I don't feel like talking, Kathy." And he walks away from her, heading for class. She trots to keep up with him.

"How come you haven't been calling me for sex lately?"

Dave shrugs. As well as he knows Kathy, she still has the ability to shock him with her straightforward remarks.

"You remember my number?"

He shrugs again.

"Here, I'll give it to you." She rips a corner from a page in one of her textbooks and scribbles the number of the telephone in the guesthouse. Then she writes something next to the number and hands the scrap of paper to Dave. The message reads: "Anytime you want it, just call."

He looks at the note, looks at her. Then he laughs.

"What's wrong? You laughing at me?" Her face and throat have flushed red.

He laughs again, enjoying her discomfort a little, recognizing the small, mean rush of power.

"You dick! Fucking asshole!" Kathy's voice carries through the hallway. Dave can see kids looking toward the windowed doors of classrooms as he and Kathy move past them. As they reach the door leading out to the grounds, he crumples the note and tosses it at her.

"I don't need this. I can get laid any time I want."

Walking fast, he moves away from her. She runs to catch up with him and when she gets near enough, she kicks him, hard, on the leg. The past couple of days have been hot—temperatures in the high nineties—and Dave is wearing shorts. He looks down at his leg. It's bleeding.

"Look what you did! What the fuck's wrong with you?"

Kathy is crying now, gulping in air.

"You're an asshole, Adkins!"

The tears get to him; that's the way it always is. As soon as somebody cries—Kathy, his mom, even Missy the bitch—he softens up. Now he reaches down and scoops up the note. Kathy yanks it out of his hand.

"I don't want you to have it now!" There is real pain in her eyes.

Dave takes her hand, the one holding the ball of paper, and, even though she tries to pull away, he doesn't let go. When he speaks again, his voice is soft.

"Hey, Kathy. Let me have your number—I'm gonna call you tonight."

Kathy's fingers loosen. She stops crying.

"You are?"

Dave takes the note, smooths out the creases, and slides

it into his pocket. When he looks at Kathy again, she's smiling.

An hour or so later both of them are waiting in the principal's office to collect their tardy slips. Kathy is elated now, reaching out for Dave's hand, whispering softly to him.

"All your problems are cured now, duder. You're gonna be calling me."

Dave knows exactly what Kathy is thinking. She assumes they're back together again. He starts to say something, he knows he should set her straight about this. One of his mother's most unyielding laws is that he does not see Kathy Macaulay; if she finds out that Dave has even begun to talk to Kathy again, there will be trouble. And Dave is still on probation.

He thinks about saying something and then he shrugs. What the hell.

. . . .

"I heard you were back with Macaulay."

Bradley Wong has stopped Dave between classes. The expression on Bradley's face is amused, expectant. Like he's waiting for the punch line to a dirty joke.

"Where'd you hear that?"

"I don't know, dude. Somebody told me."

"Well, it's bullshit, dude. I'm not going out with anybody."

At noontime he spots Kathy sitting at one of the outside tables with some other girls. He signals for her to come to him; she's on her feet immediately, trotting in that kiddish way of hers.

"How come you told a bunch of people we were going out?"

Kathy giggles, looking up at him flirtatiously.

"I only told a couple of people."

"Well, fuck, man—tell 'em it's off. Because I'm still on

probation, and if my mom finds out I'm going out with you, it'll be a violation of our rules, and I could get sent back." He looks closely at Kathy. The truth is he's sorry he even started up with her again. "So just tell everybody it's off. I'm serious."

If Kathy's feelings are hurt this time, she's not about to show it. This time she nods her head and goes for a grin.

"Okay. Cool."

....

Pam Adkins's voice, at the other end of the line, sounds frantic. She tells Sandie Wells that Dave is out on the streets somewhere; he took her ATM card from her wallet and used it to get three hundred dollars from her account. Now he's out there, and nobody knows where. Can Sandie help her to find him?

It took three days. Dave wasn't at any of his regular haunts. And none of his friends knew—or would admit to knowing—where he might be. Not even Jason Cheever. Then, as Sandie drove along Fair Oaks in the late afternoon of the third day, she spotted Dave Adkins standing at the curb, ready to cross the street. She could tell, when she pulled over and opened the passenger door, that he was glad—no, relieved—to see her.

According to Sandie, when she called Pam to tell her she had found Dave and he was with her, Pam stated, unequivocally, that Sandie was to take Dave to her place. Pam didn't want him in her house.

Sandie made use of the time with Dave to convince him to meet with a drug counselor. The counselor suggested that Dave join ACT, a teen drug-counseling program. Dave agreed, and he asked Jason Cheever to go with him. Jason said okay, it sounded like a plan.

"I told Dave he could stay with me, providing he stayed on the program, attended school regularly and, in general, straightened himself out." Sandie smiles sadly. "I remember that I told him I would help him with his homework.

"Dave positively glowed in the atmosphere of a normal home. He was so proud of everything he was learning." Sandie pauses, then goes on. "He *did* cut two classes ..." She says this almost apologetically, as if she feels responsible for the lapse. "But he told me about it, and he set his own punishment. He grounded himself.

"At the end of the two-week period, Pam called—furious. She said she didn't want Dave seeing Jason, even though they were both going to ACT."

The thought that had been tugging at the edges of Sandie Wells's consciousness began to formulate into action. The prospect of taking on Dave Adkins on any kind of permanent basis was frightening; but she felt, at the deepest level, the only chance the kid had was for her to assume guardianship.

Sandie and Dave went together to see Dave's probation officer. He listened carefully, then told them Dave had to go back to his mother until a hearing could be set. Sandie drove him to his mother's house.

She goes on. In a matter of hours Dave and Pam were clashing again. Dave called and asked me to come pick him up at Jason's house. And I did. We talked to the probation officer again, the next day, and we were told, again, that Dave had to go home. So I took him back to Pam's house.

"He ran away as soon as I left. It was only a few days until the hearing, and Dave called me every day, but he wouldn't tell me where he was. I only found out when I picked him up before the hearing, because he refused to go to the proceedings with his mother. Dave called me the night before and asked me to pick him up at 'this guy's house in South Pas.' "

Sandie pulls in a deep breath, sighs it out. This is difficult for her, this retelling of events. It is clearly painful to speculate—again—how close she might have come to averting the tragedy of March 21, 1991.

"I went to the hearing armed with letters from school and from the minister of my church proclaiming me to be a good candidate for foster parenting. As I said earlier, I *was* nervous about taking on Dave Adkins, but I really knew this was his only chance. He had made such an improvement during the two weeks he was with me.

"At the courthouse Pam was nearly hysterical. She was sobbing and saying, to anyone who would listen, that *no one* was going to take her son away from her."

According to Sandie Wells, Pam Adkins took Dave aside, there in the courthouse, and told him that if he agreed to go home with her, the court would not send him to jail for violation of his probation.

"Dave came up to me and asked me not to present my case for his custody. And I agreed. *Much* against my better judgment."

The way things turned out, Dave Adkins didn't go home with his mother or Sandie Wells. Believing that Pam Adkins had no control over her son's behavior, the judge sent Dave to placement at the Boys Republic in Chino, California.

Vinnie, left with only Jason Cheever as an on-and-off friend, managed to get a part-time job, cleaning up in a gas station near his mother's apartment. His sister, Tiki, had worked there for a while and she recommended Vinnie to the owner. It was as good a way as any to pass the time while he waited for Dave Adkins to come home.

....

Dave sticks it out at Chino for a couple of months. Then, despite good reports from his counselor there, he AWOLs. He is picked up, and this time he is sent to the Masada Group Home in West L.A. Masada is the name for a series of foster homes in which small groups of boys live under the supervision of counselors or, in some instances, a married couple.

SMOKED

The boys are bused, daily, from the West L.A. Masada to the Masada School in Lawndale.

It is Kathy Macaulay who comes to see Dave every day. She has a car of her own now, a twelve-year-old T-Bird she calls "the Hooptie." The Hooptie's interior is tagged with streetwise graffiti and cluttered with empty beer cans and crumpled cigarette packs. The exterior of the car sports an array of stickers and decals: Iron Maiden, the Grateful Dead, Sex-Wax (the brand name of a surfboard wax). Masada allows visitors, but Dave and Kathy take it a step further, driving in to South Pasadena every chance they get.

After the guesthouse up at Kathy's parents' home, Andrea Tynan's garage apartment is as safe a place as any for Dave. All the kids in their crowd go there to party. It was, according to a later conversation with Dave, all about "sex, drugs, cards (a game called Spades), and rock 'n' roll. Way more than at Kathy's."

On one of these outings, Vinnie and Heather are already at the garage when Dave and Kathy arrive. Andrea and her boyfriend of the moment slide over to make room at the card table; a shoebox lid filled with cleaned pot and rolling papers is within easy reach in the center of the table. Eight or nine half-empty twelve-packs of Bud Dry and Keystone beer are on the floor. Dave begins to roll fat joints and Kathy pops a couple of cans from the case she and Dave brought with them. The cards are dealt. An early Cure tape plays at top volume.

People are smoking, passing two and three joints around at a time. The card game has everyone's attention and they play without speaking. Then, without apparent reason, Heather begins to laugh. In a second or two Andrea joins in.

Dave and Kathy exchange glances.

"What's so funny?" Dave's voice carries an edge of annoyance.

Heather and Andrea don't even look at him; it's like he

hasn't spoken. He looks at Vinnie. Vinnie shrugs uneasily. Now Dave leans forward in his chair.

"Don't you two have the fucking balls to tell the rest of us what's so funny?"

Now Vinnie pipes up. "Yeah. What's so funny?"

Heather looks at Vinnie for a long moment. Then, taking her time, she places her cards, one by one, facedown on the table. She never takes her eyes from Vinnie's, not once. When he tries to outstare her, she laughs again, softly this time. Everyone is watching the two of them.

"I asked you what the fuck was so fuckin' funny?" There's an edge of swagger in Vinnie's tone. Heather has made no secret of the way she feels about him; she hates him.

"Are you sure you want to know?" Heather's voice is flirtatious.

"Fuck, yeah, I wanna know."

"You're sure?"

"Yeah, bitch. I'm sure."

Now Heather smiles sweetly. "Well, it's this, twit-wit: You're the ugliest motherfucker I ever saw in my life."

Andrea erupts into a braying laugh; Heather giggles loudly. Andrea's boyfriend smiles and reaches down for another beer. Neither Dave nor Kathy can hide their amusement.

"What the fuck you mean, you fuckin' bitch?" Vinnie's voice is high-pitched with rage. "You're the ugly one, you fuckin' slut! You look like a man, and you got them pictures, them tattoos and shit, all over your hands." He looks down at his cards dismissively. "Fuckin' slut."

He doesn't see Heather as she picks up the heavy glass ashtray from the center of the table. Andrea makes a grab for it, but before she can connect, Heather hurls it straight at Vinnie's face. But her aim is off and the ashtray sails past his head to slam into the wall. Ashes, cigarette butts, and roaches scatter everywhere.

Kathy tries to lighten the moment. "Shit, Heather. You got ashes all over the fuckin' cards."

Vinnie leaps to his feet and storms out of the garage, knocking over a coat rack near the door. Everyone at the table can hear him as he kicks his way through some plastic toys left in the backyard by Andrea's younger brother. Then there is the screech of rusting gate hinges and Vinnie's voice, yelling:

"FUCKIN' BITCH!"

Kathy and Andrea begin to clear up the mess. Heather goes into the bathroom. Andrea's boyfriend is fussing with tapes.

Andrea glances at Dave. "Go tell that asshole he can't ever come back here."

Vinnie is on his bike when Dave gets outside.

"Why'd you go off, dude? You know how bitchy Heather is."

"Yeah? Well, fuck her. I'm outta here." He pedals toward the corner, slows, stops, turns to look at Dave again.

"They're all bitches, man. Don't you know it yet?"

. . . .

"Kathy was into some bad stuff. A lotta drugs. They all were."

Two more boys have joined us around the table at the Cheever house: Eric Bonworthy and Michael Cruz; they are both seniors at South Pasadena High. Eric is redheaded, tall, but not outsized in the way of most football players. There is about him a rather careless grace; he looks as if he knows that he will fit in wherever he chooses to place himself. The other boy is shorter and rather shy. He sits awkwardly in his chair, but with a loose-hung individuality. He defers often to Eric, and to Jason, but in an easy way, without apparent rancor. Now he adds his comment to Eric's assessment of Kathy.

"She did a lotta coke, lotta acid, lotta pot smoking and

drinking. She, like, knew all the most popular people—the football players and stuff—but she also knew the other people, the outlaws. And she chose to get closer to *them*. She chose to hang with them."

I ask if Kathy's drift toward another crowd might not have been caused when the jock crowd dropped her. Eric speaks up quickly.

"I always talked to her. Always."

Mike Cruz continues. "This town is just fucked up from the beginning. It's the way people view things around here. The way they act." He hesitates for a moment, looks at Jason and Eric, then looks back at me. "It's acceptance."

Eric nods his head. "Yeah. If you're not a football player—or whatever—then you can't really be cool. And then, there's some people"—he glances quickly at Jason, and then at Mike, as if he needs their approval to finish his thought—"well, the girls. There's a lotta back-stabbing."

Jason names three girls in rapid succession. "Girls like them, and some of their friends. Those girls are bitches."

"Yeah, they are. And if you don't dress right, and if you don't get the right guys, and if you're . . . overweight, those girls will just give you so much bullshit." Mike sounds as if he might be having trouble believing what he just said.

"You know what, though? Kathy didn't take shit from *anybody*. Kathy was *down*. And Heather? Heather was the craziest girl I've ever known in my life." Eric employs the adjective as if it is a rare compliment; his voice has risen in excitement.

"She tried to fight this guy once. An alcoholic—big time. And, he's got this problem, see? He thinks he's invincible when he's drunk. This is a huge guy, too: he's like six two, about two hundred thirty. Huge." Eric smiles fondly now. "And Heather—who's not even five feet, who weighs in at about eighty-five pounds—Heather tries to fight him."

He is silent for a long moment. "I remember when we

were all in the eighth grade and Heather got her first tattoo. She was just so proud of it.

"And all those different haircuts she'd get? All those Mohawks and punker shit, and all those different dyes she'd put on it?" Mike is smiling now, too.

"A lot of people were scared of Heather Goodwin. But you know what? I think she was just one loony girl."

. . . .

Heather Goodwin and Al Binder were inseparable after that first night. He can remember how smitten he was, how wonderful she was to be with. "Heather was just so damn smart. She was always either one step ahead of me, or right next to me. I had never met a girl who could keep up, let alone move on ahead the way Heather did."

But his shyness about kissing her continued until well into the second week of the relationship. Then, one night, as they were walking in the small park near South Pasadena High, Heather slowed her pace and looked up at Al.

"Fuck it."

And she kissed him, reaching up with both arms to draw his head down to meet hers.

They made love, there in the park. Al Binder was fifteen years old, Heather Goodwin was fourteen; they each knew what they wanted.

"We were side by side, every day, all day, from then on."

Al is at my house; he has come over after an afternoon class at Pasadena City College. At the age of twenty, Al Binder has gotten serious about his life. He is making A's and B's in all of his courses, preparing for pre-med in two years. He also works on his drawing; Al has a real talent for art. He has brought some of his work with him today, to show me. Meticulous, intricate stuff, reminiscent of Escher.

There is little left, in the way Al looks now, to remind you of his punker days. The tattoos, maybe. And the anarchy symbol that Heather carved into his arm that first night. The scar has since been reinforced with a deep red tattoo. There are other scars, too: shiny, white tissue left on his chest and stomach by random acts of self-mutilation. A thick, pink line moves diagonally across the inside of his left forearm. And if you look closely at his face, you can see a series of holes punched into the cartilage of both ears, and the hole drilled above one nostril where he used to wear a ring. But if Al didn't point out the scars to you, you would never imagine that this handsome, clean-shaven young man in the khaki trousers and plain black T-shirt had ever presented himself in any other way.

I ask him about Heather's parents, how they reacted to him when they first met. He smiles thinly. "Mimi Goodwin always trusted me—she saw beyond the look. She was like another kid to me, one of my peers." The smile broadens slightly as he thinks about those first months with Heather. "The first time Heather spent the night with me, I called her mom. To let her know so she wouldn't worry." His expression sobers now. "I never really got to know Heather's father. None of her friends did, he didn't even speak to any of us. Dave told me he bumped into Heather's dad in the hall at Heather's house one time, and Dave said 'Hi' and Mr. Goodwin just walked right on by like he didn't see Dave."

Al shakes his head, grinning slightly, sadly. "I guess you could say he was kinda remote. I know Heather always felt rejected by his remoteness. She used to say she didn't know what she was gonna do when her older brother moved out of the house. She could at least talk to her brother."

Al remembers that Heather did get the transfer from San Marino to South Pas in the fall of 1988. But then, during the first quarter, she dropped out of school.

"It wasn't about school for Heather. It was all about getting outta the house and onto the street."

Al didn't like many of Heather's friends. Dave was okay

and Jason, he told her, but most of her girlfriends, like Kathy, or Andrea, were too shallow. So Heather began to hang out with Al's crowd, in Pasadena.

"We would party in the parking lot near the E-Bar, next to the railroad tracks. That whole setting made a good backdrop for the attitude we had then. The broken wall and the tracks and all."

Some of Al's friends, kids on the drift like him, lived in a communal fashion in a garage (of the house belonging to one of the group's parents) in Pasadena. There were sleeping bags and mattresses laid out on the floor; the walls were covered with posters and anarchistic slogans. Sid Vicious, of the Sex Pistols, was a particular hero. Heather and Al spent a good deal of time at "the Garage," as the people who gathered there called it. It was the place where, in a later conversation, Al Binder would say they "got to know each other." The place where one of Al's friends would teach Heather how to do tattoos, where the same boy would give her the nickname "Tinkerbell," where she would pierce Al's nose.

There was another group, this one from South Pasadena, who rented an apartment in Pasadena. These were slightly older kids, from South Pas Continuation classes, about ten people in all. Al describes them as "shorthaired, regular kids who fried every weekend." And he and Heather put in time with them, too.

Dave Adkins and Kathy Macaulay were not included in either group. Neither was Vinnie Hebrock.

By the early months of 1990, things were "getting too hectic with drugs and stuff" between Al Binder and Heather Goodwin. He says, now, that they were "fighting a lot. Then we'd make up, have sex, and go to sleep at about three A.M. Then we'd wake up, have sex, go out, fight, go home, fight, have sex, and sleep. It was just too much of a vicious cycle, and it got dull. Both of us felt trapped in the monotony of the situation, but each of us was jealous of the other. And

Heather had gotten so aggressive by then that I felt she had turned into *me*. Me, in a dress. And that wasn't good, either."

Finally, they broke up, with Al telling Heather that she'd be "better off back in South Pas."

They didn't see each other for six months. Then they got together—and got drunk—at a party in San Marino and made love in the front yard. The mutual attraction was still potent, but it simply wasn't possible to get back together. Al had already begun to move in a different direction. He was drifting less and Heather Goodwin seemed more lost than ever.

. . . .

One evening, during one of the forbidden outings from the West L.A. Masada home, Dave and Kathy drop in on a party in South Pasadena. Missy Gillette is there, too. Dave confronts her and tells her "not to run and snitch to my mom." He tells her to "be a grown-up." Missy turns swiftly and strides away from him. A few minutes later one of the South Pas stoners, a guy Dave doesn't know, calls him a dick, repeating it several times for effect. Dave sets down his forty-ouncer and walks over to the guy.

"Shut the fuck up, dude."

The guy turns to look at him, affecting surprise. "What'd you say, dickhead?"

"You heard what I said. I told you to shut the fuck up."

The guy swings at Dave. It's a wild haymaker that falls short of the mark.

Dave unleashes a solid right to the jaw. It catches the guy flat-footed and it nearly sends him crashing into a glass door. A couple of girls scream and people move in close to watch.

One of the guy's friends, another stoner, comes at Dave with an empty beer bottle. Dave manages to wrench it out of his hand, then Dave pulls back and brings the bottle down, hard, on the stoner's head. The guy slumps to the floor, a thread of blood welling at his hairline. There is a sharp intake of breath from the people standing near the action. Dave doesn't seem to notice; he is already walking away.

The next day Pam Adkins calls her son at the Masada house. She knows all about the party in South Pasadena, all about the fight. Dave and she argue until he hangs up on her. Within days Dave has been transferred to another Masada home. This one is further away, in Redondo Beach, a two-hour drive down the coast. There's no way the Hooptie can make that trip twice a day.

No problem.

Within a short time Kathy has a new car, a Ford Bronco given to her by her mother. Now she can drive down to see Dave every day. Sometimes the two of them walk a few blocks away from the house, down to a place they call their "main hangout," a quiet spot in a secluded area of the beach. Other days Kathy drives Dave back to South Pasadena and he spends the night with her in the guesthouse. On those occasions Kathy drives him, the following morning, to the Masada school in Lawndale. Neither her mother nor her stepfather know about these arrangements. Only Heather knows. And Heather can be trusted not to tell.

One weekend they go to a party at Jason Cheever's house. Everybody there is surprised and happy to see their buddy, Dave. People crowd around him; icy beer cans are piled in his arms, and soon everyone is pounding back drink after drink. Tightly wrapped joints are brought out and passed around. Somebody brings out an eighth of coke. Somebody else adds to it. The house is packed with kids, music is blasting, people are enjoying themselves.

"Missy Gillette's outside! You better hide or she'll snitch on you to your mom." Two girls have run in, breathless with the news.

Dave looks at Kathy and gets up to leave. His friends clamor for him to stay where he is—no way will Missy be allowed into the house.

Jason and three older, bigger kids he has hired as bouncers go outside to confront Missy. She is standing on the front porch with three of her satellites.

"You guys can't come inside. It's too crowded." Jason doesn't like Missy enough to bother with small talk.

"Oh. I get it." She turns to her girlfriends. "Dave's here with the slut." She takes a step forward; Jason moves to stand in front of her, effectively barring entrance to the house.

"Hey! He ain't here, and you can't come in."

Missy Gillette isn't about to engage in a shoving match. She saunters off to sit, pouting, on the hood of a car.

Jason and the three guys go back into the house. In a few minutes Dave appears on the porch.

"Hi, Dave . . . " Missy's delivery is sing song, teasing.

"Why do you have to snitch to my mom?"

"Why do you have to act like an asshole?"

"Hey, just mind your own, Missy."

Now Kathy has stepped out on the porch. She slips her arm around Dave's waist in a possessive gesture. "C'mon, duder. Let's go back inside."

Without a glance at Missy, Dave turns to walk back inside the house.

"Hey, fuck you, Dave!" Missy's voice carries clearly across the lawn. Kathy turns to look at her.

"You better shut your mouth before I kick your fucking ass."

Dave has already stepped inside the house. Now Kathy walks in behind him and shuts the door with a resounding thump. Heather is upon her immediately.

"Who was that?"

Kathy shrugs; it isn't even worth talking about. Heather turns to Dave.

"Who'd she tell she was gonna beat up?" It's a demand as much as a question.

"Nobody. Forget it, Heather." Dave doesn't want any more trouble.

But Missy has moved her act around to the backyard, and when Dave and Kathy go into the kitchen, they can hear her voice. She is talking about them. At top volume.

Kathy takes the bait.

"I'm gonna go kick her ass."

"If you do, I'm outta here."

Kathy delivers a slow, steady look that approaches contempt. Then she tosses the keys to the Bronco to Dave.

He is halfway to the front door when he hears people yelling:

"Fight! Chick fight!"

Dave races around to the backyard. Kathy is holding Missy in a headlock as she punches the taller, slimmer girl in the face. A crowd of kids has formed a loose, noisy circle around the two girls. Heather is leading the cheers for Kathy.

Missy manages to break free of the headlock, then she pulls back and connects with a right to Kathy's eye. Kathy punches her back, hard. Missy falls, chipping her tooth on the edge of a stone bench. Heather launches a roar of approval.

The fight's over. Missy sits on the ground, crying; both hands are cupped at her mouth. The three bouncers move in on Kathy, to put her out of the party, but people begin to yell their disapproval. Everyone wants Kathy—and Dave—to stay. Throw that bitch, Missy, out.

Kathy resolves the situation. "No, it's cool. Me and Dave are gonna bail. We want some time alone, anyway."

When Dave gets back to Masada the next morning, his mother has already called. Missy told her about Kathy, the party, the fight. When Dave calls home, Pam is still angry, and even though he brazens it out, things between them are more strained than ever.

For Kathy Macaulay, things are great. She's seeing Dave Adkins every day.

I was backed up against the garage door when Kathy and Missy were going at it. I had a can of beer in either hand, and I remember standing there, thinking, 'Oh, man—they're gonna hit *me* . . . ' " Eric is speaking.

I ask Eric if he had a date with him at the party.

He nods his head, yes. I ask if she and Kathy got along.

"Nuh-uh. No way. 'Cause Kathy liked *me*—for years."

Jason and Mike nod their heads now, affirming this statement, and Eric continues.

"She'd come up to me at parties and tell me, right in front of my girlfriend, that she loved me. One night—right in this house—Kathy tried to fight Robin, that's my girlfriend, and Robin was just terrified. 'Cause Kathy had Heather and some other girl with her."

"And his girlfriend is a mean little fighter, too." Jason grins as he says this.

"Yeah, she is. But she was scared." Eric lights a cigarette and sighs out a long plume of smoke. "Like, one night Kathy had a party, and Robin was all 'Please, don't let's go up there—let's just go to the movies.' And I was, like, 'Okay, we'll do whatever you want.' 'Cause Robin was literally terrified. She didn't want any part of that crowd; she didn't want to get her ass kicked." He takes another deep drag on his cigarette. "To tell the truth, though, Robin was mostly afraid of Heather and Andrea. Not Kathy."

Leaning forward in his chair, he stubs out the cigarette. "I'll tell you something else about those girls; they were deeper into their music than anyone else I ever met. I mean,

I'm into sports, okay? I play football, or baseball, four hours a day, six days a week. When I'm not doing that, I'm doing homework, and when I'm not doing homework, I'm hanging out with my friends. My music is classical rock—the Doors, Hendrix. Sometimes I'll listen to this Death Rock band, Ministry. *They* liked the Cure and Motorhead and the Dead. Heather even put a Cure tattoo on herself. Her and Kathy and Andrea were just ... *involved* with their music; it was playing all day long, all night."

Eric pauses for a couple of beats, then he goes on. "You know, to me, singing a love song because you're upset over a girl is one thing, but to literally live your life by this music ... " He shrugs eloquently. "There was just *always* the music."

Jason has been listening intently. Now he clears his throat before he speaks. "It was when Heather was going with Al that she got into Metal."

Eric grins. "Yeah. Al ... crazy Al."

Jason is grinning, too. "Al was in my grade up until Freshman or Sophomore year, and he was like this little surfer person. And then he ..."

Eric cuts in. "He was even a water-polo player ..."

Jason nods in agreement. " ... he moved to the desert. And then he came back, and he was ... "

Eric finishes the thought: " ... a skinhead."

Jason doesn't agree with that assessment. "More of a punker. Completely changed. Wearing all black, and combat boots, his head shaved. Then he had twin 'hawks. Then he shaved off one of the 'hawks and his hair was just growing down one side and shaved off on the other."

"Then Heather started going out with him and she got a 'hawk, too."

Both boys are talking fast now, breaking in on one another's sentences.

"And then, remember? *She* got twin 'hawks"—Eric nods

his head, he remembers; Jason goes on—"one was pink and one was green."

"And earrings. Lots of earrings."

Jason nods his head again in a fast little gesture. "And she and Al used to talk about walking down the street, and if they'd see a pin lying there, they'd pick it up and he'd stick it through his ear. Just to do it."

"And how about the lighters?" He looks at Jason. "You got your lighter?"

Eric had lit his own cigarette with a wooden match; now Jason hands him one of those brightly colored plastic lighters. Eric fiddles with it for a second, then he flicks the wheel and the flame springs up a couple of inches, burning hotly.

"They'd turn the flame up high, see, like this, and then they'd turn it on and hold the lighter upside down, till the metal end got really hot, and then they'd burn it into their hands and arms to make a little smiley-face brand."

Eric hands the lighter to me, and when I look at the business end, I can see that it would burn a rudimentary smiling face into the skin if someone got it hot enough. And pressed it down long enough.

"Two or three at a time." Jason takes back the lighter and pockets it again. "They'd sit in her room and do it, over and over." Then, in afterthought, "And Heather pierced Al's nose. And his nipple."

Mike Cruz has been listening with rapt attention, turning his head to look at each boy as he speaks. Now, when Jason mentions the piercing, Mike winces and sucks in air through his teeth; it makes a hissing sound.

Eric glances at him for an instant, then he looks at me again. "Most of us made a smiley-face burn at one time or another, but with us it was a game of chicken. With them, it was to hurt themselves."

"Yeah. It was. Like, they'd put out cigarettes on their arms. Or they'd press their arms together and stick the end of a lit cigarette in there, and the first person to move their arm would be the chicken." Jason looks down at his hands which are folded together on the tabletop. One of the dogs in the backyard begins a series of staccato barks. Jason looks up at me again.

"I saw Al in the summer of '91, and he's totally changed. Totally straight and sober. He went to AA, he's going to school . . . " His voice trails off and he shakes his head in the same slow movement he used earlier. "I remember they got in a fight once, him and Heather, 'cause he was in one of his depressions, or something. It happened right in front of this house. Anyway, they were fighting and he took out this knife and just slashed himself across the arm. Just a *huge* gash, really deep and wide. It was totally disgusting—there was blood everywhere."

A year later, Al himself would tell me what happened that night. "It was true; I guess I was depressed. Because I *was* isolating, but there was no fight. We were kicking back at Jason's house, just the three of us—me, him, and Heather—in his room. And we had all been drinking, hard liquor, and Jason and Heather were talking. Small talk, this and that, nothing in particular. I was maybe saying 'yeah' or 'no' every once in a while, but they were the ones having the conversation.

"Heather and Jason stepped outside for a minute— there's a big window in Jason's room that you can walk in and out of, we were always doing that. Anyway, they were standing just outside the room, talking. It was a mellow evening, outside of what was in my head."

His eyes shift focus for an instant; you can see his thoughts travel back in time, then return again to the present. "Jason's Swiss Army knife was on the table—I'd been playing with it, checking out all of the parts while they were talking." Now he grins crookedly.

"With me it was always, 'fuck it.' That was my motto.

My . . . 'whatever.' And so, here's this knife"—Al's hands carve the air, miming a many-bladed knife—"and I opened it to . . . the smallest blade, actually, and I slashed my arm. Zip. Like that . . . " His index finger traces a fast, diagonal path across the inside of his forearm. "No reason. Well, maybe a reason. Back then I wasn't looking too deep. The actions just came around."

"Man, I'm not into that stuff at all." Eric's voice is very soft now. "The reason why my friends didn't hang out with those kids is because they were into things you just don't do." He makes a short, dismissive gesture with one hand. "Not because Kathy Macaulay was overweight—or whatever. I mean"—he is speaking hesitantly now, searching for the words he needs—"they were into things you just *don't do.* I mean, we all used to hang out at the Roundtable 'til about ten at night. And all of us were having family problems, we were all kind of tripping out.

"But nobody dropped Kathy because she got fat. She was always kinda chubby. Always. And she was always popular. She got dropped, if that's what you want to call it, because she started doing cocaine. And hanging out with people who other people didn't want to be associated with. She just went"—Eric points his left hand in one direction—"that way, and we went *that*"—his right hand points in the opposite direction—"way. Her girlfriends became cheerleaders and Kathy became a partier and a stoner."

Now Eric leans forward on both arms, looking directly at me. "Those kids were into things you just . . . *do not do.* People knew about them, they knew what they were like, but nobody spoke about it. It was like . . . unspoken secrets."

Eric's eyes shift to Jason. And both boys nod their heads in tacit agreement. "Yeah. Unspoken secrets."

Then Jason looks at me again. "I used to say one thing to Dave, and I said it a *lot,* from the time we first met Vinnie. And it was that Vinnie was either going to wind up dead or wind up in jail. And that he was going to take Dave down with him. I remember saying that so much: 'He's gonna bring you down, man.' " Jason pauses for an instant. "And Dave would listen, like always, and then he'd kinda shrug, like always, and he'd say, 'Whatever.' " Another short pause. "Like always."

....

Thanksgiving rolls around and, although Dave tells his mother that one of the Masada officials will drive him to Pasadena, it's Kathy who picks him up in Redondo Beach and drops him off at home. Missy Gillette and her younger sister, Meredith, are at the house when he walks in. Dave hugs his mother and greets Dan and Meredith warmly; he nods coolly to Missy. Then he pulls up his shirtsleeve to show Dan his new tattoo of the ace of spades.

"Did you cover up *our* tattoo?" Missy's tone borders on outrage.

Dave yanks his shirt up higher to display the red heart surrounded by his and Missy's initials.

"See? It's still fuckin' there, bitch!"

He's not really angry; Missy has just shown him that she still cares about him, that she can still be moved to jealousy. Pam comes out of the kitchen, insisting that Dave apologize for his language, then she shepherds everyone to the table for Thanksgiving dinner.

After the meal, after the singing and the cake—it's Dan's birthday—the four youngsters go out to the backyard for a joint. In a few minutes things begin to warm up between Dave and Missy. The only problem is she's going out of town for two days. So is Pam; she'll be caring for the toddlers of the family she works for, going on vacation with them.

The following day Dave and Dan travel to Orange County for another holiday meal with their grandmother, Pam's mother. But it's too quiet out there for the boys; after dinner,

Dave calls Kathy and asks her to come pick them up. She arrives less than two hours later with Heather and Andrea, and the five of them go back to Fairlawn Way.

Kathy's older brother, Michael, is home from Stanford for Thanksgiving. One of his dorm buddies is with him for the weekend. Which means that the two guys will stay in the guesthouse while Kathy goes back to her own room in the main house. But for now, everybody goes up to the little apartment over the garage to get high before dinner. The plan is for Dave to go with Kathy, Michael, and his guest to the main house (for a second Thanksgiving feast), while Dan, Heather, and Andrea stay up in the guesthouse. Then, later, some more kids will come over and everybody will party.

The party is still going strong at 1:00 A.M. Some of the boys have moved the speakers from the guesthouse out to the balcony and music is blasting into the night. People are jumping into the pool from the roof of the main house just outside Kathy's parents' room. At some point, Kathy's mother calls out the window:

"Katherine! What's going on out there?"

"Oh, we're just swimming and diving, Mom."

"Okay, but keep the music down. It's late."

People start to leave soon after this exchange; Dan, Heather, and Andrea pile into the Bronco with Dave and Kathy. Dan has been flirting unsuccessfully all evening with Heather and Andrea in turn, and now, as the car pulls up in front of the Adkins house, he looks at Kathy.

"You guys comin' in?"

Heather nudges Kathy, hard. Kathy smiles sweetly at Dan.

"Nuh-uh. We're still way wired. See ya, Dan."

And the Bronco takes off. Kathy drops off Heather and Andrea, then she and Dave go back up to Fairlawn Way.

For the remainder of that long holiday weekend, Dave spends most of his time at Kathy's house.

SMOKED

He's surprised at the way Kathy behaves toward her mother. It seems like no matter what her mom says to her, Kathy's got some snotty little remark ready. Dave is aware that he's disrespectful to his own mother a lot of the time, but this situation between Kathy and her folks seems more intense than that. She pretty much ignores her stepfather, but that's no surprise; after all, she refers to him as "the Lame." What Dave didn't expect is Kathy's always telling Mrs. Koss off—and her mom taking it.

Dave's theory, unshared with Kathy, was that Mrs. Koss didn't want to get in Kathy's way. It seemed as if she was afraid of Kathy, or of what Kathy might do. Dave had seen the same look of panic in Pam's eyes when he and his brother Dan got into one of their punch-outs: she'd sidestep the issue, just look away until things calmed down.

At some point before his trial, Dave recalled a screaming match between Kathy and Mrs. Koss. He says he told Kathy to "chill out," and that Kathy simply yelled, "*Fuck* her!" right in front of her mother. The incident itself isn't what stunned Dave. What he found so difficult to understand was that, moments after the face-off, Kathy asked for—and got—fifty dollars from her mother.

When Missy Gillette came back to town after Thanksgiving, Dave knew he would have to choose between her and Kathy Macaulay, but it was simpler to ignore the situation. He wouldn't make a decision, he simply let things stand as they were, allowing himself to be passed back and forth like a kitten between these two overtly aggressive girls.

It was an uneventful time and when he went back to Placement, Dave was told that he would be allowed, from then on, to go home every weekend.

Missy was thrilled by the news. She had no way of knowing that Kathy Macaulay would continue to make her daily drive to Redondo Beach.

Shortly after Thanksgiving, something happened between Kathy and Missy Gillette that shocked even Dave: the two girls talked to each other at school one day, and when they discovered that Dave had been seeing both of them, they forged a truce between themselves.

On the afternoon of Christmas Eve, 1990, Dave was told that he would be allowed to go home for Christmas vacation. He left the Masada house with the firm understanding that he would return by noon of the 31st, New Year's Eve. Pam Adkins went out of town the day after Christmas to baby-sit.

Everybody in Dave's crowd started to give parties: Kathy; Missy; Jason. Dave took advantage of his mother's absence to throw an open house.

The year was over; 1990 was about to turn into 1991.

. . . .

Every party-down kid at South Pasadena High is invited to Richie Andrusco's New Year's Eve blast at the Andrusco house on Grand Avenue in Pasadena. Richie Andrusco is twenty years old, but he still lives at home and he prefers the company of high school kids. The Andrusco house, a vast, three-storied Dutch Colonial built in the 1920s, is the perfect party arena.

Dave isn't about to miss New Year's Eve with his friends. And for once, with this so-called truce between Kathy and Missy, he figures they can all be in the same place at the same time without any hassles.

By eleven o'clock it looks as if it's going to be a peaceful celebration.

Just before midnight, people start walking up toward Orange Grove Boulevard where the Rose Parade floats are being set up for the next day's parade. Orange Grove is mobbed: entire families have staked out space along the curb; people are settling into sleeping bags for the night, they're eating picnic suppers and drinking champagne. The sounds from hundreds of boom boxes and portable TV's clash in the crisp night air.

As the South Pas group rounds the corner next to the old Wrigley estate, a mammoth Italianate villa surrounded by formal rose gardens, a bunch of kids from La Cañada High (a long time rival of South Pas) bears down on them. Insults are thrown out; insults are returned.

"Fuck La Cañada!"

"Fuck South Pas!"

A guy wearing a "La Cañada" letter jacket saunters up to stand in front of Jason Cheever, who has on his letter jacket from South Pas.

"What's up?" It's the classic gang challenge.

"What's up?" Jason lobs the immediate classic comeback. These are all white kids, from privileged communities, but the language is that of inner-city gangs.

Now the guys from South Pas are ambling toward the La Canada crowd. La Cañada rushes forward. Nobody has thrown a punch yet, but everybody is in everybody else's face. It's all about "fuck you, fuck your school."

Just as the bells and whistles start to ring 1990 into 1991, things reach a fever pitch. It's on: fists and bottles are the only weapons, but after the fight is over, after the police have surrounded the field, an ambulance is called for a couple of kids who have sustained injuries.

Back at the Andrusco house everybody compares bloody knuckles and broken fingers. Dave has a sprained pinky on his left hand, but when Kathy Macaulay tries to comfort him, he pushes her aside. He and Missy, Jason and his date, go outside to sit on the hood of Jason's car. They're sharing a joint when four guys from La Cañada round the corner of California and Grand.

"Which one of you assholes fucked up my little brother?"

"What?" Dave acts like he doesn't know what the guy's talking about.

"You from South Pas?" The guy gives Dave a fast once-over.

"Yeah."

Missy cuts in. "No! He's not."

The guy doesn't even look at her. "I asked which one of you fucked up my little brother?"

Jason slides down from the hood of the car. "It was a fight, dude. If he couldn't handle it, he shouldn't've been there."

Dave slides off the hood, too. As he hits the ground, the La Cañada guy pulls a snub-nosed revolver from the waistband of his jeans.

"Hey, dude, put the fuckin' gun away." It's one of his buddies, clearly unwilling to let this beef accelerate into gunplay. The guy with the gun starts to put it back in his waistband.

Jason takes a step forward.

"I fucked up your little brother."

Dave moves in front of him.

"No, I did."

The kid with the gun pulls it out again, only his buddy, the one who told him to put it away, is too fast. He grabs it and sticks it in the back of his own waistband, under his jacket. Then he zips up the jacket and looks, for a couple of long beats, at Dave and Jason.

"You guys are real assholes." And he and the other three kids with him turn and walk back up California Boulevard. Dave and Missy, Jason and his girlfriend, go back inside to join the party.

When Dave calls Masada the next day, New Year's Day, there is no answer. When he calls again on January 2, he is told that he is no longer acceptable at Placement.

"Shit, what am I supposed to do now?"

"You could get a job."

. . . .

"Two nights after the New Year's Eve fight, me and Dave were at my house talking about it. About fifteen people had come over, and me and Dave went out on the porch, just me and him for about twenty minutes. I asked him what he did, 'cause I heard he really laid into some guy. And me and this other guy, Terry, we gave some dude a pretty good beating too."

Eric Bonworthy is speaking. We have ordered pizza and Cokes and now we are eating as we sit around the table at Jason Cheever's house. Jason's father has come home from work; after introductions are made, he goes into another room to catch the early news.

"So we're talking about what we saw, and what we did, and how crazy it all was, and how our beef with La Cañada had been going on for so many years that it doesn't even have that much to do with any of us now. And then we started talking about jail and stuff." Eric polishes off his second slice and pops another can of Coke. "I told him I hadn't been arrested for a long time, and the last time I *was* arrested was when I was in a drunk-driving accident when my friend was driving. I told him how my charge got dropped, and Dave said, 'Yeah, I wish I never . . .' and then he kinda shrugged. I mean, we were both saying how we *never* wanted to get into trouble again."

The table goes silent for a moment; we are all probably thinking the same thing.

Then Eric goes on. "I remember asking him about his experiences in camp, and we started talking about how, when you go in there, you have to prove to other people that you're tough. How you just can't go in there and not do anything, 'cause then they're gonna run your life."

Now Mike Cruz, the quiet kid, speaks up. "I remember that night, dude. I was at your house, too. I came outside to have a cigarette and I remember you guys were standing there talking. I remember Dave was dressing like us then. He had a Stussy jacket on."

"Yeah. Kathy bought that for him." Jason picks up some of the empty Coke cans and takes them into the kitchen. He continues to talk in there, raising his voice slightly to be heard. "They'd go in the mall with her mom's credit cards, or whatever, and when they'd see something they liked, she'd be all 'Oooooh, that'd look *cool* on you.' "—Jason is back in the dining room now; he sits at the table again—"and then she'd buy it for him. Like I said, she was Dave's lifeline."

I ask what Mike meant when he said that Dave was "dressing like us."

"Well, it's that acceptance thing. You know, dressing casual, not looking like a stoner or an outsider. See, everyone in South Pasadena knows each other, and some stuff is just not . . . it's just less socially acceptable." His voice trails off.

"Look, there's two acceptable groups at South Pas: there's always been us—the jocks, the football players and the cheerleaders, like that—and we've always been acceptable. And then there's the rich kids"—Jason names five or six recognizable family names—"who have been here forever. They're the old guard."

Eric picks up the thread. "It was, like, cool if you went to one of their parties. People talked to you, and accepted you, you were cool. You were accepted. But, it's, like . . . South Pasadena sticks together. No outsiders."

Jason agrees with him. "Everyone dressed like us, casual. And all it was was beer drinking and some stoning. But you went with a date, it wasn't like you'd go with the attitude, or 'Okay, man, who are *you* gonna get with tonight?' No way was it like that."

I ask about the party at Andy Simon's house; the one

where Dave Adkins met Kathy Macaulay. Eric is the first to speak.

"Well, see, I wouldn't have been there. I know all those people, but I wouldn't feel good going there. I feel like my parents are going to know that I ... " He glances at Jason; the look is almost apologetic. "I'd just feel bad, that's all."

Mike Cruz shrugs. "See, everybody in South Pas knows each other and it's just that ... it's less socially acceptable, that kind of party."

Jake Cheever has been out of the room for the past half hour or so; now he comes back in time to hear Mike's comment about parties. Jake doesn't sit down again; he stands in the doorway between the living room and the dining room, leaning easily against the jamb.

"What you need to know is that South Pas is known more for parties than for anything else. Parties and girls. People buy two twelve-packs each to go to a party."

Eric delivers a small laugh. It has a rueful edge to it. "Beer's the drink of choice around here. My brother's at college, getting a 4.0 average, and he goes out to bars with his friends every night. And the kids who go to school with me? All good students with good attitudes and they *still* go out drinking every night."

Jake laughs too, only he doesn't sound regretful. "When I was in my last year of school, playing football, we didn't worry as much about the game as where the parties *after* the game were gonna be."

"And most of our parents know we drink. My dad said to me: 'Just be sure you don't ever drive when you drink.' " Eric is leaning forward to look intently at me.

Jason has been listening quietly; now he speaks up. "But still, most of our friends have at least one DUI on their records."

Eric slumps back in his chair. "Yeah. I got one, and even though nobody got hurt, my dad was really mad. He told me if I drink and drive and kill somebody, that *he'd* kill *me.*"

We talk about beer drinking and pot smoking for a few minutes. Eric says he doesn't smoke pot. "Me and my buddies mostly drink. We'll start at like seven o'clock, and end at one. But, I'll tell ya, we'll be fully hammered by one o'clock, we're done deals. And that's without *pounding* beers."

Jake nods his head solemnly. "It's just what people do around here."

. . . .

In January of 1991, Dave is back living at home with his mother and Dan. He has been reenrolled in Continuation classes and at the end of the school day, every day, Vinnie Hebrock shows up to wait for Dave. Now, more than ever, Vinnie has become Dave Adkins's shadow self, complete only when they are together. The relationship between them has taken another turn; now it is Vinnie who looks up to Dave.

A friend of the Hebrock family, a woman who has asked for anonymity, made the following comment about them:

"From what I observed—and I saw quite a bit of those two—Dave represented everything that was desirable about South Pas. He was a longtime resident; he was in with the 'in crowd'; he knew how to charm the girls. And, best of all, Dave Adkins had that reputation—he was a bad boy. Instant gratification was what he was interested in. And he knew how to get it. He could outreach you and he could outrun you."

Vinnie waits faithfully every day. He sits on the low stone wall across from the building that houses the school, unmindful of the looks he gets from passersby, deaf to any remarks made by other students.

Whenever Dave and Vinnie are not together, Dave goes out with Missy Gillette and, because of the truce that Missy and Kathy have declared, he is able to keep his relationship with Kathy going as well. The three of them go out together, often. To the park. To drink beer, to get high on weed. Dave, content to be passive, likes the arrangement. It's cool, two girls, both crazy about him, saying to any guy who might hit on one or the other of them, "Oh, no—I'm with Dave."

But there is undeniable pressure, too. Kathy never lets up on the sexual innuendo. If she comes to pick up Dave and Missy in the Bronco, she generally has some comment, teasing them about "looking . . . ummm, *tired.*" Or she will call Dave at Missy's house and ask, "What're you guys doing, hmmmm?" Everything she says is laced with some sexual reference.

And there are other annoyances. If Dave says, "I love you," to Missy in front of Kathy, or if he compliments Kathy in Missy's presence, he can count on repercussions. The two girls act like friends when they're together, but each girl will talk against the other whenever either of them manages to get Dave alone.

"I hate it when Kathy puts her arm around you when we walk down the street. You're *my* boyfriend."

Or, "I hate it when Missy just leans over and kisses you."

By mid-February, Dave Adkins and Missy Gillette have broken up.

Now Kathy goes into high gear, driving over to Continuation whenever she feels like it, urging Dave to cut classes and go somewhere with her. Sometimes it will be Heather who comes in to fetch him.

"Hey, go outside, dude. Kathy has a surprise for you in the car. It's real important."

Dave will tell the teacher he'll be right back. Then he goes outside to where the Bronco sits idling.

"What's up?"

"Remember those sunglasses of yours I broke? Here's a new pair."

"Bitchin'!"

Then Kathy will begin to wheedle. "C'mon, duder, we're going to the beach. Come with us." N.W.A. roars out of the speakers. Heather will join in. "C'mon, Dave. It'll be cool—we got herb."

Finally the lure is too great. Dave gets in the car, his promise to return to class forgotten.

Outings like these usually take them to Venice Beach, where Dave might borrow a board and do some surfing. And, very often, over Heather's strong objections, Vinnie Hebrock will come along.

Dave begins to spend more and more time up at the guesthouse on Fairlawn Way. Kathy has made the space pretty much her own, and Heather has stored a few cartons of her belongings in a corner of the entryway; the sides of the boxes are marked with her nickname, "Tinker." Someone starts to make a collection of empty liquor bottles on the top shelf of the bookcase. Drained fifths of Gilbey's gin, Smirnoff and Absolut vodka, Heradura and Cuervo Gold tequila, Jack Daniel's. About twenty bottles in all. Lots of partying goes on in the guesthouse, lots of hanging out. Cayle Fiedler is there, sometimes; Vinnie Hebrock, often. Kelly French, Jason Cheever, and Andrea Tynan are regulars. Peggy Shurtleff comes and goes. And, always, Heather Goodwin.

By the beginning of March, Dave is living up at the guesthouse in a full-time, party-out atmosphere. Kathy's stereo blasts out the Eagles, Pink Floyd, Ratt, the Dead. People drop over to play cards, to drink and get high.

Dave will tell the following story, a year and a half later, just before the trial: One afternoon, he was lying on the couch watching television. The phone rang and he picked up.

"Missy just called here for you. She said she needs to talk to you real bad." It was Kathy, calling from the main house.

Dave sighs, hangs up, calls Missy. The instant she hears his voice, she's ready with a question.

"How did Kathy get to you?"

"She called me."

"You're not at her house?"

"Nuh-uh." He is determined not to be trapped into a lengthy conversation. Missy always wins when she can turn a face-off into a discussion.

"I need to talk to you. Bad."

"Go ahead."

There is a long pause; he can almost hear her thoughts.

"Well . . . I'm pregnant."

"Wow. Who by?"

"Who do you think?" And, unnecessarily, "You." Muted outrage in her voice now; she doesn't want him to hang up on her.

"I don't think so, man. And why're you trying to play this game with me? When we broke up, you were on your period."

"I just told you that—it wasn't true."

Dave actually takes the receiver away from his ear and looks at it. "What the fuck, Missy. Why'd you lie?"

Nothing from the other end.

"Okay, what do you want me to do?"

"I want you to give me three hundred dollars for an abortion."

Dave doesn't miss a beat. "Okay, I got the money. You want it now?"

It takes a second for it to register. Then, "How do *you* have three hundred, just like that?"

"Hey, don't worry about it. I'll have it brought to you at school."

"Fuck you!" And he hears the sound of the receiver slamming into the cradle.

Two or three days later Dave is waiting, with Vinnie, in the Bronco, to pick Kathy up at school. He has begun to drive her to classes every morning. He and Kathy leave the guesthouse by the back entrance and walk down the hill to the driveway, to avoid being seen by Kathy's mother. Now, sitting in front of South Pas High, he sees Missy walking toward the car.

In a single, fluid move, she leans in the driver's window, kisses his cheek, and nips his earlobe with her teeth.

"You waiting for Kathy, hmmm?" And, in afterthought, "Hi, Vinnie."

By way of greeting, Vinnie passes her the joint he's smoking. Eazy-E's voice fills the car.

Dave wonders when she's going to mention the pregnancy.

Now Kathy comes up to the car, tossing her backpack into the backseat.

"Hi, Missy. What's up?"

"Hey, Kathy. How's it going?"

"Oh, man. I've really got bad cramps."

"Yeah, that's fucked, isn't it?" Missy folds her arms over her stomach. "I got 'em too." And, in a stagey whisper, "I gotta go get some more Tampax."

"You do, huh?" Dave has been sitting quietly, eyes straight ahead; now he turns his head to look at Missy. She stares back coolly.

"Yeah. I do."

And she's gone.

A couple of days later Vinnie Hebrock moves into the guesthouse. Kathy lets him have the couch at night, setting up the Japanese screen to separate him from the bed where she and Dave sleep. She begins to cut classes. Less rest. More partying. If Kathy's mother is aware of the constant stream of traffic, she doesn't let on. Mrs. Koss is pleasant to any of the kids she might see, but for the most part, everyone keeps to the guesthouse. Out of the way. Out of sight.

It's Dave who picks up the phone when Missy calls.

"When are you gonna give me that money for the abortion?"

"What the fuck?"

Kathy looks up from the lid of grass she and Vinnie are cleaning.

"Who's that on the phone?"

Dave holds up one hand, tells Missy he'll call her back. Then he hangs up and tells Kathy about Missy's demand for money. Vinnie delivers an option.

"Fuck her, dude. Forget it."

"Is it *yours?*" Hurt and anger all over Kathy's face.

"She's trying to muzzle you for money, dude. Or else she's trying to set you up with your mom . . . " Vinnie seems amused.

"David, *is* it your baby?"

" . . . or the probation officer."

Kathy's and Vinnie's voices collide over Dave's head. He sits, slumped in the chair, eyes on the floor in an attitude of martyred surrender.

"So is it yours or what?" Kathy is close to tears.

"I don't know! She's fuckin' lying, anyway!"

Kathy storms out of the guesthouse. Dave moves to the balcony, watching her as she crosses the pool area and walks into the main house. Then he turns back into the room and picks up the phone, punching in Missy's number angrily.

He's talking as soon as she picks up.

"Missy, this is fuckin' bullshit! You told me three days ago you were on your period."

"I was spotting." And now she's crying. "I just wanted you back!"

Dave grimaces; Vinnie catches the look and laughs silently. Dave flips him the finger.

"Forget it, Missy. I'll call you next week."

It is already the third week of March 1991.

A few days later Kathy Macaulay is driving along Fair Oaks with a girlfriend from school. Suddenly a car pulls up behind them, horn honking. It's Missy Gillette and she is signaling frantically for Kathy to pull over.

According to the girlfriend, who has asked for anonymity, Kathy did pull over and Missy screeched to a stop behind her. Then Missy jumped from her car and ran to the driver's side of the Bronco.

"Kathy! Check it out—Dave is really on a rampage. He threatened he was gonna kill me! I'm fuckin' scared, and I just want you to know, he's fuckin' outta control."

Kathy is barely listening. She has begun to yell at Missy, ordering her to keep away from Dave. Saying that Missy is jealous of her and Dave, screaming at Missy to stop trying to break them up. When the third girl tries to get Kathy to calm down and listen to Missy's warning, Kathy turns on her, too.

"You never liked Dave either, so stay the fuck outta this!"

Missy looks at Kathy, looks over at the other girl. Then she shrugs and walks back to her car.

What none of the kids know is that the Pasadena police are looking for Dave Adkins and Vinnie Hebrock.

. . . .

Sandie Wells remembers a call she got from Dave at the beginning of March 1991.

"He told me the South Pas police were looking for him—and Vinnie Hebrock—because Vinnie's mother had called them, saying that Dave stole some money out of her purse. I remember his exact words, 'I had to run away from home, 'cause I'm in trouble with the cops.' I said that running away wasn't the answer, that the police would catch him anyway. I suggested very strongly that he turn himself in."

When Sandie asked Dave where he was, he told her he was staying at "Kathy's apartment in Pasadena." That confused Sandie; she thought Kathy Macaulay still lived with her parents in South Pas. Then Dave told her that he would be going to Mexico soon, to live there. She got the strong feeling, however, that he was angling for her to tell him to come to her. "I couldn't do that. And not just because he was on probation and had been ordered to live at home. By this time I'd given up on Dave Adkins. I'd had enough."

*I*t is mid-afternoon when the tan Bronco pulls up in

front of the apartment house where Cayle Fiedler lives with his father, Mike. They have lived together ever since the divorce, when Cayle's mother moved to Washington State, first in South Pasadena and now in the neighboring city of Alhambra. Cayle had attended school at South Pas until he dropped out. Now, in March of '91, he is enrolled in Continuation classes, which he rarely attends.

Anyone seeing Cayle Fiedler for the first time that day would imagine him to be at least two years older than sixteen. Only five eight or nine, he weighs close to two hundred and twenty pounds. His round, rather moonlike face is made fuller by the surround of thick, dark hair that has been cropped close to the scalp for a punkish effect. The most youthful thing about his appearance is the glint of metal at his mouth when he speaks. Cayle wears braces.

It has been raining, on and off, for a few days; the San Gabriel Mountains are veiled in snow. Earlier in the week Cayle, Kathy, Dave, Heather, and Vinnie had gone up into the Angeles Crest Forest. The drifts there were awesome, Heather said, and the pine trees looked just like the ones in Christmas tree lots, with every branch dusted in white. The five teenagers had loaded the backseat of the Bronco with twelve-packs and they rolled some joints before they left. They also took with them the Mossberg 12-gauge shotgun and a bag of Peters Brand shells from the closet in Kathy's parents' bedroom. This was not an uncommon occurrence; they had played with the gun before, usually firing it at night, to see the flare of orange sparks from the barrel. Dave and Vinnie had posed for Polaroids with the gun earlier in the month; each boy hefting the weapon while looking straight into the camera.

Today, Thursday, Cayle is feeling a little wasted. They had gone up to the mountains last night again, and the night before he had gone, with Kathy, Dave, and Vinnie, to the Griffith Observatory, to see the Pink Floyd laser show. They had all taken 'shrooms, to heighten the effect.

And now, another get-together has been planned.

It rained again, earlier in the day, and as the Bronco screeches to a halt in front of him, Cayle steps back nimbly to avoid getting splashed. Then, as Heather opens the passenger door, he climbs into the backseat.

"Heyyyy. What's goin' on?"

Kathy flashes a smile into the rearview mirror. "We're gonna go pick up a girlfriend of mine—Danae Palermo. You know her, don't you? She lives in Alhambra."

"Seen her around."

"Yeah, well, she told me she's got some awesome herb. And she's gonna pay for the liquor."

"Cool."

Danae flicks a glance at Cayle and smiles shyly as she gets into the backseat next to him. She is a strikingly pretty girl with dark, curling hair and thick eyebrows that wing dramatically above her eyes. She directs Kathy to the bank, hopping out of the car to collect forty dollars from the automatic teller. Then the three kids head back to Pasadena. They make only one other stop in Alhambra: Cayle goes into a liquor store to buy a fifth of Jack Daniel's and a case of Bud Dry. He has bought supplies here before; the clerk never asks for I.D.

As the Bronco pulls up in front of the guesthouse at Fairlawn Way, Danae notices Kathy's mother's dark red Mercedes in the driveway.

"Is your mom home?"

"Nuh-uh. She's in Chicago at some medical convention.

Cayle, you take the beer upstairs, okay? Me and Heather and Danae are gonna go in the house for ice and stuff. We'll be up in a minute." Cayle hoists the case of beer and walks upstairs to the guesthouse.

Dave Adkins and Vinnie Hebrock are sitting at the table scraping through a shoebox lid that holds the residual sticks and seeds of a former pot cache. Cayle sets the beer on the floor and tells the two boys that Danae's in the kitchen and she's got some weed. Then he goes back down the stairs and crosses the pool and patio area to the main house.

The sliding glass doors that lead to the living room are open; Cayle walks through to the kitchen. Kathy and Danae are deep in conversation, clearly catching up; Heather has placed a bowl of ice, a couple of lemons, and the bottle of Jack Daniel's on a tray, ready to go. Now she picks up the tray and she and Cayle walk back up to the guesthouse.

By the time Kathy and Danae join the others, they're involved in a drinking game called Quarters. The object of the game is to bounce a quarter on the tabletop so that the coin drops into a shot glass filled with liquor; if you make it, you get to drink all the liquor in the glass. The game continues for a short time with all six kids playing. Then the whiskey runs out. Danae brings out the bud of marijuana she brought with her and they smoke that, sitting around the table. Then Dave and Kathy go over to the stereo and begin to make copies of CD's—a couple of B-52's albums and some cuts from the Specials.

At some point Danae says she feels sick and goes into the bathroom; the others can hear her vomiting in there. When she comes back she lies down on the bed, next to the wall. Rain falls intermittently and by the time the case of beer is finished, it's dark outside. Cayle peers out of the window; the automatic lights at the end of the driveway have come on.

"Fuck it. We need some more beer."

Dave is lying on the floor, his head on Kathy's lap. He looks up at Cayle. "Shit, dude, I'm too fucked up to drive."

Kathy shrugs. "I'm cool to drive." She gets to her feet and walks over to the bed.

"Hey, Danae, where's the money for the liquor? We're gonna make a beer run."

Danae reaches down to the foot of the bed for her bag, takes a couple of bills from her wallet, hands them to Kathy. Then she lies down again. Heather is sitting at the foot of the bed, stripping the cellophane from a fresh pack of Marlboros. Vinnie is on the couch, trying to scrape up enough leftover weed to roll one more joint. Kathy grabs a David Lee Roth tape from the top of the stereo and she, Dave, and Cayle are out the door.

As the Mercedes pulls out of the driveway, Roth's version of "California Girls" resonates through the car. In the backseat Cayle Fiedler gets to his feet and sticks his head out of the open sunroof, bellowing into the night.

The first stop is at a large drugstore on Colorado Boulevard. Cayle picks up two twelve-packs of Keystone Beer, a cheaper brand than Bud Dry, but when he takes them to the cashier, the guy won't sell to him without some I.D. as proof of age. He scores at the next place, a liquor store a few blocks away.

Now Kathy says they need to get gas. She pulls into a station and Cayle jumps out of the car to pump. He doesn't notice he's at the Full Service island, and when an attendant tries to tell him, Cayle ignores him. Then the cashier begins to rap on the glass of his booth. Cayle turns to look at him. In his testimony at the trial, Cayle will say that "he was giving me hard looks, and I gave 'em right back."

He also gave the guy some lip. "If you can give me a look like that, then come on out here. Rock my world."

But Cayle is drunk enough for the cashier to stay where he is, behind the glass partition of the booth.

Cayle will also testify, later, that Dave Adkins was ready to back him up if there had been a fight.

Kathy pays for the gas and suggests that they stop for

something to eat. Both boys agree and Kathy pulls into a taco drive-through. After a fast meal, they head back to Fairlawn Way. Kathy is driving fast, the way she always does when she gets behind the wheel of the Mercedes. Cayle will remember, later, hanging his head out the window to feel the wind on his face. He will also remember that "Kathy and Dave seemed to be getting along."

When they get back to Kathy's house, Cayle and Dave carry the beer upstairs; Kathy is right behind them. When they walk into the guesthouse, they walk into an atmosphere charged with tension. Vinnie is nowhere to be seen and Heather and Danae are clearly agitated. Danae is still on the bed, sitting up against the pillows; Heather is kneeling on the floor with both elbows on the bed. Both girls are very drunk. Cayle will testify, at the trial, that he was still fairly drunk, too. But "not as much under the influence as I was at the gas station. I was fresher, not as 'Heyyyy, what's going on?' "

Heather starts talking the instant they walk in the door. Her voice is slurred by the alcohol she has consumed, but what she has to say isn't difficult to comprehend.

"Fuckin' Vinnie started in hitting on me after you guys left. Man, he is such a *total* asshole.

"I finally kicked him one right in the balls. *That* fuckin' stopped him." Heather's tone is smug.

"Oh, man ... " Kathy is interrupted by Danae, who says she got into it with Vinnie, too. She is speaking in a high, shrill voice, and even though Cayle isn't really listening, he can see that Kathy's angry. Arguments between Vinnie and Heather are common occurrences; everybody's used to them going at each other. They were capping* on each other earlier, when they played Quarters. Everybody was. But this is

---

*An exchange of insults. The object of this exercise is to relieve another person of his or her self-esteem by one-upping them. Vinnie was capped on often, but all of the kids in Kathy's crowd participated in capping sessions.

the first time Cayle can remember them actually coming to blows. And Heather would kick Vinnie's ass. In a minute. Vinnie only talks tough—Heather's the real thing.

It is a scene one must visualize in one's mind: Vinnie Hebrock, the butt of all the jokes, the catch all for every snide remark, drunk enough to make a grab for Heather. They were alike in some ways: both of them were so small physically, and they both worked hard at creating an outlaw image. It is easy to imagine Heather's response: too many people have spoken about her hair-trigger temper to assume that she would have reasoned quietly with Vinnie if he put his hands on her. She would have gone to fists immediately, pummeling him with as much force as she could muster.

Vinnie probably went after Danae first. She was, after all, a visitor to the inner circle; she and Vinnie were comparative strangers. And she was softer than Heather, less combative. Vinnie might have taken his chances with Danae. But she fought him off, and he hit her. At that point Heather jumped in, and now the three of them, all of them staggeringly drunk, swung and clawed at each other on the floor of the guesthouse.

Cayle notices that Heather keeps touching her forehead, probing gently at the skin around one eye. Now she gets up and goes into the bathroom and Cayle can see her standing over the basin, peering at her face in the mirror. There's no way to close the bathroom door any more. It got kicked in a few weeks ago at one of Kathy's more intense parties.

While Heather is in the bathroom, Kathy turns to Dave, telling him she's not too pleased about Vinnie messing with *her* friends in *her* house after she let him stay there because he didn't have anywhere else to go. Dave's not saying much, but when Heather comes out of the bathroom and goes to sit at the table with Kathy, he picks up a couple cans of beer and walks out the sliding glass door. Kathy doesn't say a word; she just watches him go. Heather's too drunk to even notice.

Cayle pops a beer, drinks it down fast, pops another can. Then he drops heavily onto the edge of the bed, next to Danae. She edges closer to the wall. He can't get over how pretty
she is.

"Hey . . . you don't have to move so far away from me." He slides a little bit closer to her.

One of the tapes Kathy had gotten made, with her favorite tracks from different albums, is playing. The long cut of "Truckin' " by the Grateful Dead has just ended. The next track is "Gangsters" by the Specials. Kathy and Heather are still going on about Vinnie and the fight. Heather seems particularly proud of having kneed Vinnie in the groin.

The beer is beginning to hit Cayle; he can feel himself getting drunk again. He leans unsteadily toward Danae. She giggles—it's a tiny chirrup of sound.

"You're drunker'n me, even, dude. You should lie down for a little while." Her words are slurring, one into the other.

"Right here? Next to you?" He's flirting openly now.

"Yeah. Just for a nap, though. I gotta sober up—I don't want to get sick again." She turns away from him to face the wall again. "I'm gonna sleep some more."

Cayle drops the empty beer can on the floor next to the bed. Then he lifts his feet and relaxes into the softness of the mattress, lying on his back with both hands clasped behind his head. Kathy and Heather's voices are a soothing counterpoint to the beat of the music. He can feel himself dozing. He is only dimly aware as Kathy gets up from the table and moves to the stereo.

The music starts again but he is asleep before he recognizes who is playing.

Cayle is brought swimming back to consciousness by a pair of closely spaced blasts. And he will say, to the police, that the first thing he saw when he opened his eyes was Dave Adkins with the loaded shotgun in his hands.

Michael Fiedler, Cayle's father, will remember that he was watching the 11:30 P.M. syndicated showing of "Cheers" when his son got home on the night of March 21. He will state, at the trial, that Cayle came into the apartment in a "panic situation." And he will further testify that the first thing Cayle said to him was, "They killed 'em all! Vinnie and Dave just killed the girls! They blew their heads off. Everybody's dead! All my friends are dead!"

Fiedler could smell liquor on his son's breath, but Cayle was walking normally and his speech was not slurred. This was not drunken rambling, nor was it some kind of ghoulish joke. This was for real.

By 12:30 A.M. Cayle Fiedler was at his grandmother's house in South Pasadena, brought there by his father. The grandmother, Mrs. Marilyn Fiedler Davies, will later testify that Cayle was "in a hysterical condition," saying over and over, "All my friends were shot!"

Nobody had, as yet, notified the police of the murders on Fairlawn Way.

A call was placed, from Mrs. Davies's house, to Cayle's mother in Washington State. And it was decided that Cayle would fly up there and stay with her until Mike Fiedler had the time to think about what was to be done. In his own testimony at the trial, over a year later, Mike Fiedler would say that he decided to send Cayle to Washington because he was afraid for his son's life. He would also state that he didn't call the police that night because "It seemed better to regroup and then come forward. To come back later and stand"—here Fiedler stumbled over his words, recovered, and finished his statement—"stand and deliver."

After the calls to Cayle's mother, Cayle and Mike Fiedler went back to their apartment. At this point Cayle told his father he needed to talk to a close friend, a girl named Peggy Shurtleff. Mike agreed to drive Cayle to her home. They would meet back at Cayle's grandmother's house, later.

. . . .

At 12:50 A.M. on March 22, 1991, Sandie Wells was awakened by the frantic barking of her dog and the sound of someone pounding on her front door.

She will remember, later, that she was "surprised, pleased, and shocked" to see Dave Adkins and Vinnie Hebrock standing there. Then, thinking about it, she will add that she wasn't pleased to see Vinnie, "because I didn't like Dave and Vinnie together. Whenever they got together, they got in trouble."

Sandie opens the door and lets the boys in. Dave puts both arms around her immediately, hugging her hard, kissing her on the cheek.

"We were on the freeway and when I saw the Roxford off-ramp, I just had to come see you and say goodbye."

"Yeah, he made me come see you." Vinnie stands awkwardly, looking around the apartment.

"Well, come on in." Sandie feels a ripple of unease. She's not afraid; she just can't figure why these boys have come here at this hour.

"Yeah . . . " Dave seems somewhat distracted. "We're driving Vinnie's uncle's Mercedes up north." He gestures vaguely in the direction of the parking lot. Then he grins broadly. "Can you imagine me driving a Mercedes?" He hugs Sandie again.

"Do you guys want something to eat?"

They follow her into the kitchen. Dave opens the refrigerator and bends down, with both hands on his knees, to peer
inside. Vinnie moves nervously around the room, picking
things up to look at them, setting them down again.

Finally, Dave closes the refrigerator door. "I don't see
anything I want. How about some of that coffee stuff with the
chocolate in it?"

Sandie makes three cups of Swiss Mocha and they go
into the living room. She sits on the floor and the two boys
drop down on the sofa facing her. Dave talks some more
about driving the Mercedes, then he seems to run out of
words. There is an uncomfortable silence; Sandie stirs her
coffee, waiting. Vinnie fidgets.

"All the problems I had are straightened out now," Dave
says suddenly.

Sandie looks up at him, surprised by the non sequitur.

Vinnie speaks up quickly; Sandie senses that he is im-
provising. "Yeah. My mom dropped the charges."

"What charges?"

Vinnie smirks. "Oh, she said I stole some money from
her."

Sandie has been noticing that both Dave and Vinnie are
behaving in a manner that she will describe to me, later, as
"superagitated." She will say that "Dave's eyes were too wide,
too bright. He couldn't seem to relax back on the couch. Vinnie was the same. They were wired. On the move."

"Are you guys on something?"

Dave giggles. "I'm clean. But Vinnie had a little something." Now Vinnie laughs too.

Sandie has also noticed that Dave is sporting more jewelry than he ordinarily wears: the usual assortment of tiny
crosses and studs is arrayed in both ears, and he is still wearing the silver bear-claw ring Sandie gave him at his eighth-
grade graduation, but now there are rings on every finger of

his right hand. And he's wearing a couple of silver necklaces. One more than usual.

"Where'd you get all the jewelry?"

"What jewelry?"

"Well, that necklace, for one thing."

Vinnie laughs again. "Oh . . . he got that from a *very* special girl."

Dave flicks a fast look at Vinnie. Vinnie stops talking; his eyes begin to move around the room again. Dave clears his throat.

"After we drop off the car, we're gonna go to Texas. We got jobs waiting for us." Then, in afterthought, "But I'll keep in touch with you."

If Sandie knows only one thing, it's that nobody's going to Texas—or anywhere else—for "jobs." Dave Adkins's pattern always runs true, bringing him back to South Pasadena. And the girls who live there.

"Well, we gotta bail." Dave gets to his feet and reaches for Vinnie's mug of untasted coffee. Then he takes it and his own mug into the kitchen. Vinnie stands up and moves to the door; he will neither look at nor speak to Sandie Wells again.

At the door, Dave kisses Sandie on the cheek once more. "Don't worry—we'll keep in touch."

Sandie walks outside with them. Dave makes a point of showing her the dark red car.

"See the Mercedes?"

One more hug and the two boys get in the car; Dave is behind the wheel. As he pulls out of the parking lot, he waves one last time to Sandie Wells.

. . . .

Peggy Shurtleff is in the garage apartment of her parents' home, drawing, when she hears a knock on the door. Peggy is eighteen years old, Kathy Macaulay and Heather Goodwin's age, and she has lived in South Pasadena all her life. She and Heather have known each other since they were eight years old. She and Kathy have been close friends and schoolmates for seven years. She has known Dave Adkins for almost as long a time. Danae Palermo is a more recent acquaintance, as is Vinnie Hebrock. Three years, maybe. Cayle Fiedler is a new friend, too; they met about four years ago. But next to Kathy and Heather, Peggy considers Cayle to be one of her closest buddies.

Peggy will say, at the trial, that she "partied, every day of the week," with most of these kids. That each person would usually put away a twelve-pack of beer. And that they would also smoke weed and do coke when they had it.

Now, at one-thirty or so in the morning, she is pleasantly surprised to see Cayle Fiedler standing at her door.

"Heyyyy, Cayle. What's up?"

"Everybody's dead!" He brushes past her, moving fast, turning to look at her, as if it's important to keep eye contact. He looks terrible—his skin is ashen, his hands are trembling. His eyes seem to have sunk into their sockets, and they're bloodshot, as if he might have been crying.

"What? Who's dead?"

"Kathy—Heather—Danae! They were all shot in the head!" His words are tumbling, one over the other. "Dave and Vinnie did it!"

"What the fuck are you *talking* about? Are you fucking nuts?" She looks more closely at him. "Are you frying? Is this, like, some fucked-up acid shit?"

"I swear to *God* I'm telling you the truth, Peggy! I fuckin' ran from Kathy's house! They're all dead!"

"How?"

"We were all just on the couch having a good time, and me and Danae were making out ... "

"But what would make them do this?" Peggy is leaning in to him, staring intently. She has begun to cry a little.

"Heather was shooting off her mouth and talking shit to Vinnie, like she always does."

"Yeah . . . ?"

"And Dave went down to the main house, and came back with the gun and shot Kathy and Heather and Danae."

"*Dave* shot everybody? You said . . . "

"Dave shot the first two, and then Vinnie took out the other girl, Danae." His eyes are nearly glazed over now. "Then Dave pointed the gun at me, and said, 'Are you down or are you dead?' "

At the trial there will be many questions, from all of the attorneys, about what Cayle Fiedler said to Peggy Shurtleff in the early morning hours of March 22, 1991.

"How do you know they're dead? Maybe they only got wounded. I'm gonna call Kathy's house."

Cayle grabs Peggy's arm as she reaches for the receiver. "No! Don't call on this phone. Maybe they'll trace it!"

"But what if they're still alive up there? I'm calling, dude."

"Peggy, I saw their fuckin' brains! Believe it—they're not here!"

"I'm still gonna call Kathy's. There's a pay phone up the corner."

Peggy calls the guesthouse. Then the main house. The hollow sound of unanswered telephones ringing, again and again, convinces Peggy of what she must do next. Shivering a little in the chill March air, she turns to face Cayle.

"I'm gonna call Heather's mom."

"No! Keep your mouth shut! Don't call anybody!" Cayle's face is a defiant mask. Then, in a sudden shift of energy, his shoulders lift in a weary shrug. "Hey, dude, do what you gotta do. I'm gonna bail."

The two teenagers hug each other, there on the corner. Then Cayle Fiedler moves away, melting into the darkness, and Peggy Shurtleff turns back to the pay phone to make her call to Mimi and Darrell Goodwin. To tell them that something terrible has happened up at Kathy's house.

. . . .

Sandie Wells's clock radio awakens her on Saturday morning, March 22. The news station she generally listens to is filled with reports of a triple homicide in Pasadena. No names, pending notification of the families. It is not until the afternoon, when she is driving in to Pasadena for a meeting with another realtor, that Sandie will hear that it is Kathy Macaulay, Heather Goodwin, and Danae Palermo who have been murdered. And that two of the suspects have fled in the dark red Mercedes-Benz belonging to Kathy Macaulay's mother.

"Oh, my God."

It is a phrase that Sandie Wells will repeat often, like a mantra, in the days to come.

When Sandie gets home that evening, she checks with the security guard at the complex where she lives. Visitors' license plates are always entered in a ledger by the guard on duty. The license plate of the car belonging to Kathy Macaulay's mother has been written down, and the time: 12:50 A.M., March 22, 1991.

Sandie does the thing she has known, all day, that she must do: she calls the police.

. . . .

"Did you smell that?"

Vinnie's voice sounds even more strained than it did last night, in Sandie Wells's apartment. This is the first thing either of them has said in a long time; they have been driving in silence.

Dave nods his head. He will say, later, "We both knew what he meant. I could still smell the blood and burnt flesh and singed hair."

The miles continue to unroll. The radio is tuned to classic rock stations; as the frequencies change, Dave will adjust the dial.

Later still, after they have stopped for gas, stopped for food, Dave will tell me he turned to Vinnie.

"Why'd this shit happen, dude?"

But Dave says that Vinnie had no reply, that he looked out the car window.

Dave says he tried again.

"Should we go back, bro'?"

And he will say that Vinnie shook his head. "Nah. The cops'll just shoot at us."

They continue driving.

Dave says that by the time they got to Grant's Pass, Oregon, Vinnie was worrying about the death penalty. And Dave will say he offered a solution.

"Fuck it. Let's just blow our heads off here and now. I'll do it for both of us." He will also say, almost two years later, that he was "for it [the suicide] 'cause Kathy was dead and I was going to jail for it. I really didn't want to live. I was fucked. Might as well kill myself before the system killed me."

But, Dave will say, Vinnie didn't like that plan. Vinnie told him to keep on driving.

When the money ran out they began to trade the jewelry Dave was wearing, for gas.

"I traded a bitchin' silver bracelet at one station. Kathy bought it for me at the Pasadena swap meet. It was cool—all ornate loops. I got her a silver necklace with a shark's tooth on it. For good luck. That guy I traded my bracelet to really got a good deal."

. . . .

Jason Cheever's older brother Jake was home on Spring break on March 22, 1991. He had been out with friends for most of the day but by mid-afternoon he was kicked back in the living room, watching TV. He had heard nothing about the murders.

"I happened to look outside, and what I saw was some police officers running down the sidewalk in front of my house. I guess they thought nobody was at home, because two guys came up the stairs carrying a battering ram, and another bunch was in front of the house. Then I heard somebody say, 'There's someone inside.'

"They all drew their guns, pointed them at me, and said, 'Open the door!' I opened the door immediately and they grabbed me, put me down on the ground, handcuffed me, and sat me up. I said, 'What's going on?' and somebody said, 'We have a search warrant for your house. We'll tell you what's going on later.'

"They led me inside and sat me down on the bench in the dining room. Then they asked me where Jason's room was."

Jason Cheever is listening quietly as his brother relates the events of that afternoon. His eyes move from Jake's face to mine; he is clearly interested in my responses.

Jake goes on. "Right at that point I heard my dad's car pull up, and then he was inside the house, asking what all the police were doing there. Most of them were already in Jason's room, looking around because, we found out later, they thought Dave might be hiding in the closet. But there was a guy in the living room, and he informed my dad about what was going on. The murders, everything. That was the first I heard about them.

"Then my phone rang, and one of the cops accompanied me to answer it. To make sure it wasn't Dave calling. They completely tossed Jason's room. They ripped panels out of his closet, they threw beads—from necklaces he and my mom were making—all over the floor.

"When they told me there had been a triple homicide, they asked me if I knew Dave Adkins. I said I did, and they told me they had been watching the house all day. They said,

'You left at such-and-such a time, in a black Jetta.' Which was true, and they asked me, 'Who were you with? Where did you go?' I told them I had been with a friend of mine, that we'd gone and picked up some other friends at school.

"Later on, after the police had left, I saw the whole thing about the murders on the news. And that really got to me." Jake pulls in a deep breath. "But I'll tell you what really scared me. Not many people have looked down the barrel of a police officer's gun, and *that's* the thing that really scared me, man. I was shaking."

....

At about 8:30 P.M. on March 22, 1991, Control Officer Steven Bellshaw of the Salem, Oregon, Police Department went, with Officer Selina Barnes, to the Greyhound bus station. They had been dispatched to that location after a call came into the police station, informing the officer on duty that two teenagers wanted by the California authorities in connection with a triple homicide were waiting for a relative to pick them up at the Greyhound terminal. The caller was Dave Adkins's aunt; her husband was the person the suspects were waiting for. The aunt also told the duty officer that Dave's mother, Pam Adkins, had called her earlier to tell her both boys were wanted for murder.

Officers Bellshaw and Barnes walked through the waiting room and covered all the transit malls, but they didn't locate the suspects. They gave general descriptions of Adkins and Hebrock to the bus station employees and then drove back to the city bus station, to check it out. By 9:05 P.M. they were back at the Greyhound station, and this time they got lucky.

The officers approached the two teenagers. Bellshaw told Dave Adkins he wanted to speak with him; Barnes talked to Vinnie Hebrock. Both boys were told there had been a call about loiterers at the station, both were asked for I.D. and handed over copies of their birth certificates.

At the trial, a year and a half later, Officer Bellshaw would testify that they spoke "at length, mostly general conversation," and that Dave Adkins stated that he and Vinnie had come to Oregon from Pasadena and were going on to Colorado, to get factory jobs.

In a later conversation, Dave Adkins would say that he "played the part with the cops. Shook hands with 'em, joked around, answered the questions." The same way he answered mine: all wide, innocent eyes and straightforward grins.

"Do you live around here?"

"I used to."

"Well, we got a call from the Pasadena police. Are you guys runaways?"

"No way. We're on vacation."

"Uh-huh. Well, why do you think the Pasadena authorities would want to talk to you?"

"I have no idea, Officer. I'm clean."

At the same time, Officer Barnes is searching Vinnie Hebrock for weapons. She glances over at Bellshaw, shakes her head. He reaches down for Dave's backpack.

"Hey, what're you doing?" Dave's smile has vanished.

"I've got to search for weapons, Dave."

"Why don't you just ask?"

Bellshaw simply looks at Dave. One long look.

"Okay, fuck it. Search."

"Put your hands on top of your head, please."

"Why?"

"Just do it."

Dave is patted down. No weapons on him, either. Now both boys are handcuffed and taken into custody. They are told only that the Pasadena authorities want to talk to them. The triple homicide is not mentioned.

Adkins and Hebrock are driven to the Salem police station in separate cars. Dave goes with Steve Bellshaw; Vinnie with Selina Barnes.

In Bellshaw's car, Dave watches the computer screen mounted on the dashboard. And he sees his name as it comes up, followed by the words: "Wanted for 187."

"Hey . . . "

Bellshaw turns partway around in the front seat and looks at Dave.

"Yes?"

"What's '187'? What does that mean?"

"Runaway."

Dave has a pretty good idea of what those numbers stand for. "187" is the penal code for Homicide.

. . . .

Drs. Linda Macaulay Koss and Michael Koss, Kathy Macaulay's mother and stepfather, came back from Chicago on March 22, the day after the murders. Michael Koss had gone to Chicago to give a course in surgical pathology, and his wife Linda had joined him there nearly a week earlier. Michael Koss was not a full-time resident at Fairlawn Way. For the past several years he had been dividing his time between his position as a tissue pathologist in Washington, D.C., and his home in Pasadena. As a rule, he was able to be with his family in Pasadena for one weekend a month, and holidays. Dr. Linda Koss ran a diagnostic lab at one of the largest L.A. area hospitals. They had been married for over ten years.

Linda Koss joined her husband in Chicago on March 16; when she walked into her home a week later, she faced an unimaginable ordeal. During the days and weeks to come, she would be kept busy making inventories of stolen items and answering the onslaught of questions attendant to a murder investigation. There had to be a massive cleanup in the guesthouse. Funeral arrangements had to be made. Relatives had to be notified. And, through it all, she was kept aware of the progress being made in tracking down her daughter's suspected assassins.

....

After Cayle Fiedler left Peggy Shurtleff at the pay phone on the corner a block from her home, he went back to his grandmother's house. He will testify, at the trial, that he was afraid of what Dave Adkins and Vinnie Hebrock would do to him if he went to the apartment he shared with his father and they found him there. At Mrs. Davies's house, he had two more shots of liquor and then went to bed. His father, Mike Fiedler, woke him at 6:00 A.M. Cayle will recall that although he was no longer drunk, he was "still confused." He had slept in his clothes, the same jeans and T-shirt he had been wearing the previous day, and now, on the morning of March 22, he kept them on. There was, he will state later, no time to shower, no time to change. He had to catch the first flight up to Seattle.

They still did not contact the police.

Cayle's mother met him at the Seattle airport; she had brought her therapist with her. The first stop was a restaurant near the airport and it was here, over breakfast, that Cayle told his mother—and the therapist—the details of what had happened the day before, on Fairlawn Way.

After the meal, Cayle asked to go to his mother's house, but she preferred to take him to a nearby motel, for more talk. They spoke several times, from the motel, to Mike Fiedler, and although the need to talk to the authorities was discussed, the police were not called until late that afternoon. Cayle will recall turning on the television in the motel room. "By that time we [Cayle, Dave Adkins, and Vinnie Hebrock] were on the Most Wanted list. It was all over the TV."

Cayle Fiedler remained in Seattle for two days, "watching TV most of the time."

SMOKED

At approximately 11:10 P.M. on March 22, Dave Adkins and Vinnie Hebrock met the officers who would conduct the initial interview in Salem, Oregon. Sergeant Larry Stephens sat down in one room, with Dave; Sergeant Michael Luyet was in another room, with Vinnie.

Sergeant Stephens advised Dave of his rights and read to him the "Consent to Search" card. Dave listened, then signed both cards. Next, Stephens went through Dave's backpack, listing the items he found inside. Lying loose among the underwear, T-shirts, and shoes was a set of keys. Dave told Stephens they belonged to his ex-girlfriend, that they "didn't work anymore." There were also some cards and letters from a girl who signed with the name "Kathy." Dave said she was an old girlfriend, named "Kathleen," whom he had last seen the previous month. As Stephens went through the backpack, Dave began to complain about the way he had been spoken to by another officer at the station. Dave felt the man had been unduly harsh.

"It's not like I killed somebody. It would've been different if I would've killed somebody."

Dave told Stephens that he left Pasadena the previous week and had visited friends in Grant's Pass, Oregon, before going on—by bus—to Salem. He could not, however, recall the names of his friends in Grant's Pass.

A GSR (gunshot residue) test was performed and photographs were taken. Before the test, Dave said he "hadn't fired a gun in months." He did have a couple of questions, though.

"Would it [the test] determine if a person fired a gun into another person? And if it shows I haven't, can I be charged with anything?"

At the conclusion of the interview, Dave Adkins was informed that he was being accused of murder. Sergeant Stephens will say, in his testimony at the trial, that Dave was "real casual" when he was given this information. His reply was a single word:

"Oh."

Dave Adkins did not ask for an attorney during the interview. No recording was made of the conversation. The Pasadena police had requested that there be no formal questioning; they were on the way.

Vinnie Hebrock's interview with Sergeant Luyet was uneventful; he too was read his rights and signed that card and the Consent to Search card. At some point he informed Luyet of his inability to read or write. He did not request an attorney or say that he did not wish to speak to the officer.

Luyet went through Vinnie's backpack: underwear, T-shirts, a pair of sneakers. And the Polaroids of Dave and Vinnie with the shotgun. Luyet sets the photographs to one side.

"How did you get to Oregon?"

"Me and Dave came up here on the bus. We were at some other place in Oregon way earlier. We left California day before yesterday."

Luyet has noticed a number of small scrapes and abrasions on Vinnie's face and neck. Now he asks about them.

"I got in a fight with some guy who was bigger than me. In L.A."

Luyet picks up the Polaroids again.

"Are you a bird hunter?"

"Huh? Oh, you mean the gun. Nuh-uh—that belongs to my brother. I never even shot it."

At the end of the interview, Michael Luyet informed Vinnie Hebrock that he would be held overnight in connection with a homicide.

Vinnie sat quite still, staring, for a long, long moment. Then, "Homicide is murder, isn't it?"

The police officer nodded his head.

"Well, I didn't murder anybody." Another long pause.

"What's this murder about? Is it about some basketball player getting killed by gangbangers?"

While Vinnie Hebrock was in the interview room with Sergeant Luyet, Selina Barnes was cleaning out her squad car. She performed this task routinely after every arrest, to make sure all evidence was assigned correctly. Now, after Vinnie's arrest, she found, under the backseat, as if shoved there, an eight-inch steel dagger covered by a leather sheath. The dagger had not been in the car before Dave Adkins and Vinnie Hebrock were arrested at the Salem Greyhound station, and no other officer had used the vehicle since that time.

Vinnie was photographed and given a GSR test. Then he and Dave were taken, in separate cars, to the Salem juvenile detention center for the night. The two boys would be kept apart there, as well.

When Dave and Vinnie were brought back to the Salem police station the next morning, March 23, Detectives Mike Korpal and Timothy Sweetman of the Pasadena police were waiting for them. Korpal had already spoken at length with Peggy Shurtleff and Cayle Fiedler; he had their statements.

It had been decided that Detective Sweetman would wear a concealed body mike in order to record the interviews with Adkins and Hebrock.

Both boys were taken to separate interview rooms. Korpal would question Vinnie first; he sat down on the other side of the table and nodded politely. Then he read the Oregon rights card aloud and advised Vinnie that although California rights cards are worded in a slightly different language, the rights covered are the same. Vinnie nodded his head. Korpal persisted, asking Vinnie if he understood.

"I already heard my rights about seven times already." Almost impatient. Korpal and Sweetman exchange a glance.

Finally, satisfied that Vinnie Hebrock does understand, Korpal allows him to sign the rights card. Then Vinnie agrees, verbally, to give up his rights to silence.

"You understand, fully, that you do not have to talk to me at this time if you don't want to?"

"I understand everything. I just can't read."

"Not at all?"

"Well, stuff like 'the' and 'and' and 'cat.' Like that. I didn't go to school all my life." Vinnie sighs softly. "But I couldn't read those cards or nothin' now, anyway."

"Why not?"

"I ain't got glasses on. I got really bad eyes."

The detective shifts his bulk in the narrow, state-issue chair. He is a big man, six feet seven inches tall; he weighs just over three hundred pounds. His size will be made much of by one of the defense attorneys at the trial.

Now Korpal flicks a glance at Sweetman and the business of interrogation gets under way.

"Vinnie, we'd like to ask you a few questions. I'm going to read you your rights again."

Korpal begins to read aloud and, as he does, Vinnie recites along with him. As if he is trying to show off a little for the detective, trying to show Korpal that he does, indeed, understand.

"Do you willingly give up your rights to have an attorney present?"

"Sure."

"We're here to determine what happened at Kathy's house."

"What happened?"

"That's what we're here to find out." Korpal takes a deep breath. "And I know it's weighing on you, too. We're here to find the truth. And you'll only have one or two opportunities to tell the truth like this. Other times, people will be judging you. This is the time to get what's on your mind off your mind."

Vinnie Hebrock sits quietly in his chair, looking down at his hands. There is a rind of dirt all the way around each fingernail. The scratches on his neck and face are beginning to crust over. His hair, which has been hacked unevenly on top and allowed to straggle into a longish tail in the back, lies dully against his scalp. As always, he is squinting nearsightedly.

"They told me some stuff yesterday. Told me I was under arrest for homicide." Now he looks up at Korpal. "I'm supposed to have killed somebody?" He glances at Sweetman;

the younger detective's face is impossible to read.

Korpal's voice is soft, unthreatening, as he answers the query. "We found three bodies up at Kathy Macaulay's house. Do you know Kathy Macaulay?"

"Yes! That's Dave's girlfriend!" Vinnie's eyes are wide open now.

"What does she look like?"

"She's blonde ... " He hesitates. " ... Well, she dyes it. And she's kinda heavy."

He tells Korpal that the last time he saw Kathy Macaulay was when she drove him and Dave Adkins to the Greyhound station in Pasadena, between noon and four o'clock on Tuesday afternoon. When Korpal asks how Vinnie knew it was Greyhound, Vinnie tells him he recognized the "red and blue dog." He says he guesses that Dave Adkins bought the bus tickets.

He says that after leaving Pasadena, he and Dave "stopped at a few towns, I don't know nothing about their names." He also says they "visited some people—just some people," but he doesn't know their names, either.

When Korpal asks why Vinnie came to Oregon with Dave Adkins, Vinnie tells him, "I wanna get my own place, go to night school, get a good job and pay the bills."

When Korpal asks Vinnie to tell him again when he last saw Kathy Macaulay, Vinnie repeats his story. This time he adds a comment:

"Dave's gonna go fuckin' *nuts!*"

"Why is that?"

" 'Cause that's his girlfriend. And you said she got killed."

There is a long beat. Korpal glances at Sweetman; the younger detective returns the look, then he makes a note. Korpal looks at Vinnie again.

"Yes. She was."

Now Korpal asks Vinnie about the last time he was at

Kathy's house. Who else was there? Vinnie says it was just himself, Dave, and Kathy. He thinks Kathy's mom was "at work." Korpal asks if Kathy's mother has a car.

"Yeah, a Mercedes." He hesitates. "No—a Porsche. And Kathy's stepdad—or some dude who lives there—has a Mercedes."

"Have you seen that car?"

"The Mercedes? Oh, yeah. I've rode in it."

Korpal asks if Vinnie has ever driven the Mercedes.

"Kathy wouldn't let *nobody* drive that car."

Korpal asks Vinnie about the last time he was in the Mercedes-Benz; who else was in the car with him?

"Kathy, Heather, and Dave."

"Who's Heather? Is she your girlfriend?"

"Nuh-uh."

Korpal asks Vinnie about girlfriends. Does he have one?

"I got two or three. But none of 'em are really my girlfriend."

Korpal asks him about safe sex.

"Well, if I got a condom, I use it. If I don't"—he shrugs slightly—"I don't."

Korpal asks Vinnie about the bruises and scratches on his neck, and a larger bruise beneath the tattoo on his arm. Vinnie glances down at that one.

"I didn't know *any* of 'em were there until Dave said something."

"Dave's your homie, isn't he?"

"Uh-huh."

"You and Dave kick it together pretty much?"

"Uh-huh." There is a moment of quiet. Korpal sits, waiting. Sweetman coughs softly into his fist. Vinnie looks down at the floor.

"Dave's a pretty good friend." Long pause. "He's pretty much my only friend."

Mike Korpal has been on this case, as chief investigator,

since the early hours of March 22. He was one of the first detectives to arrive at the guesthouse on Fairlawn Way. It was he who made the call to Linda Macaulay Koss in Chicago with the news that her daughter and two of her daughter's friends had been murdered. It was Korpal who spoke to the Goodwins and the Palermos. To Cayle Fiedler and his father, Mike. To Peggy Shurtleff. And now, sitting across the table from Vinnie Hebrock, his voice is as even and his manner as courteous as it was with any of those people.

"Would you lie for Dave Adkins?"

Vinnie keeps on looking down. He shakes his head, muttering softly.

Now Korpal asks about the shotgun Vinnie and Dave are holding in the Polaroids. Vinnie says he has no idea where the gun came from. Says he thinks Dave got it from Cayle.

"Who's Cayle?"

"Some Mexican."

Vinnie goes on to say that the snapshots were taken about a month ago, at Kathy's house.

"Were Kathy's parents home at the time?"

"Kathy's parents are never home."

Under Korpal's careful probing, Vinnie continues to talk. He says he doesn't know where the shotgun is now. He says he has no idea if the gun was loaded when they took the pictures. He last saw it three weeks to a month ago, when they took those pictures. He adds that he got the one with Dave holding the gun because Dave didn't want it.

Vinnie has begun to tremble.

"Is that the shotgun that killed the girls? They were shot by a shotgun? I had no idea . . . " His words trail off into silence.

"You don't know if that was the shotgun that killed the girls?"

"No."

"Do you know where that gun is now?"

The famous
1991 Polaroids,
taken about one
month before
the murders.
Vinnie Hebrock
and Dave Adkins
each pose with
the shotgun they
would use in the
multiple killings.

Cayle Fiedler with the shotgun at the trial. (JONATHAN ALCORN)

Dave Adkins *(center)* at his eighth-grade graduation.

Dave with his teacher
Sandie Wells. (SANDIE WELLS)

SMOKED

Kathy Macaulay, age seventeen.

Danae Palermo.

Heather Goodwin,
age sixteen, and
Heather with
Al Binder.

OPPOSITE: An aerial view of the Macaulay house on Fairlawn Way. Circles indicate the garage/guesthouse and the pool area. ABOVE: Inside Kathy Macaulay's garage apartment where the murders took place. Whited-out area indicates where one of the victims' bodies was found. (PASADENA POLICE DEPARTMENT)

The L.A. County coroner removes one of the bodies from the murder site in March 1991.
(WALT MANCINI, *PASADENA STAR-NEWS*)

Dave Adkins at
his trial in 199{
(PAUL MORSE)

Vinnie Hebrock at
his trial in 1992.
(NANCY NEWMAN-BAUER)

"No."

"Is Heather Goodwin your girlfriend?"

"Nuh-uh. Heather is Kathy's best friend. Like me and Dave." His right hand moves in a jerking spasm to clutch at the left hand.

"I'm shaking like a leaf."

"Well, Vinnie, lying won't stop that shaking. Honesty will stop it. Telling me exactly what happened up there that night will stop it." Korpal leans forward on both elbows and his voice, when he speaks again, is almost gentle.

"You know, Vinnie, you don't strike me as a cold-blooded murderer." There is a long moment of silence. Vinnie's head is down; it is impossible to tell if he is crying or not.

"Why don't you tell the truth now?"

Slowly, Vinnie Hebrock looks up at Mike Korpal.

"Cayle had the gun. He walked in there and shot them. There was blood everywhere. *Everywhere.*"

While Mike Korpal was questioning Vinnie Hebrock and Dave Adkins on March 23, Dr. James K. Riebe, Deputy Medical Examiner for L.A. County, was performing autopsies on the bodies of Kathy Macaulay, Heather Goodwin, and Danae Palermo.

Dr. Riebe began with Kathy. He noted that she was wearing black shorts and a black shirt that exposed her midriff. Noted that she had a tattoo on her shoulder and one on her ankle. Noted her age, her height, weight, hair color. Then he removed her clothes and took fluoroscopes and X-rays. Next, he performed an internal examination, and then he began the dissection, taking specimens for toxicology and other tests.

Dr. Riebe noted that Kathy had sustained a shotgun wound to the back of her head; he recovered thirty-three bird-shot pellets from her brain.

Blood collected from Kathy's heart showed results of .03 alcohol level—subclinical intoxication; no visible impairment. Tests on her liver showed positive for marijuana, negative for LSD.

The same procedures were then performed on the body of Heather Goodwin. Riebe's findings noted that Heather had suffered a massive head wound. There was also external evidence of blunt-force-trauma injuries on her hands, legs, and neck. And bruises to the left eye area, as well as the forehead and brow.

Riebe noted that there was a cigarette butt stuck in the

top of Heather's brain. He removed "a number of shotgun pellets" from the brain as well, which had been delivered to the laboratory in a separate envelope.

There was an insufficient amount of blood for Heather's toxicology tests. Almost all of her blood in her body had drained out at the crime site. The tests were performed on her spleen and liver. They showed a blood alcohol level of .20—a significant degree of intoxication, indicating severe impairment of judgment and motor control. Marijuana tests showed positive, LSD negative.

Danae Palermo had also sustained a close-range contact wound to the back of her head, near the neck area. Dr. Riebe noted a "great deal of blast injuries to the head with destruction of the brain and great damage to the scalp and skull." Shotgun pellets and shell wadding were removed from the brain.

Like Heather Goodwin, Danae had bruises on her hands and a "small contusion" on her left eyelid. The kinds of scrapes and bruises she (and Heather) would have gotten from being hit by someone's fists.

The toxicology tests showed positive for marijuana, negative for LSD. Danae had a .19 alcohol reading.

....

At 3:04 on the afternoon of March 23, Mike Korpal and Tim Sweetman sit down to talk with Dave Adkins. Dave looks at both detectives in turn. Then he smiles politely. Korpal tells him there are some questions that need to be cleared up about Dave's whereabouts in connection with a homicide that took place in Pasadena.

Dave leans back in his chair. Even with three days of travel on him, Dave Adkins retains his good looks. He is still the California golden boy. Mike Korpal will say, at the trial, that Dave appeared to be "comfortable and confident."

Korpal asks if he has ever been in trouble.

"Yeah."

"Are you on probation now?"

"Yeah. For breaking and entering in L.A. County a long time ago."

Now Korpal reads Dave's rights to him again and asks if he understands. Will he talk to Korpal now? Yeah. Does he want an attorney present? No.

The manner in which Dave gives these answers seems to imply a question: Why would he need an attorney when he hasn't done anything wrong? He glances occasionally at Sweetman, as if to include the younger detective in the conversation. He has already told both men that he doesn't think "you guys are gonna dick me around." He is serving up the easy charm that always works for him.

Korpal gets down to cases. He asks Dave to tell him, "basically, where you've been the past few days. Start with Wednesday."

Dave tells the detectives he was at his girlfriend's—Kathy Macaulay's—house the previous Wednesday morning, March 20, but had gone, with Vinnie Hebrock, to Ontario that afternoon. Spent the night there, went to the Ontario mall on Thursday, went back to Pasadena.

Then what, Korpal asks.

Dave says that he and Vinnie were only briefly in Pasadena before they left for Bakersfield.

Korpal asks how they got there. Dave tells him they went with "a friend." Korpal asks for a name. "Jim." Dave doesn't know Jim's last name, or his telephone number.

Now Korpal asks Dave how he got the money to get around.

Dave shifts uneasily in his chair. "From my mom. And odd jobs—cleaning up, painting. Stuff like that."

Dave's words have become so muffled it sounds as if he is in another room. Korpal says that he (Korpal) has a bad cold which makes it difficult for him to hear. He asks Dave to speak up; he says it's very important for Sweetman and himself to hear everything. Dave nods his head, clears his throat.

"We went to Bakersfield on the Greyhound. We just pretty much walked around when we were there. We were basically going up to Oregon. To get jobs."

"How much money did you have when you left Bakersfield?"

"Not much. We ran out of money in Redding."

Now Dave begins to ramble, talking about some other friends whose names he does not recall. His voice has softened into a slur again, and, again, Korpal asks him to speak up.

"We got off the bus and we were sitting at the bus stop, talking, da-da-da-da-da-da. So then we got a ticket to Grants Pass. We got there about three o'clock on Friday, and went to visit another friend." He is silent for a long moment. Then, "Aaron." Another lengthy pause. "I think."

Korpal asks if Dave can provide a number for Aaron.

"Nuh-uh." His hands have been folded on the table. Now he begins to tap out a dull, persistent tattoo with both index fingers. And he begins to ramble again. They ran out of money. They met someone else. Another friend. "Not of mine." His words are running together, melting into a drone.

Then he says something that rivets the attention of both detectives. He says he didn't steal the Mercedes-Benz.

"I never mentioned anything about the Mercedes being stolen." Korpal's voice is very soft. Dave's fingers stop tapping.

Another thread of silence winds itself around the three people at the table. Korpal allows it to play out. Dave clears his throat. Sweetman coughs again. Korpal pours a cup of water, takes a sip. Then:

"Who do you know in Salem?"

Dave replies eagerly, as if relieved, "My aunt and uncle." He gives their names. "I called 'em from the bus station and they said they were gonna come and get us. We waited and waited. Then I called again. Then we waited some more and then the police picked us up." Dave looks at Korpal with an aggrieved expression. Then he glances at Sweetman.

"They didn't tell us shit, you know. I told them, 'I'm a minor but I *do* have some rights.' "

"When did you last visit Kathy?"

Dave takes so much time before he answers the question that Korpal will wonder (and say, later, at the trial) if Dave was responding slowly—as he will continue to do—in a calculated effort to distract. Finally, Dave tells Korpal that he was at Kathy's house the previous Wednesday. He says that he had been "staying at Kathy's house for quite a while," but that he did not call her on Thursday, March 21, or the following day. When Korpal asks why not, Dave shrugs.

" 'Cause she told me how me and Vinnie couldn't stay up there any more 'cause her mom was coming back. Her mom had been gone for about four days." His tone is surprisingly pious.

"Are you guys boyfriend and girlfriend?"

"Well, not really boyfriend and girlfriend. We're just—" Dave pauses, searching for the words that will effectively describe his relationship with Kathy Macaulay—"seeing each other."

"Is it physical?"

"Yeah." In a tone that implies "so what?"

"When was the last time you slept with her?"

"About a week ago."

"Safe sex, I hope."

Korpal sits quietly; he simply looks at Dave. Dave tries to meet the detective's steady gaze, can't hack it. Korpal leans forward on his elbows again.

"Aren't you curious about this homicide?" Dave's eyes snap back to look at Korpal; his face remains impassive.

"We've been sitting here for twenty minutes and you

haven't asked anything. Not a thing. Aren't you curious?"

"Hell, yeah, I'm curious. But they just pulled me in—I don't know anything."

"Do you know Heather?"

"Goodwin? Yeah ... "

"How long since you last saw her?"

"I saw her last Monday or Tuesday. Me and Kathy and Heather went to get something to eat. Vinnie and Cayle went along too."

Korpal nods his head. His face gives away nothing. Dave looks at Sweetman. The younger detective's face is a blank.

"Do you know Danae?"

Dave's eyes slide back to Korpal's face. "Uh-huh. Known her for years."

"She's a good friend of yours?"

"Uh-huh." Dave assumes an expression of curiosity. "Why? Do you know something about her?"

"Unfortunately, I do."

Nothing from Dave. He sits, waiting. Korpal sighs softly.

"Look, I'm not here to trick you, David. That's not my job. My job is to get to the bottom of a tragic occurrence. I can't sit here and not share facts with you. You say you haven't read a newspaper, seen TV, heard a radio news station. So there's no way you can know that Kathy and Heather and Danae are dead. That somebody blew their heads off."

Korpal sits back, waiting for some kind of response. Nothing.

Korpal needs this boy to tell the truth, and to that end the detective's voice is soft. But the urgency is clear.

"Who do you think would have so much anger to have done that to those girls? Was someone after them?"

Dave slumps forward, resting his elbows on both knees. "A lotta people were after them."

"Who?"

Dave shrugs. "Anyone. Like I said, a lotta people were after them." His voice has gone to a whisper.

"Look, Dave, if you're protecting someone, forget it. You only get one opportunity to tell the truth in a case like this. Start that process now. Get the burden off your shoulders."

Dave keeps looking down at the floor; his head moves from side to side.

"Don't let your feelings of friendship cloud this issue." Korpal waits. Then, raising his voice a notch, "Dave."

Dave's head comes up. He looks at the detective.

"Would you lie for Vinnie?"

Dave's eyes shift to one side again.

"If it wasn't important." Dave's voice sounds as if his throat is closing up on him.

"Do you think murder is important?"

"Yeah . . . " Leaden acceptance in his voice.

Then, just like that, everything changes. Dave sits up a little straighter in the chair; his voice, when he speaks again, has gathered, from somewhere, more strength.

"If somebody was there, okay? If somebody was—just there—would that person be guilty?"

"Where?" A fast glance at Sweetman.

"Where . . . they got killed."

Korpal takes a beat before he replies. "Well, if that person knows something, if they were hiding under the bed or something, then that person wouldn't be responsible. But if that person was connected to the crime in another way, then they would be responsible. There are variables here."

"But if I didn't *do* anything. If I was just . . . *there*."

Now it's Korpal's turn to shake his head. "David, that's for the courts to decide." He takes a hard look at the boy sitting across the table from him. Dave Adkins is sixteen years old and now, in the greenish glare of fluorescent lighting, he looks even younger.

"Were you there?"

Dave nods his head, yes.

"Then why did you tell me that other story?"

"I wanted to protect Vinnie and Cayle from getting nailed."

Dave pulls in a deep breath, lets it out. Breathes in again. He seems preoccupied, as if he might be listening for the sound of air as it moves through his lungs. Then he begins to speak.

"We were up there, partying—me and Vinnie, Kathy and Heather and Cayle. And Danae . . . " Dave's voice trails off. He looks at Korpal. He licks his lips.

"Do you need some water?"

"Yeah. Please."

Korpal fills another cup, places it in front of Dave. Dave's hand is shaking enough to spill some of the water as he lifts the cup to his lips.

"I don't know . . . " He brushes droplets of water from his shirt absently. Takes another sip. Sets down the cup. "Oh, man, I really don't know what happened. I was tripping." He looks at Korpal.

"First thing I knew, Cayle stood up and started knocking things over. And then Vinnie jumped up and started yelling at Danae."

"Yelling what?"

"Stuff about her being a dick tease, and shit."

Dave's hands grip his thighs, then the fingers relax slightly and he rubs his palms, hard, against the faded denim of his jeans.

"What did Danae say to that? Was she yelling, too?"

"Oh, man . . . " Dave shakes his head slowly. "I was in my own little space. But Vinnie was all 'You fuckin' bitch!' and 'you liar' and Cayle was all 'Fuck this!' and 'Yeah! Come on, let's go!' And then they were gone, outta there, and then . . ." Dave makes a small procedure of taking another sip of water.

Korpal asks if the girls were upset at this point. Dave shakes his head, no.

"All I know is ten minutes later Cayle and Vinnie came in with the shotgun and pulled it on me and told me to lay down on the floor. And I did. And then I heard the shots." Dave sets down the cup and rubs his hands together as if it were cold in the room. "And then, right after that, Vinnie pointed the fuckin' shotgun at me and said, 'Are you down?' And I said, 'Down on the floor?' And he said, 'Down to die.' "

. . . .

Dave Adkins told me, at different times, two different versions of the murders. What follows is the first version. I have made no attempt to edit; these are Dave's words, just as he spoke them.

Me and Vinnie and Cayle were sitting down, partying, and the three girls were partying too. Then me and Kathy and Cayle went out to get beer. We stopped for gas at a Full Service station and Cayle pushed the guy away and said, "I'm gonna full service your ass," when the guy tried to fill up the car. We were in the Mercedes and Kathy had the radio on really loud. We paid for the gas, though.

We had to go to two stores before we scored the beer. Then we went back to the house and pulled into the garage. Vinnie was downstairs, walking down the driveway, yelling "you bitch" back toward the house. I got him to calm down and go back upstairs with me.

Back up there me and Kathy started in kissing, so did Heather and Vinnie. Cayle grabbed Danae and tried to start kissing her, but she didn't want to, she had a boyfriend. So Cayle started in calling her a dick tease, and shit like that. So Heather grabbed a beer bottle—this little chick is *down*—and started in yelling, "You can't call my girlfriend a dick tease! I'm gonna fuck you up!"

So Kathy got all mad and told Cayle to get the fuck outta there.

So Cayle left, and about ten minutes later he comes back with the shotgun. [At this point Dave makes the sound of a shell being pumped into the chamber.] First he shot Kathy, and she falls up against the stereo. Then he shoots Heather. Then Danae.

I was sitting at the table with a magazine in my lap, cleaning and rolling weed. Vinnie was next to me, picking out the sticks. When Cayle started in shooting, I pissed my pants.

After he shot Danae, Cayle looked at us and said, "Don't look at the bodies. The first time you see something like this, just look away and it will be okay."

Kathy looked like she was asleep, there on the stereo. But you could hear her blood dripping down from the top of the stereo; it sounded like a heavy rain.

Heather had her head hanging down off the end of the bed. She had been lighting a cigarette and it was still lit, and you could see the end of the cigarette burning the flesh on her fingers. The blood was just *pouring* out [he makes a gushing sound] and it was just in huge puddles around three feet around her. Really thick puddles of blood. And you could see her brains lying on the floor under her head.

Danae was facedown on the bed. There were just chunks of bone and brains all over the wall and the bed. It was a king-size bed, and the blood just covered it. Her head was wide open and you could look in there and see her brains.

I went over to Kathy and shook her elbow, 'cause I still thought I could wake her up. But it was . . . dead. Like . . . *dead.* And her blood sounded just like rain.

Then we started walking around the room, and I stepped on something hard, and it was a round piece of bone—a big piece—on the floor. It was all red and white on one side, and there was a whole bunch of Kathy's blond hair on the other. And the room had a real thick smell in it. Of blood. 'Cause it has a smell, you know.

Then we left, and Cayle told Vinnie and me to go to Mexico, and to call him from there, he'd take care of everything. So we dropped him off at home, but then we decided to go to Oregon to see my aunt, 'cause we weren't gonna go someplace where they didn't speak English or anything.

I have a lotta dreams about Kathy and Heather and Danae. And they're always asking me why Cayle went off like that.

*T*he 12-gauge, pump-action Mossberg used to kill Kathy Macaulay, Heather Goodwin, and Danae Palermo was bought in 1983 by Dr. Michael Koss, Kathy's stepfather, for home protection. It was purchased at a gun store in Rosemead, and Koss will state, at the trial, that it was kept hidden, along with a bag of cartridges, in the closet of the master bedroom. His wife Linda will testify that she didn't want a gun in the house, and so she put a gun lock on the weapon soon after purchase.

Koss will go on to state that during the spring of 1989, shortly after the family moved into the house on Fairlawn Way, he came home early one afternoon to find Kathy hosting a pool party. As Koss walked across the poolside area, he noticed that one of the kids was holding the shotgun. At the trial, three years later, Koss will say he "made a sharp left and confiscated it."

Koss will also testify that he "took part in a joint discussion with Linda and Katherine later that evening. I asked Katherine how she knew the gun wasn't loaded, and she said, 'I looked down the barrel.' Or something equally stupid."

The shotgun was moved. This time it was placed in another closet, also in the master bedroom, but now it was hidden behind the clothes and a device for storing shoes. Koss will go on to say that the weapon was never fired after it was relocated.

They never found out who removed the safety lock.

. . . .

The small interrogation room is very quiet. Vinnie's eyes move from Korpal to Sweetman, as if he is pleading with them.

"I was only thinking about getting out of there without Cayle seeing us. He was on PCP—fuckin' tripping *big time*!" Vinnie's voice has gone hoarse again.

"Cayle walked in—I saw him standing in the corner— and I looked up and said, 'Fuck!' And he started in yelling, 'I'm gonna kill you all! You were fucking with me!' "

Korpal says nothing; he is simply listening. Sweetman makes the random note. Vinnie goes on.

"But we were all fucking with the girls. We were all trying to get pussy. Me and Heather and Danae were just wrestling, fooling around—I was trying to get up and they were pulling me down and stuff." He pauses, thinking. Then, "We were all playing with the gun that same night, jacking shells. But we only fired it by the pool.

"But then I seen Cayle up there with it, and then there was just blood everywhere, and him screaming he was gonna kill us all." Vinnie's eyes are in flight around the walls of the interrogation room. "I fuckin' bailed, I booked outta there. And Dave was right behind me and he was all 'He fuckin' shot my girlfriend!'

"Then we looked in the house and grabbed our clothes. Dave started losin' it. He was all"—here Vinnie acts out his idea of personal agony—" 'Oh, no-o-o-o-o-o!' I fuckin' grabbed the clothes and we bailed. And Cayle was in the driveway with the gun, all 'I'm gonna kill you!' "

He is breathless from the telling. Korpal nods his head, then he sits forward; his eyes and Vinnie Hebrock's eyes connect.

"Cayle Fiedler told us a considerably different story." Vinnie slumps in his chair; his head droops.

Korpal goes on. "Take a little break, collect your thoughts. I need to know the truth, every bit of it. And you need to make peace with yourself. You need to make peace with Kathy's parents, Heather's parents, Danae's parents. They *deserve* to know what happened. *Your* mom deserves to know. The people you left behind need the entire truth. That can be the beginning of healing for everybody." He pauses for a moment. "Tell me the truth, Vinnie."

Vinnie is very close to tears now. He looks desperately at both detectives.

"It's all a fuckin' blur. All I know, I was in the house and Cayle was on the bed and the shooting started ... "

"We need every bit, Vinnie."

"Okay, Kathy has this shotgun. It's in the closet in her mom's room. Me and Dave played with it a million times— just fuckin' around." Vinnie is controlling the urge to cry, but the tears remain close to the surface. "Anyway, Dave told me to go in through the window and get it. I went in through the glass door in the kitchen and I got the gun. And Dave got the shells and told me, 'Load the gun,' and I did."

Vinnie looks earnestly at Korpal. Looks at Sweetman.

"He told me he was just gonna scare 'em." Vinnie's voice is a bleat.

Korpal stares at Vinnie in disbelief. "With a loaded shotgun? C'mon ... "

"He walked in there and said, 'Fuck you all.' And then he popped a shot."

"But what did Kathy say when she saw him standing there with the shotgun? She must have said something, like ... I don't know ... 'Fuck you, Dave.' Something ... "

Vinnie shakes his head in a short, brisk movement. "No, she just stared at him. She was looking dead at him." And then, in afterthought, "I looked away when he shot her."

There is utter silence in the room. Not a creak of wood, not a cough. Nothing.

"Then who did he shoot?"

"I don't know. Either Heather or Danae. Then he pointed the gun at Cayle and said, 'Are you down with me?' "

"Why not call the police, Vinnie? Did that occur to you at all?"

Vinnie thinks about that one for a moment. "Dave's my homie. If he could shoot his own girlfriend, he could shoot me. I was scared." Vinnie's hands clench into fists. "Honest to God—I didn't shoot *nobody!* I only shot the gun outside the house, like I said."

"Did you know the back of Danae's head was shot off?"

Silence fills the room again; it is like a separate entity. And Vinnie has to get rid of it.

"Honest to God! I didn't shoot *nobody!*" He is panting now, as if he has been running. "He did all the shooting himself!"

The calm in Korpal's voice is ominous.

"We have different versions, Vinnie."

"What're they saying? *I* shot 'em? *I didn't shoot nobody!*"

"Come on, Vinnie. Tell the truth."

Now the tears come. Soft, snuffling sobs. Vinnie swipes at both cheeks with the heels of his hands. And, finally, he begins to speak.

"I had to shoot his girlfriend . . . "

. . . .

What follows is Dave Adkins's second version of the murders. Like the first version, it is verbatim.

We're partying upstairs. We had all taken acid,
except for Cayle, but the fry had went away. We went
swimming in the pool and used the Jacuzzi, and
then we went back upstairs. We were all kicking
back at the table in the middle of the room, and
Danae gets sick and runs into the bathroom. When

she came out, she went and laid down on the edge of the bed. Cayle says, "Fuck it, we need some more beer." And I said, "Shit, I'm too fucked up to drive." But Kathy says, "I'm cool to drive."

So we take the Mercedes and Cayle's hanging out the sunroof, drinking beer. When we got to the station, Cayle starts to pump the gas, but it won't go on. So Cayle's all "Fuck!" And he says to the attendant, "What the fuck's the matter with your gas station, man?"

Kathy gives the dude her credit card, and now the other attendant is telling Cayle to move. And Cayle says, "Who the fuck are *you* to tell me to move?" And I'm like trying to make peace, and Cayle's all "I'm gonna fuck him up!" The attendant hears him and says, "I oughtta kick his ass. Fucking kids!" And Cayle says, "Fuck you! Come on, dude!"

And I'm just watching, kinda surprised, because I always thought Cayle was quieter than this.

We finally got the credit card back and we go to the drugstore to get the brew. Cayle goes in 'cause he looks older than anybody else, and me and Kathy are in the car and we see two guys get out of a car and follow Cayle into the store. So I get out of the car and tell Kathy that if anything happens she should honk the horn.

Inside the store, the two guys are hitting on Cayle for change and he's all pissed off. Plus the clerk won't sell him the case of beer—Bud Dry, it was. So Cayle drops the whole case on the floor and we walk out. We scored at the next place we went, a liquor store. Then we went to Del Taco and Cayle just really started hogging out. He almost got in another fight there, and me and Kathy were just chillin'. She had partied with Cayle before; she knew how he could get. I knew him since the ninth grade, when we had a P.E. class together, and we used to sneak off for smokes, but we'd never really partied before.

As we drove back up the driveway of the house, we saw Vinnie walking down the driveway. I stuck my head out the window and said, "Hey, bro'—what's happening?" But Vinnie just kept on walking. We parked the car in the garage and I ran after Vinnie and told him to hold on, I'd be back in a second. Then I went upstairs. Heather was still there and she had a black eye, and Danae was all drunk and excited. Heather told me she got in a fight with Vinnie. Cayle was already starting in on the beer. I grabbed a couple and ran back downstairs to get Vinnie's story.

I said, "Hey, bro'—what's up?" and Vinnie just started to yell up at the guesthouse:

"You fuckin' bitch! You cunt!"

And I handed him one of the beers, and he said, "Fuck these bitches."

And I'm all "Whaddaya mean, dude?"

And Vinnie said, "Let's smoke 'em."

"*What?* Are you fuckin' *crazy?*"

"No, man. That fuckin' bitch kicked me in the nuts, and Kathy wants me to leave, and I got nowhere to go, and we did all them burgs and scams, man . . . "

He was talking about dealing and robbing a radio and stuff, and I said, "You want to just walk away from all this madness." And then we figured we'd just go in the main house, only I didn't want to go upstairs and ask Kathy. But she had told me about a sliding window there that was unlocked, you know? So I could always get in if she wasn't home. So we went in that way.

I went to the refrigerator and started to eat something, and I was just rambling away there, thinking Vinnie was behind me on the bar stool. But first thing I knew, Vinnie was behind me with the

shotgun and shells, saying, "Here, hold these." And I
shoved the shells in my pocket, all "What're we
gonna do, Vinnie?"

"We're gonna go shoot."

"Cool." I thought he meant in the backyard,
because it was dark and we could see the sparks.

So we went outside and Vinnie says, "Let's go
fuckin' blow 'em away. Fuckin' Heather kicked me in
the nuts. Fuckin' Danae won't get with me. And
fuckin' Kathy told me to fuckin' get out."

I had this sandwich in my hand and I set it down
on a table there in the backyard. I still thought we
were just gonna shoot up in the air, like we always
do. I took the shells outta my pocket and put them
on the table, and then I looked around and no Vinnie.
I looked some more and there's Vinnie up at the top
of the stairs [of the guesthouse]. I started in grabbing
the shells and the cigarettes, and shoved 'em back in
my pocket. I was still thinking that Vinnie's just
gonna shoot off the balcony, so I went on up.

Vinnie's next to the door with the gun, Rambo-style,
at his side. And he tells me, "Open the door, man."

I tried to open the door, and it was locked. And I'm
thinking, "What the fuck's *my* door locked for?" I
can see Cayle through the glass, so I said, "Open the
fuckin' door, dude." And he does.

Vinnie runs past me, around Cayle. Then he cocks
the gun [Dave makes the sound of a gun cocking]
and aims it at Kathy. She said, "What . . . ?"

And Vinnie blows her shit all over the place.

Then Cayle grabs the gun outta Vinnie's hands
and says, "I'll do this one!" And he blows Heather's
shit out the other side.

Then Cayle kills Danae and points the gun at me.
But I knew the gun only holds three shells. Then
Vinnie walks in between us and says, "It's over."

And I say, "What the fuck you mean? It ain't over!"

I go over to Kathy and shake her elbow, and I'm thinking, "This can't be real, I'm still frying." And Kathy's blood is pouring like raindrops on the stereo.

I looked at Heather, and her head is hanging down from the bed and blood is just *pouring* all over the rug.

Then I looked at Danae and she had a big fuckin' gash in the back of her head. And when I turned around I kicked this piece of head with skull and flesh on it, all white and red with blond hair hanging off it. And then I looked around again and those heads looked like three squashed pumpkins.

I had pissed my pants.

And then I said, "*Fuck!* What're we gonna do?"

And Cayle said, "Just don't look at the bodies. It'll be cool. I been through this before—just turn around and walk away. It'll be cool."

And I yelled, "It *won't* be cool, man!"

I was in a haze, a complete haze, and I picked up my jacket and started to walk out the door when Cayle said, "Get the beer. I paid for it."

I started to hit Cayle, but Vinnie stopped me. We just grabbed our stuff and went down to the laundry room. Cayle was holding the shotgun now, and I wasn't saying anything. I was just tripping.

After we left the laundry room, we went to the garage and sat in the Mercedes, and I said, "Okay, where do you want me to take you guys?"

We started to drive down the hill and Cayle says, "Take me home. You guys leave the state. Don't worry about anything, just fuckin' *go*."

But Cayle also keeps telling me, "You just shot fuckin' Heather and Danae!" And I kept saying back to him, "What? Fuck you, you're tripping."

Anyway, we dropped Cayle off at home, and we drove on up to Oregon, 'cause that's where my aunt lives. And that's where we got busted.

· · · · · · · · · · · · · ·

On March 22, the day before they flew up to Washington State, Detectives Mike Korpal and Tim Sweetman went, with search warrants, to Mike Fiedler's apartment and then to Mrs. Davies's (Cayle's grandmother's) home. They spoke briefly with Mrs. Davies but there was very little she could tell them. At the Fiedler apartment they collected articles such as a shower curtain, towels, and clothing. And a call was placed to Cayle (at his mother's house) in Washington. Korpal and Cayle spoke at length, and Korpal urged Cayle to come back to Los Angeles immediately. The conversation was not recorded.

When he got off the phone, Korpal spoke with Mike Fiedler. The detective emphasized two points: this case was being investigated to the fullest extent possible, and how important it was for Cayle to get back to town. Fiedler seemed uncomfortable talking to the police, and although he gave Korpal his ex-wife's telephone number, the detective did not press him for her address. Korpal was working within a strict forty-eight-hour time limit.* The focus had to be placed on Dave Adkins and Vinnie Hebrock.

· · · · · · · · · · · · · ·

"Afterwards they made me drive, and I kept saying, 'We gotta go back! We gotta go back!' "

Dave's voice is louder now, as if the relief he feels at being able to tell the truth, finally, has strengthened him.

"When we got to Cayle's house he said, 'You guys go to

---

*Once a suspect is in custody he must be arraigned before a judge within a forty-eight-hour time frame. Otherwise he must be released from custody.

Mexico.' And I said, 'Why do *I* have to go to Mexico? *I* didn't do anything.' And he said, ' 'Cause you're an accomplice.' And then, driving to the freeway, later, I told Vinnie we should go back and tell the cops. Do whatever it takes. Fuck . . . !" The final word is delivered in an explosive rush of self-righteous anger.

"What did Vinnie say to that?" Korpal's voice is maintaining a soft, almost nurturing tone.

"He didn't want to." Dave's voice has dropped again.

"Because he shot someone?"

"Yeah . . . "

"Who?"

This is too direct for Dave. His whole body backs off; he seems to shrink into the chair. So Korpal tries another approach: he makes a little small talk. About his work as a cop. About guns.

And Dave seems to loosen up again. "You were at Kathy's house, right?"

Korpal nods his head; he was there.

"Okay, you know that little table near the couch?" Another nod. "Well, I was sitting there. And Kathy was over here, playing the stereo." Dave's hands move briskly, pointing, as he talks. He is like a retired general reenacting a battle on a tabletop. "And Heather and Danae were over here. Next thing I knew, Vinnie and Cayle came in the door. Cayle had the gun. They walked in, saying, 'Get down!' And I got down on the floor and then Vinnie came over and put his foot on my back." He sucks in air. "And then, *bam!*" He pauses dramatically. "And then his foot came off my back, and I was shaking and crying, and I heard two more quick bangs."

"Where was Cayle standing with the gun when Vinnie told you to 'get down'?"

Dave is ready with his reply. "They both said, 'Get down!' And Vinnie came over to me. And Cayle cocked the gun."

"But you told me Vinnie shot someone. How do you know that?"

This answer comes nearly as fast as the one preceding it. " 'Cause they were tripping about it in the car." Dave's voice changes eerily, taking on the pitch and delivery of another person. " 'You got one and I got two.'

"And then Cayle put his hand on my shoulder and said, 'Yeah, we're all in this together.' "

"Did he say, 'I got two and you got one'?"

"He said"—Dave makes an obvious effort to remember— 'I got two and you got . . . ' No . . . " He stops, shakes his head in a brisk movement, goes back. "He said, 'I got one, you got two.' "

"Cayle said this to Vinnie?"

"Yeah."

"Did you ever try to reason with Vinnie?"

"Yeah. Later, when I pulled over and said, 'We gotta go back, dude.' " And Dave begins to reenact that moment, taking both parts again. "He put the gun to my head and said, 'I'll fuckin' blow you away right now. I don't care if you are my friend. I'm not going down for this.' " Dave goes on to say that the dilemma was solved when he suggested they go to Oregon, instead of Mexico as Cayle had ordered.

"Why Oregon? Because of your relatives up there?"

"Well, if we'd gone to Mexico they probably would've pulled us over."

"Yeah, but that would have been good for you. Right?"

"No. It wouldn't of."

Korpal persists. "But if the cops pulled you over, it would have given you an opportunity to get out of there. You would have had every opportunity to tell them what happened. Why didn't you think about that?"

" . . . I don't know."

Nobody says anything for a while. Korpal blows his nose, wads the tissue, throws it away. Sweetman turns back a few pages in his notebook, checking something he has written. Dave sits looking down at the floor. Then:

"Where's the gun, Dave?"

"Out in Grants Pass." Then, very softly, almost wistfully, "I learned to ride my bike in Grants Pass."

"Where did you leave the gun in Grants Pass?"

"I couldn't tell you that."

"Why did Vinnie keep hold of the gun all the way up there?"

"He was in charge of it. Like when we'd stop for gas, he'd be all 'You just do what I tell you, da-da-da-da-da-da.' But all the way up there I was telling him, 'If you don't want to take me back down [to L.A.], then we're going to my relatives and tell them exactly what went down.'" Dave looks straight at Korpal now.

"It was intense being with him. You know, the fact of knowing what he did."

"Killed your girlfriend?"

Dave looks down at the floor again. "Yeah." Korpal mentions his cold and the deafness it is creating. He reminds Dave that he must speak up.

"Where'd the gun come from, Dave?"

Dave tells him the gun came from Kathy's house, that he had seen it before, handled it often. That the first time he shot it, he was with Kathy.

"When would that have been?"

"Gimme a minute to think." Dave looks off, running events past his memory. "I'm sixteen now, and I been going out with her since I was twelve ... so about four years ago." He pauses again.

"Okay, we didn't go *out* for all four years, but we stayed friends. And *all* Kathy's friends handled that gun."

That single statement will prove to be the only thing upon which all three of them—Dave Adkins, Vinnie Hebrock, and Cayle Fiedler—are in complete agreement.

SMOKED

The interrogation continues. Dave tells Korpal that he, himself, drank three cases of beer on the night of the murders. And that he took two tabs of acid, "they had little stars on them," provided by Danae. He says they all took the acid earlier in the day, "under that bridge near the Arroyo, where everybody goes." But, he continues, they went back to Fairlawn Way "when it began to get dark."

And, Dave says, that's when the trouble started. That's when Cayle and Vinnie began to fight with the girls. When Korpal asks what the fight was about, Dave tells him he doesn't know.

"All of a sudden, it was just on. And Kathy was all 'If you guys want to fuck around, then fuck around outside.' And Cayle was all 'Fuck you! We'll fuck around!' And then he and Vinnie went out."

Both Korpal and Sweetman are listening intently.

"I thought they were just fooling around. And that's what Kathy said when they came back with the gun. 'Put that back. Stop fucking around.' And Heather and Danae said, 'Oh, they're just fools, they're just suckers.' And Cayle said, 'Yeah, we're just fools.' And then Vinnie came around . . . "

It is at this point that Korpal interrupts.

"I gotta tell you something, Dave. You're telling me some stuff here that's making me believe something else happened and is getting twisted here. I already interviewed Vinnie and Cayle. And Vinnie took a lie detector test and he passed one hundred percent."

Dave simply looks at the detective. But everything about him, his face, the way he's sitting in the chair, his hands—everything—has, without any movement whatsoever, shifted.

Korpal's voice remains soft. Almost tender.

"Look, I know you're scared, Dave."

"Uh-huh." Nothing moves; even his breathing seems to have come to a halt.

"I know your life is shattered almost as much as the

girls'. But what happened in that room is a separate tragedy. Like the girls' parents. And your mom. Separate tragedies, Dave. I've been in touch with your mom; she loves you no matter what. Make it right for everyone, Dave. Get things on the right road."

Korpal pauses, looking at Dave. Dave has stretched out one hand; the tips of his fingers are moving along the edge of the table in front of him, feeling the ridges as if they held some message for him.

Korpal goes on. "You do owe Kathy's parents—all the parents—an explanation."

"Okay." Dave draws in a deep breath, sighs it out. "We were partying under the bridge and they started in arguing. We went back to the house. They got the gun. They put me on the floor. They . . ."

Korpal breaks in. "Dave, here's Vinnie's statement." He begins to read aloud from a paper he takes out of his notebook. " 'Cayle had nothing to do with it. Cayle was on the bed with Danae. I shot Kathy. Dave shot Heather and Danae, and then he put the gun in Cayle's face. We drove Cayle home.' " Korpal looks up from the paper. "Last night I spoke to Cayle, David. Cayle took a polygraph test . . ."

". . . And Cayle passed." Dave finishes Korpal's sentence.

"Exactly." Korpal puts Vinnie's statement back inside his notebook. "I need the truth from you, man. What I got is two guys telling the same story, and one guy who's just scared to death of the consequences. *Scared to death.*" He leans in closer. "Get rid of the burden, man. Unload on me. You can't bring the girls back, but you *can* help their parents, ease their suffering a little bit."

"How would I do that?" A slight tremor works its way across Dave's face.

"Tell the truth. And say you're sorry. 'Sorry' begins the process. It doesn't really help, but it *begins* to help. One of the biggest problems with Kathy's parents is their terrible feelings of betrayal. The girl you had a relationship with died. What set it off?"

"Wasn't me. I didn't set anything off." Sullen now.

Korpal goes on. "Why would Vinnie lie? He cried when he told me the truth—telling what happened was one of the most painful things he ever did. Because he felt he betrayed you, David. He loves you. You're the only thing he has in his life. But he didn't want to blame Cayle for something Cayle didn't do." Korpal takes a couple of beats. "Do you?"

Nothing from Dave. He brings one hand up slowly, to brush the hair away from his face.

Tim Sweetman is motionless. His eyes move in steady arcs from Korpal's face to Dave's and back again.

Korpal's voice, when he speaks, is filled with quiet urgency. "I know what the truth is, man. I know how difficult this is for you. I don't want to hurt you, but you have an obligation to those girls' parents."

Nothing.

"Tell me what really happened."

Dave slumps in the chair. He sighs. He shakes his head slowly and closes his eyes.

"We . . . went on a beer run. When we came back, Vinnie and Heather and Danae had been arguing . . ." His head droops. "I don't know . . . I don't know . . ." Dave sounds as if he might be close to tears. But he is not crying.

"What happened, Dave?"

"We went out and got the gun, and . . . we walked in . . . and Vinnie shot Kathy . . ." He is nearly choking on the words.

"Do you know why?"

Dave shakes his head vigorously. He mutters something about the fight between Vinnie, Heather, and Danae.

"Are you telling the truth now?"

Dave's head comes up with a jerk.

"Yeah!"

And then he begins to speak again.

*U*pon the conclusion of their interviews with Dave Adkins and Vinnie Hebrock on March 23, Detectives Korpal and Sweetman flew back to Los Angeles.

On Sunday, March 24, Mike Fiedler drove his son Cayle to the Pasadena police station and Cayle surrendered to Mike Korpal.

On Monday, March 25, a complaint charging Dave Adkins and Vinnie Hebrock with three counts of murder was filed by head deputy District Attorney David Disco. The complaint was filed in adult court so that extradition papers could be issued to bring the suspects back from Oregon.

On Tuesday, March 26, Disco assigned the case to deputy D.A. Nancy Naftel. That same day Mike Korpal and Tim Sweetman flew back up to Salem.

By Tuesday afternoon, March 26, after waiving extradition, Dave Adkins and Vinnie Hebrock got into a rented car with Detectives Korpal and Sweetman. Korpal took the wheel, with Vinnie in the front passenger seat. Sweetman and Dave sat in the back. Packed in separate cartons, in the trunk of the car, were items of evidence taken from both suspects' backpacks and persons: clothing, necklaces and rings, snapshots, letters, a pair of shoes, and the Oregon GSR reports and rights cards.

The reels of Dave and Vinnie's taped interviews are in Korpal's pockets. These tapes are central to the case and Korpal does not want to take any chances with them. He has heard other stories of magnetically taped interviews and confessions being inadvertently erased by airport security measures. The contents of the cartons in the trunk of the car are important, but what is on the tapes is crucial.

The trip from Salem, Oregon, to the Portland airport takes about an hour and a half. Adkins and Hebrock, Korpal and Sweetman, will then board an Alaska Airlines flight back to Los Angeles.

It's quiet in the car, nobody is saying much of anything. Then Vinnie turns around to look over the back of the seat at Dave.

"They got us, dude."

"Yeah, I know." Dave's shoulders hitch up in a shrug. "I told 'em where the gun was."

Vinnie smiles crookedly. He understands and accepts any and all of Dave Adkins's frailties.

"Yeah. I told 'em where the car was."

Neither detective asks any questions during the ride; what conversation there is is completely general. At some point, however, Vinnie will tell Tim Sweetman that he drove Linda Koss's Mercedes at 150 mph through Redding, California.

. . . .

Shortly past 6:00 P.M. on Tuesday, March 26, Dave Adkins and Vinnie Hebrock were booked at the Pasadena police station. They were then immediately transferred to Eastlake Juvenile Hall in Los Angeles. TV reporters with camera crews crowded the entrances of both facilities, and the triple homicides and subsequent capture of the suspects continued to be the lead story on local—and national—news programs.

On Wednesday, March 27, Dave and Vinnie appeared before Municipal Court Judge Elvira Mitchell for their arraignment. After confirming their identities and ages, Judge Mitchell suspended all adult proceedings and bound the boys over to juvenile court. Stephen M. Romero and Robert J.

Brown, attorneys who were seated on the juvenile court defense panel that day, were appointed by the court to defend Dave and Vinnie, respectively. The boys were then returned, to be held without bail at Juvenile Hall.

There had been some mention, in the papers, that the District Attorney's Office would seek the death penalty if Dave and Vinnie were convicted of the murders of Kathy Macaulay, Heather Goodwin, and Danae Palermo. Nancy Naftel swept away all doubt on this point when she stated that California law prohibits the execution of minors.

It seemed clear, however, that the state would go for convictions with Dave Adkins and Vinnie Hebrock being tried as adults. If tried and convicted in juvenile court, the maximum term for first-degree murder would be imprisonment to age twenty-five under the California Youth Authority. If tried and convicted as adults, the maximum sentence for first-degree murder would be life in prison without the possibility of parole.

The rest of their lives. In prison. Dave Adkins was sixteen years old at the time of the murders. Vinnie Hebrock was seventeen.

The Fitness Hearing that would determine whether or not Dave Adkins and Vinnie Hebrock were fit to be tried as juveniles was slated for the morning of June 18, 1991. People began arriving at the Pasadena Courthouse before eight o'-clock. The networks were well represented: news anchors with highly recognizable faces sat, with their crews, on the wooden benches that line the corridors outside the courtrooms. Reporters from the *Los Angeles Times* and the *Pasadena Star-News* took early notes. Print journalists from national and local magazines read newspapers and chatted idly. Photographers fussed with lenses and flashbulbs.

One of the earliest arrivals was Pam Adkins, Dave's mother. She seemed to be enfolded by women: Sandie Wells; two or three other friends; a couple of relatives. Dave Adkins bears a striking resemblance to his mother. They share the same burnished good looks; they both seem to radiate good health. She is overweight now, but it is not difficult to imagine Pam Adkins at eighteen, at Highland Park High School, or at the beach, taking a wave. Brian Wilson composed songs about suntanned, blond girls like Pam; she was one of the California Girls, one of the Rhondas.

Seated in a cluster near Pam Adkins are a group of Dave's friends. Jason Cheever is there, and Eric Bonworthy. Michelle Sandford, a girl Dave used to go out with, is there, with her younger sister Marci. Michelle, who is tall and blond and rather icily beautiful, keeps saying, to anyone who will listen, "Dave's innocent. He's innocent and Cayle Fiedler isn't telling the whole truth."

Michelle's younger sister, Marci, sits quietly, close to Pam, as if to draw strength from her. And, in fact, Pam Adkins does seem to possess some inner resolution that enables her to sit here, hands folded in her lap, listening carefully when someone speaks to her and answering in near whispers as she waits for the hearing to begin.

At the other end of the corridor are three other women. They stand close to each other, too, but these three are busy with conversation. They are Vinnie Hebrock's mother, Faye, and his sister, Tiki. The third woman, who seems to be running interference with the press, describes herself as "a friend of the family." Faye Hebrock looks angry; her face is closed, pinched-looking, but every once in a while her daughter will say something that amuses her, and she will laugh out loud. As the reporters and journalists approach Mrs. Hebrock for comments, she shakes her head vehemently, denying any relationship to Vinnie. She says, over and over, "Who said I was his mother?"

Neither Mrs. Adkins nor Mrs. Hebrock look at each other. There is no eye contact whatsoever between them.

At 9:30 A.M. the doors swing open and people begin to file into the courtroom. The Pasadena Courthouse is a fairly new building, built within the last twenty years. Most of the courtrooms are the same; a plain raised bench for the presiding judge, glaring fluorescent lights, rows of theaterlike seating, jury box, desks for the bailiff and court clerk.

Stephen Romero and Robert Brown are already at the counsel tables, as is Nancy Naftel. Juvenile Court Judge Sandy Kreigler takes his place at the bench. Now the bailiff escorts Dave Adkins and Vinnie Hebrock into the courtroom through a locked door to the right of the bench. This is the access to the holding cells, where prisoners are kept when they are not needed in the courtroom.

Dave is first through the door; he is wearing dark, well-pressed trousers, a white shirt, and a black tie. His hair is freshly shampooed and it gleams gold under the lights. His eyes scan the spectators as he walks toward his chair at the counsel table, and when he spots people he knows, he nods and very nearly—but not quite—smiles at them.

Vinnie has on the gray sweatshirt and bright orange jumpsuit provided by Juvenile Hall. He looks at no one as he walks in, looks neither right nor left. He seems slightly different today; something about him has changed. His hair has the same punkish styling, his posture is as bad, but there's something. Then you realize what it is: he is wearing thick, horn-rimmed glasses. He takes his place next to Dave Adkins. They do not look at each other.

The first person to be sworn in is Detective Korpal. Under Nancy Naftel's questioning, he describes the crime scene at Fairlawn Way and the condition of the bodies. He says that, upon being questioned in Salem, Oregon, "Minor" Hebrock admitted "shooting Dave's girlfriend, Kathy."

At this point the judge interrupts to say that much of the testimony in this Fitness Hearing is hearsay.

Detective Korpal continues his testimony, ending with the information that Alaska Airlines had lost one of the evidence cartons collected in Oregon after "Minor" Adkins and "Minor" Hebrock were apprehended by the police.

Cayle Fiedler takes the stand. He is rather trendily dressed in black, with an off-white blazer. His eyes are covered by a pair of wraparound dark glasses. Settling himself into the witness chair, he takes off the glasses and, at Naftel's request, identifies Dave and Vinnie by pointing at them. Then, taking it point by point, he delivers an account of the events he witnessed on March 21, 1991.

As Cayle describes the murders, both Dave and Vinnie sit, without expression, watching him.

Cayle talks for about twenty minutes; then he is excused.

The attorneys speak to the court. Romero stresses that there was no argument between Dave and Heather, "or any other girl" on March 21. He questions Cayle's actions and the fact that neither Cayle, nor his father, Mike, contacted the police. He talks about the lack of fingerprints and the lost evidence. Finally, he questions the issue: "Are Cayle Fiedler's statements accurate or are they lies told to incriminate a sixteen-year-old boy?"

Brown presents Vinnie Hebrock as a victim. He talks about Vinnie's inability to read or write, his alcoholic parents. He says that Vinnie functions as a seven- or eight-year-old child due to his learning disabilities and "cognitive immaturity." He cites psychological tests that suggest Vinnie Hebrock might be a victim of fetal alcohol syndrome. "He was lost before he started."

Both defense attorneys urge the court to find Dave Adkins and Vinnie Hebrock fit to be tried as juveniles. They cite lack of criminal sophistication, dysfunctional home settings, and prior juvenile records showing no use of weapons. Both Romero and Brown urge the judge to believe that rehabilitation is probable.

Now Nancy Naftel speaks. She states unequivocally that "nothing here suggests any method of rehabilitation." Recounting specifics of the crime, which she refers to as a "massacre," she reminds Judge Kreigler that "this was not self-defense. These minors were more than a danger to those girls." She states that "Vinnie Hebrock's inability to read is of no moment. He functions, is cooperative, and seems quite capable of making decisions." She ends her plea by saying that she "can't conceive of anything more serious than murder. No rehabilitation is possible in a few short years."

Judge Kreigler makes his decision. After citing the law in which "the burden is upon minors to prove they are fit," he goes quickly through all of the criteria set forth by the attorneys. Then he looks at Dave Adkins and Vinnie Hebrock.

"The circumstances and gravity of this offense, the grotesque enormity of this triple homicide, coupled with the knowledge that they knew very well it was morally and legally wrong, lead me to find these minors unfit for treatment in Juvenile Court."

The case against Adkins and Hebrock is then dismissed, "without prejudice," to the Superior Court of Los Angeles.

Dave and Vinnie are remanded to the L.A. County Sheriff, to be transferred to special housing (for unfit juveniles) in the L.A. County Jail. No bail pending.

The next day, at their arraignment in Pasadena Superior Court, both boys plead innocent to three counts of murder.

About three weeks after the Fitness Hearing, I went with Dave's mother to visit him in the special housing unit of the L.A. County Jail. This unit accommodates, in separate areas, not only unfit juveniles but also homosexuals and informants. Dave and I sat across from each other and spoke on telephones through a thick sheet of smudged Plexiglas.

We make small talk. The size of his living space; the movies that are rented and shown on the VCR in the unit; the fact that there are no arrangements for schooling for any of the juveniles in special handling. We talk about books. He tells me he wants to read *Where the Red Fern Grows*.

Pam Adkins sits to my left, her eyes on her son, as we sit talking. Between the two of them there is what appears to be a warm relationship. She seems to be absolutely convinced of Dave's innocence in this crime, and she is committed to his defense. She speaks often, almost obsessively, about Dave's helpfulness to her when he was growing up; she talks about the times he would bring her flowers, or do the cleaning up.

One of Pam's favorite stories about Dave has to do with Christmas of 1985. Her boyfriend, J.D., was still alive then; he would not be killed until the following June, and he had fulfilled the role of father figure for the past four years. The family had not yet bought their Christmas tree, and money was tight, even though J.D. was working as a welder. Dave was just eleven years old that year, but he had scored a part-time job on a Christmas tree lot. Two nights before Christmas Eve, the kid came home with a tree strapped to his skateboard.

"J.D.! J.D.! Look! I saved you fifty bucks!"

It is one of Pam Adkins's most treasured stories about her son Dave, and invariably, she ends it with a fond sigh and the question, "Isn't he a wonderful kid?"

When J.D. died, he took most of the family feeling with him. There was no "man of the family" now, but fifteen-year-old Dan Adkins began to assume the role of a father. He often complained to Pam that he was worried about "his little brother's friends." And he warned her: Dave would get in trouble one day, because of Kathy Macaulay and Vinnie Hebrock.

. . . .

On August 22, 1991, a preliminary hearing was held with Judge Elvira Mitchell presiding. Dave and Vinnie were escorted into the courtroom by the bailiff just before the proceedings began. Both boys were cuffed, with their hands behind their backs. Dave is wearing the same dark trousers and white shirt with a black tie. Vinnie is wearing civilian clothes, too: dark trousers, pale blue shirt, dark tie. He is not wearing glasses today. They are seated, side by side, between their attorneys, Stephen Romero and Robert Brown. Armed deputies—two for each defendant—move in to stand a few feet behind them.

Nancy Naftel calls her first witness: Dr. James K. Riebe, the deputy medical examiner. He describes his findings and identifies photographs of the victims' bodies. Both Romero and Brown cross-examine. Romero, in particular, has questions about whether or not a person lying next to Danae Palermo (at the time she was shot) would be splattered with blood and/or tissue. The reply is, "Not necessarily." Brown's focus has to do with the bruising that occurred (with Heather and Danae) before they were killed.

The next witness is Detective Mike Korpal. Nancy Naftel asks him to describe the crime scene. Then she asks about his interviews with Cayle Fiedler and, in Oregon, with the suspects. Romero and Brown cross-examine again.

There is "no affirmative defense" at this time, but both Romero and Brown make motions for dismissal. Romero's grounds are "Cayle Fiedler's obvious wrongdoing in fleeing the state, and the scene of the crime." He also bears in on what he describes as "deceit and subterfuge" in the police investigation of the murders, citing the use of "religion and forgiveness of families," and the fact that polygraph tests were mentioned but were not in fact done.

Brown talks about Cayle Fiedler "holding himself clear of responsibility, blaming Dave Adkins and Vinnie Hebrock." He urges Judge Mitchell to believe that Vinnie was "simply there." He finishes his plea by placing all three murders "squarely at David Adkins's feet."

Nancy Naftel cites the statements of both defendants, referring again to the murders as "a massacre." She states that both Dave and Vinnie "assassinated three innocent girls."

Both motions for dismissal are denied by Judge Mitchell.

Dave Adkins and Vinnie Hebrock will be arraigned on September 6, 1991, in Superior Court, on three counts of violations of Criminal Code 187: Homicide. They will both plead innocence.

....

Dave Adkins has plenty of time to reflect in jail. He will remember scoring weed in East L.A., and seeing a couple of Hispanic kids exchange shots in the ensuing beef. He will recall getting caught in cross fire when he "was kicking it with a Crip set in Altadena."

He remembers riding motorcycles at top speed to the peak of Elephant Top Mountain. And the time he drove up there with a girl he met at a party. They were in her car and

SMOKED

Dave was speeding. When a cop pulled them over, Dave told the girl to "act drunk."

"I am drunk."

"Act drunker."

When the cop asked for Dave's license and registration, Dave gave him the golden boy grin.

"I have no license, sir. But my girlfriend here is really drunk, and I'm the designated driver."

According to Dave, the cop said, "Good thinking."

Then, as the officer was about to turn away, he spotted the joint tucked behind Dave's ear, the skinny joint almost lost in the thicket of Dave's hair.

"What's that?"

Dave's smile wavers, fades. He gets serious. "Well, that's a joint, sir. I was going to smoke it after I made sure my girlfriend got home safely. And *way* after I got home."

The end of the story, according to Dave, is a happy one: the cop lets them go.

He will say he spends most of his time thinking about Kathy Macaulay. He says that, "if she wasn't dead, she'd be *tripped* out. And she'd be coming down here to see me every single day." He has a particular memory of being in Placement, in Redondo Beach, when Kathy was making that drive daily, "an hour and a half each way, man." How one day she got there and the house parent wouldn't let Dave go out, so Kathy went back home. Then, when another of the house parents relented, Dave called Kathy and she drove straight back to Redondo and took him to the beach.

He thinks about all the times Kathy took him shopping with her mother's credit cards. And he remembers life at the guesthouse on Fairlawn Way. How there were "just parades of girls in and out. Full-out, party-down people. It was just 'Bring your own dope, your own booze, and do whatever you want.'"

Toward the end of July 1991, two Hispanic kids got into

Dave's cell and beat him up. He says he had no idea how the beef came about, but he doesn't think it had anything to do with the murders. Dave got a shiner; one assailant's nose was broken.

During this time Dave saw his mother and Sandie Wells regularly. Missy Gillette came to see him often, as did her younger sister Meredith. Kelly French, Jason Cheever, and Melanie Pinkney visited him as well. Peggy Shurtleff wrote long letters.

Vinnie was visited sporadically by his mother. Once in a while one of his brothers or his sister would come along.

Although Dave and Vinnie were housed in the same unit, they saw each other only in the dayroom, where inmates pass time by watching TV and playing cards or dominoes. Dave will say that Vinnie is "real afraid of being sent to the penitentiary." Of himself, Dave says he'll "take what's coming." Even though, according to him, he is innocent of any wrongdoing.

In speaking about prison, he will say, "I heard the pen is just like a city. Like a big bazaar. You walk down the row and here's one guy's cell, and he's selling food. And here's another cell, and that guy might be selling clothes. Another cell, it's dope. Or jewelry. Everything's for sale in the pen. So I guess it's a lot like real life."

Vinnie Hebrock turned eighteen in October of 1991. This meant that legally he was no longer considered a juvenile. He was transferred to a detention camp on the outskirts of Los Angeles.

Dave Adkins remained in the special housing unit at County Jail until April 1992, when he had his eighteenth birthday.

He was then transferred to Wayside detention camp, to wait, as Vinnie was waiting, for their trial to begin.

SMOKED

....

It is the decision of Superior Court Judge J. Michael Byrne that Dave Adkins and Vinnie Hebrock be tried together, but separately, in a little known legal procedure involving dual juries. The defense attorneys cited a 1965 State Supreme Court ruling that statements made by one defendant cannot be presented verbatim if they are damaging to another defendant. Deputy District Attorney Nancy Naftel agreed; both defendants have made statements she wants to use, with each defendant implicating the other in the crime. These statements are so interwoven they cannot—and, most attorneys agree, should not—be separated.

This will be Nancy Naftel's first bifurcated trial, and it is a difficult undertaking, but all three attorneys feel strongly that it will be better for the families of all concerned if the trial takes place as quickly as possible. Out-of-state witnesses are another, though lesser, consideration.

Jury selection begins on June 23, 1992, in Courtroom F, the largest courtroom in the Pasadena Courthouse. Judge Byrne presides. He is in his early to mid-forties, slender and bespectacled. His face is intelligent and thoughtful. On appearance alone, Michael Byrne is the kind of man you would choose for a career in the law: He *looks* as if he would be fair.

Today, as the time-consuming procedure of jury selection begins, double the usual number of prospective jurors are waiting outside Room F, J. Michael Byrne's courtroom. Eighty to one hundred people at a time are led in by the bailiff.

Now Dave Adkins and Vinnie Hebrock are escorted into the courtroom. Dave has had his hair styled; it is short, and it makes him look even more clean-cut than usual. Vinnie, too, has shorter hair, and the rattail at the back is gone. They both have on the dark trousers and light-colored shirts they will wear throughout the trial. And Vinnie's glasses have made a reappearance.

Something else has changed as well: Robert Brown has been replaced as Vinnie's counsel by Rickard Santwier. Santwier and Stephen Romero, Dave Adkins's attorney, appear to be about the same age: mid-forties. Santwier is rather tall, with a heavy build; he looks as if he might have played football at one time. His face is big and long and pale; he wears glasses and his eyes are combative and intelligent.

Like Santwier, Romero is stocky of build, but he is not as tall. And where Santwier seems almost colorless, Romero is a bit of a dandy, given to crimson ties and carefully fitted suits with a good deal of linen on display at the cuff and neckline.

Deputy D.A. Nancy Naftel is a reed of a woman, standing not much taller than five feet three. Her legs, beneath the skirts of her tailored suits, look strong, like the legs of an athlete. She is probably in her early forties.

Before jury selection begins, there is a request that Judge Byrne will hear: Rex Heinke, attorney for the Courtroom TV cable network, is asking that they be allowed to televise the trial. Heinke argues that the "dignity of the court will not be compromised," and he cites the Kennedy rape trial and the Rodney King beating trial as examples of "no spectacle." He further promises that neither jury will be photographed.

Byrne is not so sure. And he's worried about the ages of the two defendants. That said, he allows the attorneys to speak.

Santwier objects strenuously and at length. He is worried about the fairness of the trial, the victims' families, the possibility that the jurors might be inadvertently photographed. He adds another concern: Witnesses may behave differently when they know they are being televised, and it can affect the testimony.

Romero also objects to televising the trial. He too is wor-

---

ried about fairness, and about the effect of the cameras on witnesses' testimony.

Naftel does not object. She says that TV is no worse than any other branch of the media.

Byrne listens carefully and then delivers his decision: Courtroom TV will be allowed to cover the trial, with restrictions. And there will be no filming during direct examination of the two defendants, due to their ages.

During this discussion and the jury selection that follows, Dave and Vinnie sit stolidly next to each other. No words pass between them, no glances. It is as if neither boy exists for the other any longer.

It will take a little over two weeks to fill the seats on both juries. Four alternate jurors, two for each panel, are also picked.

The trial is set to begin on Monday, July 13, 1992.

*P*am Adkins is one of the first spectators to arrive on Monday morning. With her is her older son, Dan Adkins, and one of several women friends who will be with her during the trial. Dan bears a resemblance to his brother, but I remember what one of Dave's friends said about him, that he is "a typical football monster." He stands quietly at one of the high windows that punctuate the corridor outside the courtroom, looking out at the street below.

As television newsmen and crews arrive, they are admonished, by the bailiff, about filming jurors.

The courtroom itself has been sectioned off, with the middle spectator section (directly behind the counsel tables) reserved for one of the juries. (The two panels will alternate every other day when both juries are seated; one panel in the jury box, one in the spectator section. They will be coded by color: the Adkins jury will wear blue name tags, the Hebrock jury red.)

The families of the victims will be seated on the left side of the courtroom after they testify. Today, that section is half-filled with grandparents, friends, and relatives. People nod to each other but do not speak. Pam Adkins, her son Dan, and her friend are seated on the right side, past the middle section where one of the juries will be seated. Print journalists and reporters are also seated on the right. There is a single video camera, which will access film to all networks, at the back of the courtroom.

Covert glances are exchanged between some of the victims' relatives and the Adkins family. No one from Vinnie Hebrock's family is here.

Judge Byrne takes his place at the bench and Dave and Vinnie are escorted to their seats at the counsel tables. They do not look at each other, but Dave's eyes scan the courtroom, as usual.

The Hebrock jury is led into the jury box. Their two alternate jurors take seats near them. The Adkins jury moves into place in the center spectator rows. Their alternates sit behind them.

The courtroom hums with contained energy.

"Ladies and gentlemen, we will now go on record."

With these words Judge J. Michael Byrne begins the trial of Dave Adkins and Vinnie Hebrock for the murders of Katherine Macaulay, Heather Goodwin, and Danae Palermo.

Speaking to both juries, Judge Byrne gives a brief rundown of the case, describing the charges against Adkins and Hebrock. He then informs the jurors that both defendants have entered pleas of not guilty.

Next, Byrne gives the juries some instructions. He relates to the standard of evaluating testimony of witnesses, talking about common sense, background, experience. He urges the jurors to remain aware that every person who testifies under oath is a witness, and he tells them they must consider "the extent of opportunity of each witness to see, or hear, and remember." He reminds them that even though they will be issued notebooks (which will be taken back every day by the bailiff), they are not here to take notes. Their job, as jurors, is to *watch* the witnesses as well as listen to them.

Finally, there is a roll call of both juries, and then the Adkins jury is excused from the courtroom with an admonition against any discussion of the case, any contact with witnesses, any investigation of their own.

It is time for opening statements. Nancy Naftel gets up and moves to a rostrum that faces the jury box where Vinnie

Hebrock's jury is sitting. She greets them politely, then takes the jury through events: the crime itself, the flight, Cayle Fiedler's role, the arrest. Who is accused of saying what, and when they are accused of saying it.

Then she wraps up.

"At the end of this case there will be unanswered questions. We may never find a motive. And I am not required to prove a motive. You must decide whether or not Vinnie Hebrock participated in this crime." A pause. "We intend to show that Vinnie Hebrock shot Kathy Macaulay on March 21, 1991, but is legally responsible for all three murders. And I will ask you to return a guilty verdict on all charges. Thank you."

It is now Rickard Santwier's turn to move up to the rostrum. But before he does that, he walks to a blackboard next to the jury box and writes a single word: WHY? Then he begins to speak.

"I would like all of us to understand what happened. And to try and understand *why*." He pauses for an instant. "All six families are perhaps different than most. There were, in those families, normal problems, of course. But their other problems—lack of supervision, lack of structure—those problems are different than we expect. And there were outside influences at work: alcohol—two cases of beer. A fifth of Jack Daniel's. A bowl of marijuana. The evidence presented will be that all six individuals were under the influence of what had been ingested.

"Who sold the alcohol to these kids? And what about the shotgun and the shells? Yes, they had been hidden [in the main house], but they had been used previously by Dave and Kathy, et al. And Vinnie had the pictures to prove it." He takes a deep breath. "A lot of things happened up there that are difficult for us to relate to. The lack of supervision. The party atmosphere and the lack of structure. These are all things that contributed to the situation which brought us to this tragedy.

"Is Vinnie Hebrock responsible? Yes, he is." Santwier's voice lifts a little now. "But who *else* is responsible?" He waits before he delivers an answer, and then his voice rings through the courtroom:

"All of us."

He points to the single word on the blackboard again.

"One of our problems is that we don't have a tape we can play back that will show us exactly what happened. So *you* must decide, and one of the ways you can do that is to listen to the testimony of the witnesses. Study the photographs you will be shown. And, in particular, pay close attention to the eyewitness, Cayle Fiedler. He is the most substantial witness, and in evaluating his testimony, you must take into consideration his point of view. What did he observe? What did he receive and what influence was he under? And what was his ability *to* perceive—and recall what he perceived—while in a 'drunken stupor'?"

The jurors are listening carefully. Once in a while somebody will make the random note in the notebooks they have been provided.

Santwier continues, talking about the differences in Cayle's previous statements, and what Peggy Shurtleff has said in her statement. The inconsistencies. He reminds the jury of the prosecution's theory: That Dave and Vinnie are each responsible for the other's actions. "Thy brother's keeper."

He talks about Cayle's fear. About his statement that "Vinnie and Dave were living up there." About Cayle's description of "a party house."

The main thrust of Santwier's opening statement seems to pinpoint his doubt in Cayle Fiedler's ability to "perceive, to recall, and to relate."

The Hebrock jury leaves the courtroom, and the Adkins jury is escorted into the jury box.

Nancy Naftel approaches the rostrum again. She greets the jury and delivers a brief summary of the case. Her words are very similar to those she spoke to Vinnie's jury. Only now, of course, the focus is Dave Adkins. Once again she talks about motive.

"You may notice I haven't asked *why* this happened. You are not required to decide why. You are only required to find if David Adkins was involved. I intend to prove that he is legally responsible for all three deaths. And that he is legally responsible for using a shotgun. At the end of this trial I will ask you to find that the defendant committed all three murders."

Stephen Romero takes a large placard from a wheeled carrier holding his briefcase and files, and places it on the blackboard. There are two carefully lettered lists on the card, which is the general size and shape of a TV cue card.

PROSECUTION		DAVID	
Theory	Opinion	Proof	Scientific
Closed	Prejudicial	Verify	Objective
Incomplete	Police	Total	Scapegoat

Turning to the jury, Romero introduces himself and thanks them for accepting "this burden." He says he agrees with Ms. Naftel; this is a horrible tragedy. He then goes on to summarize the case, stating firmly that the area of agreement is that all six people (he names them) were up at the guesthouse on the night of March 21, 1991.

Then he begins to talk about Cayle Fiedler and the contradictions in Cayle's statements to the police. "First he was tired, then he was drunk. Then he tries to convince the police that he was at his most perceptive." Romero refers to "a memory of convenience."

He says Cayle Fiedler is smart enough to tell the police a story "that sells." He talks about "a rush to judgment."

And, like the two attorneys who spoke before him, he talks at length about what was said immediately after the murders. And who said it.

He does not take the two lists on the card point by point. He looks at it, often, but for the most part it is simply there for the jurors to take note of, and to tie in with his opening statement.

He goes back to the police work, describing it as "an incomplete investigation." He cites the lost evidence box which contained some of Dave's clothes and letters to him from Kathy Macaulay.

He says that as a result of "police failure to explore all leads, we have no evidence and a questionable witness.

"The difference between Mr. Fiedler and Dave Adkins is that Dave Adkins is sitting here accused of three murders, and Cayle Fiedler is out somewhere having a good time."

Romero ends his statement by telling the jury that "the evidence will show, through placement of the bodies and blood splatters, that David Adkins could not have discharged the weapon that night. The evidence against David Adkins is purely speculative." He draws in a deep breath and looks down the two rows of people in front of him. "Nothing happens out of a vacuum. Please listen carefully, ladies and gentlemen, to everything that you will hear."

The Hebrock jury is brought back in and the prosecution's first witness is sworn in by the court clerk. It is Dr. Michael Koss, Kathy Macaulay's stepfather. He is in his late forties; a soft-spoken, balding man. Nancy Naftel takes him through the preliminary questions in which he states address, occupation, marital status, and relationship to Kathy. He identifies aerial views of the house on Fairlawn Way, and the attached guesthouse. He identifies other photographs, as well: the master bedroom; the kitchen, and outside utility area, access to the guesthouse. He describes the condition of the Mercedes-Benz when it was returned after Dave and Vinnie were arrested.

"For one thing, the radio didn't work anymore, and it was covered with fingerprint powder."

He gives a brief history of the murder weapon.

Naftel goes to the court clerk's desk, and when the clerk hands the shotgun to her, there is an audible intake of air from the spectators. As Koss catches sight of the gun, he flinches slightly; then, for the first time, he looks, for a long moment, at Dave and Vinnie. Neither boy changes expression: they simply sit there, staring straight ahead.

Naftel walks to the witness stand and puts the shotgun in Koss's hands. He glances at it, says it looks like the one he purchased in 1983.

Now Naftel produces two more photographs. Romero objects before she can show them to either the witness or the jury. Romero requests a sidebar—a discussion kept between the attorneys and the judge, but placed on the record by the court reporter, who takes her machine up to the bench. The whispered conversation goes on for a couple of minutes.

Koss sits stolidly in the witness stand, staring straight ahead, one index finger resting lightly across his lips. Dave and Vinnie sit side by side at the counsel table; Vinnie's head is down, it looks as if his eyes are focusing on the tabletop. Dave watches the discussion at the bench with idle interest. The jurors look at both boys and at the photographs that have already been placed in evidence and are propped up against the blackboard.

The sidebar ends and Judge Byrne allows Naftel to show the photographs. They are blowups of the two Polaroids found in Vinnie's backpack, the ones of him and of Dave holding the murder weapon.

Koss identifies the location of the first picture: "It appears to have been taken in the master bedroom of our house." He says the same thing about the second photograph, adding, "it looks like the shotgun from my house."

Nancy Naftel has no further questions. Romero gets up to cross-examine. Most of his questions have to do with the last time Koss saw the gun, and if he had ever seen Kathy with it.

Romero also asks Koss how often he went to the guesthouse during 1990.

"Only a couple of times, to do 'fixing jobs.' The TV set, and a broken window."

How about 1991? Dr. Koss says that he was never in the guesthouse in the early months of 1991. When Romero asks if, when he did go in there, he saw anything unusual, Koss thinks about it for a moment, then says he saw "some beer cans scattered around."

Now Rickard Santwier gets to his feet. He asks Koss about the last time he saw the shotgun shells. Koss replies that he last saw them in 1983, when he bought them.

"Was there also a .22 or .25 revolver in your house?"

Koss shifts slightly in the chair. "Linda told me there was."

"Did Katherine have your permission to drive the Mercedes?"

"She did not."

Dr. Koss is excused, subject to recall. He reiterates that he must go back to Washington in two weeks.

Now the second witness is sworn in. It is Linda Macaulay Koss, Kathy Macaulay's mother.

Dr. Linda Koss is in her forties; a blond, gently pretty woman, with a resemblance to Faye Dunaway.

Under Nancy Naftel's questioning, Mrs. Koss describes the "well-hidden shotgun and shells," and the safe in an office in the main house.

"Before I went out of town I placed my jewelry in the safe, and locked it." She describes the jewelry: gold necklaces, earrings, bracelets. She says that when she got back to town after the murders, the safe had been broken into and the shelves had been emptied. Jewelry boxes under the safe were also empty, and a diamond ring inside the safe was gone. Mrs. Koss speaks calmly, but it's costing her. Her voice is thick with the tears she seems determined not to shed here.

When Naftel asks Mrs. Koss to identify Dave Adkins and Vinnie Hebrock, she looks at them and points at each boy in turn. She says she knows Dave, says she met Vinnie only once. She says she had "absolutely no idea either of them was staying at the guesthouse."

After asking Mrs. Koss to identify photographs of the garage and guesthouse, Naftel thanks her and sits down. Stephen Romero gets to his feet.

"I have very few questions." He sounds almost apologetic.

Slowly, carefully, he takes Linda Koss through her initial encounters with Dave Adkins. She tells him she first met Dave Adkins when "Katherine was in junior high school; she would have been thirteen, and I think David was thirteen too."

She says that he was "very quiet, he didn't talk much. His demeanor was like any other boy of that age."

She says that "Katherine was good friends with David for less than a year." That "she had other boys in her life." But, she tells Romero, in September 1990, her daughter Katherine began to go out with Dave Adkins again, only "not on a regular basis. He had another girlfriend. But Katherine had other boyfriends too. She didn't hang around the phone waiting for David to call.

"After Thanksgiving of 1991, Katherine said she wasn't going to see David anymore. But I saw him in the courtyard one afternoon with his brother and some other boys. They came to see Katherine."

SMOKED

When Romero asks Linda Koss about the guesthouse, she says, "Katherine liked to call the apartment 'Kathy's house,' but we all used it. She kept her junk there, and they [the kids] used it."

Mrs. Koss tells Romero that she "went in on a regular basis. I'd pop in and see if they needed ice or something."

She is maintaining an astonishing calm.

Now, in answer to another of Romero's queries, Mrs. Koss says she was unaware of any alcohol consumption by her daughter, or her daughter's friends. She does remember offering Katherine wine at Thanksgiving. "Katherine refused; she didn't like wine."

She tells Romero that she had been inside the guesthouse, "probably the week before Katherine was murdered. I'd go up there regularly for dirty laundry and wet towels."

Romero asks if she noticed "anything different" at that time.

"Well, it was a big mess. Like always."

Beer cans?

"Yes. They were from a party my son had there quite a bit of time before. I told him that I refused to carry them downstairs. And so they stayed there."

Romero asks if Kathy's friends had access to the main house. Mrs. Koss tells him yes: the food was there, and ice. "And Katherine would cook dinner for people when I wasn't there."

When he asks if Kathy's friends had access to the office room and the master bedroom, she tells him yes, they had access to those rooms as well.

Both participants in this interrogation are performing with the utmost caution. Their behavior is beyond courteous; it is stately.

Now Romero asks about the shotgun. Mrs. Koss says she recalls being told, by her husband, "that Katherine had the gun. He spoke to her quite severely. I didn't want a gun in the first place. That's why I put the gun lock on it in 1983.

"I don't know how Katherine got the gun lock off in April of '89. I didn't talk to her about it—I was too furious. My husband talked to her."

Romero thanks her and sits down next to Dave Adkins. Dave whispers something; Romero nods his head in a fast movement.

Rickard Santwier gets to his feet. He greets Mrs. Koss politely, then asks his first question.

"Did you prepare an inventory of the safe? [after the murders]"

"Yes, I did."

He asks when she did that.

"We moved back into our house very soon. The next night, I think; a day and a half after my daughter was murdered. That's when I noticed the place was a mess and needed to be cleaned up." She mentions an ironing board with a box of pizza on it, the box "filled with pieces of brown crust."

There is some discussion about the safe and its contents. Then Santwier asks if there was another weapon in the house, in addition to the shotgun.

"Yes. A taken-apart—by me—.22 or .25 handgun, in a box." She hesitates for a moment. "I don't know much about guns."

Santwier changes the subject: he asks if the Kosses filed an insurance claim for the missing jewelry. Mrs. Koss tells him they did.

"Did Katherine throw a lot of parties in the guest-house?"

"No, Katherine did *not* throw a lot of parties in the apartment. She did, one time, but I got mad because the music was so loud. I told her she couldn't have so many kids over any more." She takes a beat. "She did throw some swimming parties. But I have no knowledge of any parties in 1991. And I was home all the time."

SMOKED

When Santwier questions Linda Koss about the Mercedes, she says Kathy had permission to drive it "only for school, and to get groceries." She had already testified that the Bronco she bought for Kathy broke down often. "Unfortunately, we didn't buy a great car."

Did Mrs. Koss talk to Kathy from Chicago?

"Two or three calls a day."

Santwier thanks her, and sits down. Vinnie says nothing. His head is down; his eyes are on the tabletop.

Romero gets up to re-cross. He asks if Kathy ever gave parties in the main house.

"Well, she had slumber parties—three or four girls sleeping over. They'd sleep in the guesthouse, but they'd come to the house to eat."

"Did they listen to music in the main house?"

Mrs. Koss seems impatient with the question. "Yes. This was Katherine's house, too." She pauses. "For loud music I'd suggest the guesthouse."

On Santwier's re-cross he asks Linda Koss if she ever knocked on the window of the guesthouse, for Katherine to come outside.

"Yes. I'd say—in my mother's voice—'Come out, Katherine.'"

"But you never saw anything inappropriate?"

"Only that they were making a mess. Spilling things. Not sitting in the chairs when they ate, eating off the counter. That kind of thing."

Mrs. Koss is excused, and after lunch, the clerk calls the next witness: Darrell Goodwin, Heather's father. It is impossible to guess his age, or what he looked like before the murders; he might have been a handsome man. Now, he has the look of a combat veteran newly returned from a terrible, lost war.

Under Nancy Naftel's queries, Darrell Goodwin says that Kathy and Heather were "lifelong friends since grade school." He says also that although his wife had met Danae on a previous occasion, he had not. Nor did he ever meet Dave Adkins or Vinnie Hebrock.

When he mentions Dave and Vinnie's names, he looks at them. A single, icy stare; it is without the rage or hatred one might expect; it is simply a look of disbelieving curiosity and revulsion.

Goodwin says the last time he saw his daughter alive, "she was in the kitchen, cooking dinner. Kathy came in and, for some reason, she was afraid to stay alone [at the guest-house] and she asked Heather to spend the night with her up there. We offered to let the girls stay with us, but they wanted to go back up to Kathy's and stay there." He pauses. "They were headed to Alhambra to pick up Danae Palermo."

Now he goes, step-by-step, through the frantic, late-night call from Peggy Shurtleff, the drive to Fairlawn Way, the drive to the Pasadena police, the arrival of the squad car, and the wait while the two officers went up to the guesthouse to investigate.

"Then the police came out on the balcony and told me to come upstairs."

The silence in the courtroom is nearly palpable.

"When I went into the guesthouse, I looked to my right. There was a young girl on the bed with a bedspread over her head. Straight ahead was Kathy Macaulay, on her back. Her eyes were open and the back of her head was blown off. To my left, my daughter's upper body had fallen to the floor. Her lower body was on the bed. The back of her head had been blown off too. That's what I saw."

Neither Romero nor Santwier has questions. Judge Byrne excuses Darrell Goodwin and recesses the trial for the remainder of the day.

. . . .

Both defense attorneys have a motion to make before the jurors are brought in the next day. They are asking the judge to disallow one of the photographs in evidence. Their grounds are that the photograph (it is of Heather's body) could be prejudicial, due to the "extreme and graphic nature of the wounds." Romero contends that the photograph "is so shocking as to incite the emotions of the jury."

Nancy Naftel argues that the position of the body, the location and nature of the wound, and the cigarette clutched in Heather's fingers all show that Heather was not acting in an aggressive manner when she was shot.

Santwier feels there are enough photographs "without the graphic nature of this particular shot." He feels it will "exacerbate."

Dave and Vinnie sit impassively throughout the arguments. Today, they are both wearing shirts that make spots of color in the courtroom; Vinnie's is blue, Dave's deep rose.

Judge Byrne announces his decision: "It *is* an unpleasant photograph. But it is relevant to the issue. And that outweighs the objections to it. The photograph will be admitted, not as evidence, but it will be shown in the courtroom so that the witnesses and juries may see it."

Now the jurors are escorted into the courtroom. The Hebrock jury will be in the box today; the Adkins jurors will be seated in the spectator section reserved for them.

The first witness is Deputy Medical Examiner James K. Riebe. He delivers a brief professional history and then, as Naftel questions him, tells the court his findings upon conducting autopsies on the bodies of Kathy Macaulay, Heather Goodwin, and Danae Palermo.

One by one, the photographs go up on the board to the left of the jury box. They are the ones taken at the site: there is Kathy, crumpled in front of the stereo shelves. She is barefoot, and you can see the gleam of an anklet on one leg; the other leg is curled beneath her. She is wearing black shorts and a black top that exposes her midriff. Another photo, a close-up of her face, shows that her eyes are closed; long lashes feather across the lower lids. The shotgun blast left a trail of torn flesh and bone, blood and brain tissue, as it plowed through the top of her head. If it were not for the terrible wound she would look like any pretty young girl, peacefully asleep.

Danae is on the bed, next to the wall and turned toward it. Bright red arterial blood and brain matter are pooled in a jellylike mass beneath her. She is wearing jeans and a red top. She was moved onto her side for the photograph and her arms are frozen into right angles by rigor mortis. Her face is unmarked except for the slight bruising over one eye. Her eyes are open, her face without expression.

The photograph of Heather Goodwin at the murder site is, in fact, a shocking picture. She is slumped, facedown, at the foot of the bed; the upper part of her body is on the floor. She is wearing faded black jeans and a tie-dye T-shirt; her shoes are off and she has on black socks. A pool of congealing blood spreads out around her head, her hair is matted with it. Heather's brain, virtually intact, rests on the carpet next to her head. A large, crescent-shaped fragment of skull is on the floor a few inches away from the brain. There is a spray of blood and brain matter splashed across the bottom of the mattress.

Heather's arms are splayed out on either side of her torso. There are silver and turquoise rings on every finger of both hands, a single ring on one thumb. The tattooed bracelet of stars, moons, and crosses is highly visible on her left wrist and, in her right hand, held fast between her first and second fingers, a cigarette has burned down to the filter.

The final photograph on the board is of Heather, taken at the morgue. It is a close-up of her face, and it is a compelling picture; seeing Heather Goodwin in death, at seventeen, it is possible to see how she might have looked at fifty. The blast of the shotgun took her youth as well as her life. The black eye she received in the fight with Vinnie Hebrock looks purple in the flat, fluorescent lighting.

During Romero's cross-examination, he asks about the bruising on Heather's face. What was the object that caused this blunt-force trauma? Was it a fist?

Dr. Riebe's reply is that any object hard enough could have made that kind of bruise when it connected.

Now Romero begins to place new photographs on the stand. He requests that the other photographs, the ones of the bodies at the crime scene, be taken down. Naftel removes them, placing them on the floor to lean against the counsel table. They are face out and a couple of the jurors take a closer look. The new photographs, six in all, were also taken at the crime site; they show different angles of bloodstains and a small puddle of vomit found next to Kathy's head, and tissue and blood splatters on the wallboard behind the stereo shelves.

He turns to Riebe. "I believe, from your report, that Ms. Goodwin was the first person shot . . . "

"I object, your Honor." Nancy Naftel.

Romero, Naftel, and Santwier move up to the bench for a sidebar.

Dave and Vinnie are watching intently. There has been absolutely no interplay between them, even when no one is occupying the chair between them. And neither boy displayed any emotion at all when the photographs of Kathy, Heather, and Danae were up on the board.

The sidebar ends; Naftel's objection is sustained.

Riebe states that he believes the vomitus is Kathy Macaulay's, and he says it occurred at that location. But he cannot say when.

Romero persists, asking the same question in different ways. Naftel continues to object.

Romero ends his cross-examination with a request that the medical examiner be kept on recall.

Santwier's line of questioning concerns the blood level of alcohol and the intoxicating effect of marijuana. Would body weight make a difference in the absorptive phase? Sometimes.

After a series of queries focusing on impairment, Riebe repeats a previous statement: "As I said before, there is a substantive variance in individuals."

Bearing in on the cognitive factor, Santwier asks if the information-gathering process is impaired at .19 and .20 alcohol levels in the blood.

Riebe states that judgment and cognition would be impaired. The ability to walk and stand straight would be affected.

Could a person's ability to recall be impaired as well?

There might be complete or retrograde amnesia, but that is caused by a late appearance of chronic alcoholism on the brain, not by the alcohol itself.

Santwier asks when redness would appear in bruising. (He is referring, it seems, more to Heather's black eye than to the slight contusions on Danae's face.) Would the redness appear in hours? Seconds?

Riebe states that redness would appear, not in seconds, but quickly.

Then what would it mean if someone did not mention seeing those bruises when they saw the bodies?

The medical examiner almost, not quite, shrugs. "Either they didn't see them, or they didn't look."

On Nancy Naftel's re-cross, she points to the photograph of Heather taken at the morgue. Would the bruising around her eye be more visible after death?

Riebe nods his head. "Yes. Because of the postmortem position—head down."

Naftel turns to confer briefly with Detective Korpal, who is sitting behind her. Then she looks at Riebe again.

"Would a .20 or .19 alcohol level in the bloodstream affect a person's ability to process information if they saw something that frightened them? If that person saw, or participated in a dramatic event, would it impair their memory?"

"It depends. Severe stress can affect cognition."

"Would the recollection of events be highly variable in each individual?"

"Yes."

Dr. Riebe is excused.

Dave's demeanor has been consistently impassive during the medical examiner's testimony. Vinnie is clearly distressed. As Riebe leaves the stand, and just before Judge Byrne calls for a lunch recess, Santwier leans in close and asks Vinnie if he wants to talk. Vinnie shakes his head in a small gesture; Santwier reaches out to grip his shoulder for a moment. Then both boys are taken back to the holding cells.

Cayle Fiedler is seventeen now, and his looks have undergone a subtle change in the year and a half since the murders. His hair is long and the braces on his teeth are gone.

There is a small wave of sound, a sigh of caught breath throughout the courtroom as he walks through the witness door next to the jury box. He is wearing a navy suit jacket with a collarless dress shirt and jeans that are so long they droop into denim puddles at his ankles.

As the court clerk administers the oath, Cayle looks out over the spectators. If he is nervous, he's hiding it well; he seems completely self-contained. He does not look at either Dave or Vinnie.

He says he has known Dave Adkins for about three years, "seen Vinnie Hebrock around with Dave." He identifies Dave and Vinnie in turn by pointing at them and describing their clothes. He says he "knew Kathy Macaulay for three years, and Heather Goodwin for a year and a half." Says that he and Danae "were associates. I knew her, but not very well."

Now he describes the events of March 21 and March 22, 1991.

He sighs often as he speaks.

He tells the court about Kathy and Heather picking him up in the Bronco before they went to get Danae. The purchase of Jack Daniel's and beer. The drive up to the guesthouse. Dave and Vinnie. The game of Quarters and smoking the bud of marijuana. The beer run with Dave and Kathy. Coming back to find Heather agitated and with a black eye, after a fight with Vinnie. Drinking more beer and lying down on the bed next to Danae. Seeing Dave slide out through the glass door of the guesthouse. Seeing Kathy and Heather at the table and Kathy getting up to change the tape on the stereo.

It is deadly quiet in the courtroom. Nobody moves. Nobody coughs.

"I got woke up by two shotgun blasts. Then I sat up in a semierect position, on my elbows, and looked over as Dave breached another load into the gun, put it to the back of Danae's head, and fired.

"Then there was a lotta commotion . . . 'Are you with us? Are you down with us? C'mon, let's go!!' And I'm, like"— Cayle's voice lifts—" 'Yeah! Let's get the fuck outta here. *Now!*'

"The gun had swung casually in my direction. I looked over and Kathy was slumped up against the stereo. Heather was at the foot of the bed, facedown. They both appeared, to me, to be dead."

Under Nancy Naftel's diligent questioning, Cayle says he got up and walked to the glass door. "They [Dave and Vinnie] were moving around, and I think they chambered another cartridge. I saw an enormous pool of blood by Heather when I was at the door. I was just trying to get it out of my head, so I could cope and get *outta* there.

"For a moment I was given possession of the gun when we went downstairs to get Dave's laundry. I didn't know if it was loaded or not, but I was trying to keep as far away from it as possible." He sighs deeply again. "Vinnie had possession of the gun on the way down—he handed it to me so they could carry the laundry. I used my sleeves so my fingerprints wouldn't get on it." He pulls the sleeves of his jacket down so that his hands are covered.

Naftel asks if there was any conversation while the laundry was being taken from the drier.

"Dave said, 'I can't believe I just killed my girlfriend.'

And Vinnie said, 'Yeah, dude—we smoked 'em all.' "

Cayle says he can't remember if there was any more dialogue between Dave and Vinnie. He says Dave was "acting like he wanted to load up."

Nothing else?

"Vinnie mentioned he was worried about the three used [shotgun] shells upstairs, that they might have his prints on them."

"Earlier that evening, before the shooting, did you hear Dave or Vinnie say anything to do with the house?" Naftel asks.

"Yes. Dave said he'd been wanting to get outta town, and he talked about robbing the house and taking the car."

"Had you ever seen the gun before that day?"

"I saw pictures of Dave and Vinnie brandishing the gun earlier in the evening. The girls weren't present then."

"Other than the pictures, had you ever seen the gun, or other weapons, before?"

A beat of hesitation from Cayle. Then, "I didn't see any other weapons that night, but I knew Vinnie carried a knife."

Cayle goes on. "After they got their laundry out of the drier, we went to the red Mercedes, to drive home. I started to get in front, but Vinnie told me to get in the back, and he got in the front seat—so he was riding shotgun."

Naftel stops him right there. "What do you mean by 'riding shotgun'?"

Cayle stammers a little as he answers, and some of the veneer of coolness cracks. "It's just a term I always use—I didn't mean anything by it." He goes on. "Vinnie was sitting in the front passenger seat with the shotgun next to his left leg. They said they were going to go to Mexico, and they asked if I wanted to go with them. I said, 'No—no, just drop me off.'

"At different times, and in different ways [during the ride], they both said, 'Don't say anything, don't tell anyone, or we'll come back and do the same thing to you.'

"I was under the impression they'd come back that night and kill me." Cayle draws in a deep breath, releases it in another weary sigh. "It's safe to say I was in fear of my life.

"When I got home, I said to my dad, 'Everybody's dead! I gotta get out of this place!' "

Now Nancy Naftel shows Cayle the photographs of the girls' bodies. He sighs and takes a long look at them, and as he does so, the corners of his mouth turn down in a tragic grimace. Naftel shows him photographs of the crime site next. He identifies the room and points out the stereo system, stating that Kathy was slumped against that area. He says he doesn't recall seeing her lying on the floor, as she is in the picture. He identifies Kathy, Heather, and Danae, delivering a soft, whispered "yes" in each instance.

He recognizes the two Polaroids of Dave and Vinnie with the shotgun. "They showed those to me that very night."

Now Nancy walks across the courtroom to the clerk's desk and stretches out her hand. The clerk passes the shotgun to her.

She walks back across the room and holds up the weapon for Cayle to identify. "Is this the same gun you saw that night?"

And Cayle Fiedler frowns as he identifies the murder weapon.

From their seats at the counsel table, Dave and Vinnie sit quietly, watching.

Nancy Naftel thanks Cayle and sits down.

Stephen Romero gets to his feet.

"Good afternoon, Mr. Fiedler."

"Hello." Leery, bordering on hostile.

"Prior to March 21, 1991, had you and Heather and Kathy gone to the mountains with the shotgun?"

"No."

"When *did* you go up to the mountains?"

"The day before. Dave, Vinnie, me, and Kathy and Heather. We drank and played in the snow."

"Were drugs included on that trip?"

"No. We smoked some pot."

"Did you do LSD?"

"No."

Both Dave and Vinnie are fidgeting in their chairs a little. Vinnie crosses and recrosses his legs; Dave's foot is jiggling.

The atmosphere in the courtroom is electric: everyone in the spectator sections; the Adkins jurors, reporters, the families—everyone, including, of course, the Hebrock jury, in the box—seems to be leaning forward to listen.

Now Romero asks Cayle about "previous drug use on other occasions." Nancy Naftel is on her feet at once with an objection. Romero requests a sidebar, stepping to one side to usher Naftel ahead of him. Although she complies, the gesture is clearly unimportant to her.

The sidebar is rather a long one. Dave's foot continues to jiggle. Vinnie sits quietly; once or twice he glances up at Cayle. Cayle sits looking down at some point near a leg of the counsel table; he sighs twice and the sound is amplified by the microphone in front of him. There is a brief racket as the court clerk sharpens a set of wooden pencils for the jurors' use. Finally, Judge Byrne sustains Naftel's objection.

Romero tries again. "How did you determine that there were no other drugs beside [the bud of] marijuana up at the guesthouse on March 21?"

"There are obvious signs."

"How would you have known?"

"I've experienced controlled substances."

"Are you familiar with the term 'magic mushrooms'?"

Naftel's objection is sustained. Cayle looks down at his hands and smiles.

Now Romero asks him to tell the court about the events

at the guesthouse on the afternoon and evening of March 21. Cayle works his way through the get-together, the beer run, the beef at the gas station, the return to the guesthouse. There is an edge of something very close to snottiness in his tone when he gives answers to Romero's questions. He seems wearily impatient with Dave Adkins's defense attorney.

Just before a short break is called by Judge Byrne, Cayle describes the conversation between himself and Heather Goodwin upon his return to the guesthouse from the beer run.

"She said that Vinnie had been hitting on her and they got in a fight and she kicked him in the balls. She said he was an asshole." He goes on to say that he had not been alarmed; arguments were a "common occurrence between Vinnie and Heather."

When Romero asks again if Cayle had been upset by the news about the fight, Cayle smiles grimly. "No, I didn't care. Heather would have kicked Vinnie's ass."

....

The courtroom is crowded with spectators after the fifteen-minute break; people are standing in close ranks along the back of the room. It is clear that word has gone out: the eyewitness is on the stand.

Now Romero takes Cayle through the murders. When Cayle talks about being handed the shotgun, Romero gets the weapon from the clerk and asks Cayle to show the juries how he held it.

Cayle gets to his feet and, after pulling down the sleeves of his jacket until his fingertips are covered, takes the shotgun out of Romero's hands into his own.

Not a sound in the courtroom except the click of a camera.

The judge allows Cayle to stand there, like that, for a moment, then he tells the clerk to take the gun. "I don't want this witness standing in front of the juries with the weapon in his hands."

"Why did you hide your fingertips, Mr. Fiedler?"

"I didn't want, in any way, to be implicated in this crime. I wanted nothing to do with it."

"Did you ever point the weapon at David?" Romero's voice changes slightly, " 'It's my turn, now . . . '?"

Cayle sighs again; his attitude now, since the break, has become more sullen than it was earlier.

"Absolutely not. I had no idea if there was a cartridge in the chamber or not."

"But *why* did you stay on *after* the weapon was handed to you?"

Cayle shifts slightly in the witness chair.

"I have no answer to that."

"Did you tell David to go to Mexico, that you would cover for him?"

"Absolutely not."

"Why didn't you stay [at the guesthouse], tell them to take off?" Romero's voice alters pitch again. " 'I didn't do anything.' "

"I have no answer for that."

"But you *had* a choice, did you not?"

Nancy Naftel makes an objection; it is overruled. Cayle is allowed to answer.

"As a matter of fact, it never crossed my mind. What crossed my mind was getting to safety. Getting away from people who had just murdered three of my best friends."

"How long were you in Seattle?"

"Two days."

"Doing what?"

"Watching TV."

"Did you go out and party?"

"Hell, no."

Romero changes his focus.

"How much money were you given? Sixteen hundred dollars?"

Nancy Naftel objects and is sustained.

Romero goes another way. "Did you receive money from the Pasadena Police Department?"

"Yes. For relocation."

"Was there a lie detector test?"

"No."

"Did you talk to Detective Korpal from Washington?"

"Yes. I told him everything."

"Was that conversation taped?"

"I wasn't concerned about that."

"Did Detective Korpal advise you that you were no longer a suspect?"

Cayle shifts position; his entire body seems impatient.

"It had been on TV already."

"What did Detective Korpal say to you?"

"He said, 'If you didn't commit a crime, you have nothing to worry about.'"

Vinnie has been sitting with his eyes closed for most of the cross-examination; Dave makes the random whispered comment to Steven Sonoro, Romero's associate counsel.

Now Romero asks permission to approach the witness. He hands Cayle the photograph of Heather's body at the edge of the bed, asking if that was the position she was in when Cayle propped himself up on his elbows after the third shot. Cayle says he does not recall.

"Were your feet stretched out?"

"My legs were to one side of the bed."

"Did you have to slip your feet out from under Heather?"

The expression on Cayle's face registers shock. For a long moment there is complete silence in the courtroom as Cayle looks at Romero.

"No. I would have remembered that."

"But you don't remember what position you were in."

Again, Cayle seems to have been rendered speechless. He nods his head in reply.

Romero has no further questions. It is now four-thirty and Judge Byrne halts the proceedings until the following day.

. . . .

Cayle Fiedler takes the stand again on the morning of July 15, the third day of trial. This time he will face Rickard Santwier, Vinnie's attorney.

The defendants are brought in from the holding cells to take their places at the counsel table. Vinnie looks straight ahead; he seems to fold in on himself, making his body into as small a package as possible. Dave sits comfortably in his chair, staring intently at Cayle. The look is not returned; Cayle, like Vinnie, is gazing straight ahead.

Pam Adkins is in her place in the front row; her friend is seated next to her. No one from Vinnie's family is in the courtroom. Kathy Macaulay's mother and stepfather, Darrell Goodwin, and members of Danae Palermo's family are on the other side of the jury.

Santwier asks Cayle if he has read the transcripts of his interviews with Detective Korpal and with Stephen Romero's investigator. Cayle says he has read the transcripts twice, and adds that he has also read statements he made at Juvenile Hall and a transcript of an interview with Nancy Naftel.

Now Santwier goes to the blackboard that stands between the witness stand and the jury box. He writes a short list of what he calls "areas" of Cayle's testimony. One of the items on the list is "reporting of the incident," and the order in which people were told: Cayle's father; his grandmother; his mother (by telephone); Peggy Shurtleff; Detective Korpal (also by telephone). Pointing to the list, Santwier asks Cayle if he told the truth to everyone there.

"Certainly."

"And you told the truth at the Pasadena police station?"

"Certainly."

"And is the transcript of the statement you made there accurate?"

"No. I recognized mistakes made by the stenographer."

Cayle testifies that he detected flaws in the other transcripts, as well: "pockets of time" is how he refers to them.

"Did you see Vinnie inside the guesthouse when you got back from the beer run?"

"No."

Cayle tells Santwier he became aware of the fight that occurred between Heather, Danae, and Vinnie when he got back from the beer run.

"Did you tell Detective Korpal, at the police station, there had been a fight?"

"Yes."

"There's no question in your mind about that?"

"No."

When Santwier asks how long it took Cayle to fall asleep when he lay down, and how long he slept, Cayle tells him he doesn't know. He does know what it was that woke him: shots. And he remembers the first thing he said after that third shot:

" 'Let's get the fuck out of here.' "

"What did you hear next?"

"The gun being reloaded."

"What did you feel?"

"Fear for my life."

"What was said next?"

" 'Are you down with us?' In unison."

"What did *Dave* say?"

" 'Come *on*—are you down with us? Are you with us ...?' "

Cayle hesitates, trying to remember the order of things said,

" 'Are you coming ... ?' "

"In that order?"

"I can't give the *exact* words—it's over a year later. Your memory changes."

Cayle's attitude with Santwier is a little more courteous than it had been with Romero. Santwier's soft voice and coldly analytical approach seem to have dispelled the too-hip impatience displayed yesterday.

"What does 'down' mean?"

"Willing to help out a friend."

"And both Vinnie and Dave said this?"

"Yes."

"How far away was Dave?"

"He was at the foot of the bed."

The Adkins jury is in the box today. Now several members of the panel make a note in the pads provided for that purpose.

"How far away was Vinnie?"

"About three to six feet away, to Dave's left."

"Dave was between you and Vinnie?"

"Yes."

"Did you ever testify that you weren't paying attention to where Vinnie was standing?"

"It's possible."

"Did you state that Vinnie said nothing?"

"It's possible."

"Is it true?"

"It's possible that I said it. I was paying more attention to Dave."

"What were your exact words after the shootings?"

" 'Let's. Get. The. Fuck. Out. Of. Here. Now.' " Each word a carefully spaced pistol shot.

Now Santwier takes Cayle through a minute search for inconsistencies in his previous statements: who stood where; who said what; did anybody run down the stairs ("Nobody ran anywhere"); was Vinnie holding something in his hand ("I believe he was holding the box of shotgun shells").

Cayle says they—all three boys—went downstairs, "after I saw Dave take something out of one of the girls' purse." And, he says, on the way down, Dave said, "I just killed my girlfriend." There is no question in Cayle's mind about that. There might have been an "Oh my God" in front of the statement, but Dave said "killed," not "shot." And Vinnie said, "Yeah, dude, we smoked 'em all." No question.

More note taking among the jurors.

Cayle says that, at one point, after the murders, Vinnie said, "She won't do *that* again." Cayle's assumption is that this was said in reference to the fight between Vinnie and Heather.

"When Vinnie handed you the shotgun, your testimony says you didn't know it was loaded. Have you also testified, 'This shotgun had a bullet in it'?"

"It's possible."

"But is that the truth?"

"It's possible."

"But, this morning you said it was re-chambered."

"I said it *seemed* it was."

Cayle is without visible nerves today. He is not sighing, as he was yesterday; he seems confident.

Santwier hands him a transcript to read. Cayle begins to read aloud. " 'I knew it was loaded. But I don't remember how many shots were in it.' "

"Is that true?"

"Yes."

Now Santwier's line of questioning goes back to the phrase, "We smoked 'em all." Cayle says Vinnie might have said, "We smoked 'em all, Dave," instead of "dude." Santwier continues to question Cayle about this until Naftel objects and they move to the bench for a sidebar.

During the sidebar, Dave huddles with Sonoro. Vinnie just sits, his face an unreadable mask. While Dave is engrossed in his whispered conversation with Sonoro, Cayle watches him closely.

After the sidebar, Santwier places a blowup of a page from a transcript of Cayle's Juvenile Hall interview dated June 19, 1991, on the blackboard. Everyone in the courtroom watches, and waits, as Cayle reads it silently. Then, pointing to the blowup, Santwier reads aloud.

"'And Vinnie said, "Yeah, dude, we killed 'em all. We smoked 'em all."'" Santwier looks at Cayle. "So this is an inaccurate statement you made while under oath?"

Cayle does not look away. "I suppose it is."

Santwier continues to question Cayle about discrepancies in his statements. The route taken, in the Mercedes, to Cayle's house. A remark made by Dave about needing gas. The exact words Cayle first said to his father about the murders. His exact words to Peggy. The sequence of the beer run. The amount of whiskey Cayle consumed. At one point in the interrogation, Cayle and Dave exchange a long look. Neither face shows any emotion whatsoever.

More questions about what Dave said. What Vinnie said. What Cayle said. *Exactly* what everybody said. Cayle reminds Santwier, over and over, about the confusion of the moment and the difficulty he has, over a year later, remembering *exactly* how things were said. Word for word.

Now Santwier asks a series of questions relating to the conversation in the car on the way to Cayle's house after the murders. Cayle says he remembers telling Detective Korpal that Dave was driving fast and that he (Cayle) was scared. When Santwier asks if Cayle told Korpal that Dave and Vinnie said, "We killed 'em, we killed 'em!" Cayle says he "was paying less and less attention. It was their conversation—I was a bit confused."

Cayle does not recall if Dave and Vinnie talked about Danae. They did talk about Heather, he says, and it was during the ride that Vinnie said, "She won't do *that* again." He tells Santwier that Vinnie was upset by the way Heather treated him: the physical abuse. When Santwier asks if Vinnie wanted to have a physical relationship with Heather, Cayle says he thinks he did, yes.

Now, Santwier turns to previous testimony again: Cayle had told Korpal that Heather and Danae were crying after the fight with Vinnie. Cayle shakes his head in a fast motion.

"Oh, no. They weren't crying—they were laughing and talking."

"You were asked why you didn't call an ambulance?"

For the first time today, Cayle sighs. "Several times."

"And you said . . . ?"

"I don't recall."

Santwier refers to his copy of the transcript. "You said it was because you 'didn't want to be involved.' "

"It's possible."

"Did you tell Peggy that Dave shot them all?"

"I don't recall."

"Did you lie to her?"

"Absolutely not!"

"Did you tell Peggy that you were kissing Danae on the bed?"

"I may have. I don't recall."

"*Did* you kiss her?"

"I don't recall."

"Did you tell Peggy Shurtleff that Dave walked up to Heather and shot her first? And that Vinnie grabbed the gun and shot Kathy, and then Dave took the gun back and finished Danae off?"

"I don't recall."

. . . .

Judge Byrne calls for a lunch break, admonishing the jurors, as always, not to discuss the case. It has been an exhausting session and there are people on both panels who seem clearly affected by what they have heard. Others have maintained more of a distance.

A code of deportment outside the courtroom has set in. The families of the victims form themselves into a loosely knit group. None of them glances at or talks to Pam Adkins or anyone with her. Both groups take separate elevators to and from the street. It is an interesting but not unexpected contrast to the behavior of the attorneys, who exchange courteous, easy greetings with each other.

Rickard Santwier and Cayle Fiedler face each other again after lunch. Cayle is asked if he was concerned about Dave and Vinnie coming back after they dropped him off at home. Cayle says that he was, indeed, concerned. And he repeats what was said to him at that time.

"Dave said, 'Don't say anything to anybody or we'll come back and do to you what we did to them.' And Vinnie said, 'Don't tell anybody or we'll kill you.'"

Santwier asks if there had been "regular parties up at Kathy's." Cayle tells him there had been several. Drinking? Yes. Kathy drank, too? Certainly.

More questions about leaving the house after the murders. Was Cayle afraid to be wasted up there? Yes. By Dave? Yes.

There are further questions about Vinnie handing the gun to Cayle "for less than a minute" and about "Vinnie piling laundry on Dave's arms" in the laundry room. Cayle does not remember, now, whether or not a shirt was dropped. And, in answer to whether or not he used the word "run" to describe movement, "I don't remember what I meant by words like 'run' a year ago."

"Had you considered if, when you got home, they would not let you out of the car?"

"No. Why would they drive me home and then not let me out?"

"You thought they would trust you?"

"I was under the impression they wouldn't hurt me in the car, since they had let me live."

"But at Peggy's house you were in fear of these guys who had let you out of the car?"

"Yes."

"Then why take the risk and walk to the corner?"

"Because I was taking a bigger risk if I didn't."

"Isn't it because you didn't think they would come back to South Pasadena?"

Cayle stares icily at Santwier.

"I didn't know *what* they would do."

Santwier has one more question for Cayle Fiedler.

"Was there a capping session going on at the party that night?"

"Yes."

Some months after the trial, Rickard Santwier will say about his client Vinnie Hebrock: "He grew up being capped on."

Nancy Naftel asks Cayle if he has talked to friends about this case, has he read newspaper articles, seen television reports having to do with the murders? He tells her yes, in all instances. And, when she asks if all of that gets confusing to him, he tells her yes, again. Is it difficult to distinguish what was said from one interview to another? Most certainly.

Naftel now asks a series of questions about the night of the murders. Did Dave or Vinnie appear to be afraid of each other? Did either of them have any trouble walking around? Did either of them fall down? Did Cayle hear Vinnie say anything before Dave shot Danae? No, to everything.

Quoting now, from a transcript of Cayle's telephone interview with Detective Korpal, Nancy Naftel asks if Cayle remembers telling Korpal, "They were gonna rob the house and I said, 'We gotta get outta here.' " Cayle says he remembers. "Vinnie said, 'We gotta get some shit.' "

"Why?"

"They needed financial help to get out."

"Do you remember Vinnie saying that?"

"Yes."

Naftel asks if Cayle ever heard Dave and Vinnie talk about leaving town. He does. He doesn't remember when he heard it, but it was before the shootings. "They both said they needed to get out of this area."

Santwier requests a sidebar.

Cayle is slumped wearily in the witness chair now; Dave and Vinnie seem tired too. The sidebar ends and Nancy Naftel walks back to face Cayle once more.

"In March of 1991, did Dave Adkins have a regular type of job?"

"No."

She repeats the same question about Vinnie. Same answer.

"Did you tell Dave or Vinnie, when they dropped you off, that you were going to Peggy's house?"

"No."

"Did either of them indicate they were going to go to South Pasadena?"

"No."

"What does 'smoked' mean?"

"Killed."

"Did you shoot anybody that night, Cayle?"

"No, I did not."

"Are you positive?"

"Absolutely positive."

Nancy Naftel sits down. Stephen Romero gets to his feet; he is holding a photograph in his hand.

"Mr. Fiedler, do you know what a pentagram is?"

There is an immediate objection and sidebar.

During the sidebar, Cayle sits looking down at the floor; his eyes never leave it. Vinnie stares straight ahead most of the time, looking down at the table for a second or two at a clip. Dave is bent over a legal pad, taking notes; he looks like a college student studying furiously for finals.

Romero walks back to the counsel table.

"No further questions."

Santwier stands.

"Did Vinnie appear to be scared that night?"

"No."

"Did you?"

"I have no idea."

"Did you have trouble walking?"

"No."

"Do you drink a lot?"

Cayle shrugs slightly. "Yeah. A considerable amount."

"Did the five of you drink a lot when you got together?"

Another shrug. "Some."

Dave looks up from his legal pad with a barely visible smirk.

"How much did you drink when you went up to the mountains?"

"A fifth of Southern Comfort between five people."

"Did you have pot that day?"

"A few quiet bowls that Dave had."

"When you were on the bed, after you went to sleep, your first awareness was of two shots. Tell us the sequence."

"Boom. Boom." He pauses briefly. "Boom."

"Did you hear a round chambered between the first two shots and the third shot?"

"No."

"Did you hear voices between the second and third shots?"

"No."

"Did you have any idea of a threat that evening?"

"None whatsoever."

Santwier looks down at his papers, looks back up at Cayle.

"Is it difficult to distinguish the truth?"

Cayle doesn't even blink.

"The truth doesn't change."

Nancy Naftel takes Santwier's place at the rostrum.

"Is it difficult to remember what happened that night?"

Cayle slowly shakes his head. "No."

Cayle Fiedler is excused. He steps down from the witness stand and walks out of the courtroom without a glance at Dave Adkins or Vinnie Hebrock.

The next witness is Cayle's father, Mike Fiedler. Fiedler looks like the kind of man whose friends describe him as "a decent, hardworking guy." He calls Nancy Naftel "Ma'am" as he answers her questions. As he speaks, he clears his throat often with soft, explosive sounds.

He says he first talked to Detective Korpal after Korpal "showed up at my mother's house." Fiedler then called Cayle, in Washington, and put him on the phone with Korpal.

After Cayle's return to L.A., and after his surrender to the Pasadena police, Fiedler states that he was "given assistance" from the Pasadena police to move away. He says that he and Cayle were "in fear of our lives, our family's and our neighbors."

Nancy Naftel asks about financial arrangements.

"Pretty much fifteen hundred bucks and a pat on the back."

"Did you encourage Cayle to talk to the police?"

"I didn't have to."

Romero stands.

"Why didn't you call the police at once, Mr. Fiedler?"

"I had no confidence in the police department. That's changed now."

"Why not?"

"Well, at the time I was growing up in Pasadena, the police didn't have a very good reputation."

Romero asks Fiedler if, after the murders, he contacted

lawyers for "legal advice." Fiedler, clearly uncomfortable with the question, admits "seeking personal advice from a friend of mine who used to be in Homicide, in Washington." The friend, he states, advised him to call the FBI.

"Did you call anonymously?"

"No, I gave my name, address, and phone number, and I told them my son had been a witness to a homicide."

Fiedler says he didn't get the name of the person he spoke with at the FBI and he cannot recall if the all-points bulletin was still in play at the time he called, or if he gave information as to Cayle's whereabouts.

Now Romero asks if Fiedler was concerned for Cayle's safety when he dropped him off at Peggy Shurtleff's house.

Fiedler says no, that Peggy is considered to be not only an honest person, but "a paragon of virtue in their circle of friends."

"Did you, at any time, consider calling the girls' parents?"

Fiedler moves uncomfortably in his chair. "I didn't think of that at the time."

Romero thanks Mike Fiedler and sits down. Santwier's questions are brief: Did Cayle say that three girls had been shot? No, not three girls. He said, "Everybody's dead—all my friends are dead." Did Mike Fiedler review interviews and transcripts before testifying today? Yes, he did.

Nancy Naftel asks if there had been any indication that Cayle had been drinking that night. Fiedler says he could smell alcohol on his son's breath, but that he was walking normally and talking coherently.

After Mike Fiedler's testimony, Judge Byrne ends the day's proceedings.

. . . .

Peggy Shurtleff is the first person to take the stand the following day. Without makeup, with her long, sand colored hair held back by a band, and her prim navy and white jumper, it is easy to see this young woman as the "paragon of virtue" described by Cayle's father. It is a more difficult task to form an image of her as an integral member of the clique that hung out at the guesthouse on Fairlawn Way. She is noticeably pregnant.

Peggy testifies that she is twenty years old now, that she has married and lives out of state.

She then describes the visit from Cayle Fiedler on the early morning of March 22, 1991. She says when Cayle told her "to keep my mouth shut and not to call anybody, I was just saying to myself, 'I gotta call *somebody.*' "

When questioned about letters written by her to Dave Adkins in custody, she says she did in fact write to him and that he wrote back, stating his innocence. Dave's letters to Peggy also stated Cayle's "involvement" in the murders, and Dave's love for Kathy.

She says she spoke to Cayle, when he called, "a few weeks later. Just to talk. Maybe five conversations in all."

At one point, Stephen Romero asks her about a letter she sent to Dave, in custody, in which she mentions "hearing in the paper that you might not have anything to do with this."

There is an objection, and a sidebar is called.

During the sidebar, Peggy sits gazing around the courtroom. It is a blistering day, and the air-conditioning in the courthouse is out of whack; many of the jurors and spectators are fanning themselves with magazines and folded pieces of newspaper. Peggy glances often, in brief, sliding looks, at Dave and Vinnie.

Dave gets most of her attention. Vinnie doesn't seem to be aware (although he must be) of Peggy's covert scrutiny; he sits, staring straight ahead, as usual. His hair is slightly punked out today—moussed into little spikes on top. Dave knows that Peggy is watching him. He rakes the back of his hair often, shaping and patting it as he keeps up a whispered conversation with Steven Sonoro. More than once he will smile and laugh quietly at something Sonoro has said.

It is a lengthy sidebar. Peggy yawns daintily and turns partway around in the witness chair to glance at the attorneys and the court reporter clustered near the bench.

Kathy Macaulay's mother is here alone today; Heather Goodwin's father has not yet arrived. Danae Palermo's family is here, in force, every day. Five or six people, as a rule.

As the sidebar ends, Judge Byrne calls for a lunch break. Peggy stands, but does not leave the witness stand; she waits, watching Dave and Vinnie as the bailiff leads them past her. There is no eye contact between her and the two boys she knows so well. As Vinnie passes, her eyes drop; when Dave walks by, she looks up at him.

After lunch Romero takes his place at the rostrum.

"Peggy, since this happened, have you told anyone that Cayle did the actual shooting?"

"No."

Now he holds up a copy of a letter Peggy identifies as one she wrote and sent to Dave on May 2, 1991. Romero reads aloud: " 'I'm hearing from people and newspapers that you might not have anything to do with this. Everyone I know is pointing the finger at Cayle.' " Romero looks up at Peggy. "Correct?"

"Yes."

Romero thanks her.

Santwier asks a series of questions in which Peggy describes her relationship with the inner circle of the Kathy Macaulay/Dave Adkins crowd.

"When you called the guesthouse and spoke to the police that night, did you say"—Santwier places a copy of the transcript on the board—" 'Dave took the shotgun from the house, came back, and shot all three'? Did Cayle tell you that Dave said anything?"

"He said Dave said, 'I shot my girlfriend.' "

"Did you tell the police that?"

"No."

"Is it in your notes?"

"No."

"Did you tell the police that Dave said anything else?"

"No."

Another page of transcript goes up on the board. Peggy looks at it, reads silently.

"Does this refresh your memory of talking to Detective Korpal at the station? You said, 'The only thing Cayle said Dave said to him was, "Are you dead or are you down?"' "

"Yes."

"But Cayle said that Dave *also* said, 'I killed my girlfriend.' So he *did* say more . . .?"

"Yes."

"At one time you said that Cayle said, 'Dave shot all three.' But at a later time he said, 'Dave shot the first two and then Vinnie took the gun and shot Danae.' Do you remember that?"

"No, I don't remember."

"Did you ask Cayle to explain the difference?"

"No."

"Cayle told you not to contact the police?"

"Yes."

"And Cayle told you that Dave said, 'I shot my girlfriend,' and, 'Are you down or are you dead'?"

"Yes."

Peggy is excused and given permission, by Judge Byrne, to remain in the courtroom. She takes a seat in a row with the families of the victims.

Sandie Wells is called to the witness stand.

In answer to Nancy Naftel's questions, Mrs. Wells says she has been a teacher in the South Pasadena School District for twenty-five years. She tells the court she lives in Sylmar and that it is a thirty-five-minute drive to South Pasadena from there.

After pointing out Dave Adkins, she gives a brief history of their relationship, beginning with their meeting in her eighth-grade English class. She says that Dave stayed with her at random times, and that she had attempted to gain custody as a foster parent. She says she does not know Vinnie Hebrock very well, but that he was a member of her English class, and of her homeroom—briefly—in 1988. Mrs. Wells points at Vinnie, too.

Now she gives the court an account of what happened when Dave and Vinnie came to see her in the predawn hours of March 22. At one point, in trying to describe the boys' apparent state of mind, Mrs. Wells says they looked "cheerful—but agitated." She says she wondered "if they were on anything."

It's that word: *cheerful.* She said it, it's out there, but you can see, looking at her, she'd like to take it back. It's a damning word uttered in this context.

Naftel goes on with her questions. Did Dave or Vinnie ask for, or did Mrs. Wells offer, money? No. Did they tell her what direction they were going on the Golden State Freeway? North.

Naftel sits down; Santwier gets to his feet.

One of his initial questions, about Vinnie's illiteracy, is objected to, by Nancy Naftel, on grounds of irrelevancy. Byrne upholds.

"You said Vinnie appeared cheerful that night?"

"Yes."

"You had seen him 'cheerful' before? This is based on some previous reference?"

"I'd seen him cheerful. I'd seen him despondent. I'd seen him angry . . ."

"Had you seen him frustrated?"

"Definitely."

"Did you and Vinnie Hebrock have a close relationship?"

"Not close. We got on in my class."

"Did you attempt to befriend Vinnie Hebrock in your class?"

"No more than any other student." Mrs. Wells goes on to say that she thinks Vinnie "may have liked and trusted me, but there was no real reason to seek me out. We didn't have a special relationship, but I was certainly more friend than foe."

After Mrs. Wells is excused, Judge Byrne calls a recess for lunch. When the proceedings reconvene in an hour, she will be seated in the spectator section, near Pam Adkins.

The first witness of the afternoon session is Deputy Dale Falikon, of the L.A. County Sheriff's Scientific Service. His specialty is crime scene evidence and photographs. The used shotgun shells and pieces of shell wadding found in the guesthouse are brought out, and, on an architectural diagram, Falikon points to where he found pieces of skull and bloodstains.

When it is Romero's turn to examine the witness, he asks about a photograph Falikon took of the bloodstain and puddle of vomit found near Kathy's body. Is that a drop of blood on top of the vomit? In his re-direct, Romero will ask about a photograph of a star-shaped design drawn into the dust on the top of an outside table. Why did Falikon take the picture? The deputy says he was simply trying to document the whole location. "And the star was interesting and unique to me."

. . . .

On Monday morning, July 20, Stephen Romero has a motion to be heard before the juries are brought in. He is asking to "suppress confession." And he needs witnesses on the stand.

Steven Bellshaw, the control officer with the Salem, Oregon, Police Department, is sworn in. Bellshaw describes the apprehension of Dave Adkins and Vinnie Hebrock at the Salem bus terminal. He says that Officer Selina Barnes was present, "a few feet away," and that Dave was not told, at that time, that he was wanted for homicide. And that at no time did he request the presence of an attorney.

The next witness is Sergeant Larry D. Stephens of the Salem Police Department. He states that he met Dave in an interview room at the station, and that he read Dave his rights as well as the "Consent to Search" card. At the conclusion of this interview, in which Stephens went through Dave's backpack, he informed the boy that he was being accused of murder. Dave's reply to the accusation consisted of the single word, "Oh." There was no request for an attorney, no refusal to talk.

The third witness called by Romero is Detective Mike Korpal of the Pasadena police. He describes his interview with Dave at the Salem Police Department on March 23, and he states that Dave willingly gave up his rights to silence.

When Romero asks whether or not Korpal told Dave that Vinnie had taken—and passed—a lie detector test, Korpal says he did tell that to Dave, that it was in fact untrue, but that he used "tactics I was comfortable with."

When Romero asks if Dave cried when the murders were discussed, or when Korpal mentioned the girls' parents and Dave's mother, Korpal shakes his head.

"Dave never cried."

After a series of questions about any "due process" violations that might have occurred, Judge Byrne denies Romero's motion.

Now Rickard Santwier makes a motion to suppress confession.

After a series of questions, to the same witnesses, about Vinnie's ability to understand what is said to him, Judge

Byrne dismisses. He rules that Vinnie Hebrock's rights were not violated, either.

Dave Adkins's jury is brought into the courtroom and the trial continues. (No part of the motions to suppress confession will be made available, as evidence, to either jury.)

Detective Bellshaw takes the stand again and describes finding Dave (and Vinnie) at the Greyhound station in Salem. He tells the court that Dave did not seem fearful of Vinnie when he and Bellshaw were alone in Bellshaw's patrol car, nor did he ask for help. He says Dave "was cooperative."

Next up is Sergeant Stephens again. He describes the initial discussion, with Dave, in the interview room at the Salem police station. He says there was a GSR test and that he conducted it. Quoting Dave's response to the news that he was under arrest for homicide, Stephens says, "He was real casual about the whole thing. He didn't seem to take it seriously at all."

Stephens was one of the police officers who went, with Dave Adkins, on March 24, to pick up the murder weapon in Grants Pass. Stephens testifies that Dave "gave specific instructions to the area, then walked, with us, about half a mile to a dump area, where we located the shotgun and a bag of shells."

Nancy Naftel asks if Dave Adkins said anything after the shotgun was located. Sergeant Stephens consults his notebook.

"Dave said, 'We didn't fire the shotgun after we killed the girls.'"

Some discussion of the boxes of evidence with items found in Dave's backpack is next (one of the boxes was lost by Alaska Airlines). Stephens testifies that there were no apparent bloodstains on any items of clothing found. "Noticeable bloodstains would have been remarked on in the report."

The Adkins jury is excused for the day and Vinnie's jury is brought in.

Officer Selina Barnes of the Salem Police Department takes the stand again. She is followed by Sergeant Michael Luyet, the first officer Vinnie met at the Salem station. Luyet states that during the photographic session after the interview, Vinnie said, "I don't even know why we killed them. She [Kathy] gave us a place to stay, and money, and she bought us clothes."

Luyet testifies, under Naftel's examination, that he went with Vinnie, Dave, and Sergeant Stephens to Grants Pass to collect the murder weapon and shotgun shells. The following day, March 25, Vinnie sent word he wanted to speak to Luyet again.

Luyet tells the court that when he met with Vinnie again, Vinnie told him a long scenario of drinking and smoking (on the day of the murders). Vinnie also said that Dave, Kathy, and Cayle "went on a beer run." He told Luyet about "the rough play" with Heather and Danae.

"Then Vinnie said that he and Dave Adkins went into the main house, and Dave said, 'Let's get the gun and scare 'em.'

"He said they walked back around, went up on the deck [of the guesthouse] and Dave Adkins handed the gun to Vinnie and 'it jerked and went off and Kathy got shot.' He said Kathy was at the stereo and Dave took back the gun and then he [Dave] shot Heather and Danae." Luyet says, also, that Vinnie told him Cayle was on the bed next to Danae. Then Vinnie drew a diagram of the crime scene, with Luyet printing the names of the victims, because Vinnie could not read or write.

Court is adjourned for the day.

. . . .

The next morning, before the Hebrock jury is brought in, Santwier sits close by Vinnie's side, rubbing Vinnie's back, whispering to him, smiling, bucking him up.

Sergeant Luyet will testify again.

Today he tells the court that Vinnie told him, on March 25, 1991, about "them [Vinnie and Dave] robbing the safe in the main house a couple of weeks before the shooting."

Vinnie had also expressed concern to Luyet. "He felt he could have saved one of the girls, but he was afraid of what Dave would do if he—Vinnie—interfered."

One of Luyet's concerns was whether Vinnie Hebrock had questions that needed answering. Vinnie did. He wanted to know if he would get "a good lawyer." He also said, "I don't mind doing my time, but I don't want to do any more time than I have to."

Sergeant Luyet is excused, Vinnie's jury is brought back into the courtroom, and there is a succession of witnesses, each one an expert in various aspects of a homicide investigation. Heidi Robbins is a criminologist specializing in biochemistry and genetics. Her field is bloodstains and residue. Robbins states that jeans found in the back of the Mercedes yielded an infinitesimal amount of blood consistent with Heather Goodwin's blood type. But that this was inconclusive: the blood could have come from anyone in that blood group.

Nothing significant on any other item tested. Not even the yellow towel, collected from Cayle Fiedler's bathroom a day after the murders. There *was* a droplet of blood on the towel, all right: it was deemed to be the kind of stain made by a shaving nick.

The next witness is a gunshot residue expert: John Bever, of the L.A. Sheriff's Department. He explains that the failure of the GSR tests performed in Salem to show residue is more than likely due to the fact that they were performed almost twenty-four hours after the weapon was fired. Tests made after only six hours can show no residue.

Now Naftel calls Deputy Sheriff Dwight Van Horn to the stand. Van Horn is a firearms examiner. He is handed the 12-gauge Mossberg, examines it quickly, and identifies it as the murder weapon. He says that when he first examined it, the plastic safety lever was missing, and the gun was "somewhat dirty but performed as it was supposed to perform."

And now he pumps the gun, to demonstrate to the court how the shells are breached into the chamber.

The sound of the mechanism explodes in the silent courtroom. It is loud and it is horrifying. This is the penultimate sound Kathy Macaulay, Heather Goodwin, and Danae Palermo heard just before they died.

A member of Danae Palermo's family, an older woman, covers her face with both hands. Heather's father does not move at all, but some small connection at his jawbone begins to pulse. Kathy's mother takes off her glasses to rub her eyes.

There is absolutely no response from either Dave or Vinnie.

Dave has been given (in his cell) a transcript of the statements he made in Oregon, to read; it is about forty-five pages long. He has said he thinks he will testify this week. When asked about Vinnie, he says that he and Vinnie do not speak, either on the bus ride back and forth from jail to the courthouse, or in the holding cells during court recesses and breaks. Dave says that Vinnie sleeps, or he sits, looking at the floor. Dave himself does push-ups in his cell and, when they are on the bus, listens to the music that plays constantly. He says the sheriff's bus has a "bitchin' loudspeaker."

The questions and answers about the gun continue. Naftel. Romero. Santwier. The photographs of the bodies as they were found at the crime scene go back up on the board. And Van Horn pumps the shotgun again and again. To show how it works, to demonstrate that even if it is jerked or thrown, it will not discharge accidentally. Van Horn testifies that the only way this weapon will discharge accidentally is if it is dropped straight down from a height of approximately thirty inches. He adds that 4¾ pounds of pressure must be applied before the gun will fire when the trigger is squeezed.

Dr. Koss is here today; as the photographs of the dead girls are placed against the board, his right hand stretches out to cover his wife's left hand. "I can't look," she whispers, without raising her head.

. . . .

Detective Mike Korpal of the Pasadena police is called to the stand the next morning. Before he testifies there is a motion made, by Stephen Romero, to keep the transcripts of Dave Adkins's statements away from the jury, even though they will be listening to the tape. Nancy Naftel feels the transcripts will be an aid in listening. Judge Byrne says that he will rule on this "at the time the jury hears the tape."

Naftel begins her questions. Korpal delivers a brief synopsis of his involvement in the case, beginning with the predawn hours of March 22, 1991. Finally, Judge Byrne asks Korpal if, after a last revision of the transcript, he went over it "word for word." When Korpal says he did, and that all inaudible parts have been marked, Byrne is satisfied. He will allow the transcript to be handed out to the jurors. Then he turns to look at them.

"This transcript is *not* to be read *as* the tape is being played. You are to listen and refer to the typed pages only when necessary."

The copies are passed out by the bailiff and then, when everything is in order, the tape begins to play. We hear Mike Korpal's voice giving us the time and date; we hear Dave Adkins's rights as they are read to him; we hear Dave relinquish his right to silence and his right to have an attorney present. Then we hear Korpal ask Dave to tell him where he, Dave, has been the past few days.

"Start with Wednesday."

We hear Dave Adkins's initial statement: that Cayle and Vinnie killed Kathy, Heather, and Danae.

We hear Korpal tell Dave that Vinnie had passed a lie detector test "one hundred percent clean."

We hear that Korpal had spoken to Cayle and believed his story.

We hear Korpal plead with Dave to set the record straight.

Then we hear Dave's muffled voice.

"We . . . went on a beer run. When we came back, Vinnie and Heather and Danae had been arguing . . . " There is a pause. Then, "I don't know . . . I don't know . . . "

"What happened, Dave?"

"We went out and got the gun, and . . . we walked in . . . and Vinnie shot Kathy . . . " He is nearly choking on the words.

"Do you know why?"

Dave mutters something about the fight between Vinnie, Heather, and Danae.

"Are you telling the truth now?"

"*Yeah!*"

"Did Cayle do anything? Or did you just put the gun in Cayle's face?"

Dave's reply to this is inaudible. The only thing we can hear clearly on the tape is a deep, bone-weary sigh. Then Dave's voice again.

"Cayle was next to me, all 'What should I do?' "

"Cayle said there was a voice on his answering machine [after the murders] saying, 'I got to know if you're down.' Was that you, Dave?"

Dave's reply is inaudible.

Korpal waits a beat or two before he asks the next question.

Then, "There's been enough tragedy, Dave. Tell me where the gun is."

"Grants Pass."

"Will you take me there?"

"Now . . . ?"

"Later. Can some kid find it and pick it up? Because we've had enough tragedies here."

Whatever Dave said next is lost.

"Who got shot first, Dave?"

"Kathy."

"What did he say to her?"

"Nothing."

"Where did he shoot her? In the head?"

"Yeah."

"Did she plead with him?"

You can almost hear the shrug before Dave answers.

"She said, 'Stop fucking around . . .' "

"Where were you standing? About four feet away?"

"Closer."

"Did the other girls say anything after Kathy was shot?"

"No . . . " He pauses. "Oh, man . . . I was tripping."

"Then what happened?"

"Vinnie handed me the gun."

"And then?"

"I pointed it at Heather . . . here"—Dave is clearly indicating some point on his head—"and I shot her."

"Where did you shoot Danae?"

"In her back."

"In the back of her head?"

"In her *back*. She had her back toward me."

Dave's voice, on the tape, seems to be devoid of any feeling other than fatigue. He sits at the counsel table now, over a year later, making idle notes on a legal pad, listening along with everyone else. The people on his jury look at him more frequently than they refer to the transcript. Dave Adkins, as a human being, is more of a mystery than any inaudible passage in his statement.

"Was there any conversation between you and Vinnie?"

"Nuh-uh."

"And after you said that ["Are you down?"] to Cayle?"

"We left."

"Who went through the purses?"

"I went through Kathy's purse."

"You went to Cayle's house?"

"Yeah."

"You still had the gun with you?"

"Yeah."

"Was anything said, by Cayle, in the car?"

"He said, 'I didn't think you guys were that down.'"

"Cayle did not have anything to do with the murders?"

"No."

"Did you keep on the same clothes as when you shot those two girls?"

"Yeah."

There is a pause on the tape; you can hear shuffling, as of sneakers on linoleum, and the soft scrape of furniture, as if someone has changed position in their chair. During the playing of the tapes there have been tears from the families of the slain girls. And, at some point, Pam Adkins has begun to weep softly into a handkerchief.

"Do you have any questions, Dave?"

"Yeah. What happens now?"

"I get the information back to L.A. and the District Attorney decides what happens next." Another pause. "Will you go back to California freely?"

"Yeah."

Now Korpal asks Dave to show, by sketching out a map, where he left the gun in Grants Pass. Dave talks, describing the area as he draws, and his voice is different now. Lighter. The terrible weariness seems to have been lifted. It comes back when Korpal says he won't mention Dave's confession to Pam unless Dave wants Korpal to tell her. Korpal asks how Dave wants this handled. The reply is inaudible.

"Well, I'll have your mom call you here."

Then we hear Dave, his voice stronger now, speak again.

"Look, what usually happens? Obviously I'm guilty. What I'm saying here is, if I went to court and said I was guilty, what usually happens?"

"In terms of the sentence? I don't know, Dave. I don't file charges—I only investigate."

"Yeah, but what I'm saying here is, could they throw me in jail for life?" There is real urgency in Dave Adkins's voice now.

"I honestly don't know. I'll ask your attorney and let you know." He takes a beat. "Thanks for your cooperation. And for the parents. You've eased their pain." Another beat. "I'm going to leave you here for a few minutes, by yourself."

The tape ends. The bailiff collects the copies of the transcripts from the jurors. There is the feel, in the courtroom, of people leaning back against their chairs.

Nancy Naftel stands. She asks Korpal one or two questions about errors in the transcript. (On page 14, "If it was important" should be changed to read "If it *wasn't* important.")

Naftel thanks Korpal and takes her seat. Stephen Romero begins his cross-examination with a series of questions having to do with Korpal's size. He even asks the detective to get to his feet. That accomplished, he takes Korpal through his earlier interviews with Cayle, Peggy Shurtleff, and Mike Fiedler, searching out and exploring the time lapses between the interviews.

Romero asks Korpal if he had "a preconceived version before you talked to Dave Adkins?"

Korpal says he had "formed an opinion after interviews with Vinnie Hebrock and Cayle Fiedler." He refers to Dave's initial statements as "First Lie" and "Second Lie."

When Romero asks if Korpal was "unhappy" because he felt Dave wasn't telling the truth, the detective says it wasn't that he was unhappy. He was simply not satisfied that Dave Adkins was telling the truth.

Romero asks about the tactics used by Korpal when he interviewed Dave. The attorney refers to them as "ruses," and he takes them point by point—the clearing of conscience, the easing of the families' pain, the "lie detector test." Korpal assures Romero that these are all legal tactics.

After asking Korpal for a physical description of Cayle Fiedler, and another mention of the lie detector tactic, Romero sits down.

Naftel goes to the rostrum again.

"Detective Korpal, did you ever beat up or threaten Dave Adkins during your interviews with him?"

"No."

"Did you refuse him food during the interviews?"

"No."

"Did he ask for food?"

"No."

She takes her seat again.

Romero asks if, by virtue of Korpal's size, he is threatening to people.

There is an immediate objection, but Byrne allows Korpal to reply. Korpal cuts right to it.

"I was *not* using my size to intimidate. I moved closer to Dave Adkins during the interview to force him to look at me."

It is the end of the day. Detective Korpal has maintained a calm civility throughout the session. His height and weight, combined with florid coloring, walrus mustache, and shambling gait, present an image more avuncular than anything else.

The Adkins jury is excused for the day. After they have filed out of the courtroom, Rickard Santwier requests that the tapes of Vinnie Hebrock's interview with Detective Korpal in Oregon be heard without the typed transcripts. He refers to the tapes as "the best evidence." Judge Byrne tells him the transcripts will be allowed, as they were with Dave

Adkins's tapes, but that the jury will be instructed to use them as "an aid only."

. . . .

Detective Korpal takes the stand the next morning. Today it is Vinnie Hebrock who must face his jury as the tapes of his statement are played.

The transcripts are handed out; Judge Byrne cautions the jurors about listening rather than reading. The tape begins to roll.

We hear Mike Korpal's voice giving us the time and date; we hear Korpal reading Vinnie's rights to him, and Vinnie reciting them along with the detective. We hear Vinnie say that he does, in fact, understand his rights, and then we hear him give up the right to have an attorney present.

We hear Vinnie's initial versions of the shootings; we hear Korpal as he tries to reason with the kid. There is some more back and forth and then we hear:

"Come on, Vinnie. Tell the real truth."

And we hear what might be sounds of crying from Vinnie. Then,

"I had to shoot his girlfriend."

"Why?"

" 'Cause he was gonna kill *me* if I didn't."

At this point Vinnie says he might get sick. There is a stretch of tape where you can hear him taking in a couple of deep breaths. Then Korpal's voice again:

"Do you feel any better? Okay, I need to understand the sequence. So let's start with the kitchen."

"Dave told me to go through the window, we were gonna rob the house. I went in and opened the glass door and he went straight through to the bedroom . . . "

"Did he know where the gun was kept?"

"Yeah. So he handed the gun to me and told me to load it."

"How many shells got jacked in?"

"Three. Then we went back upstairs."

"What did you say?"

"I didn't say nothin'. Nobody said nothin'. We went upstairs and he crammed the gun in my hands, and the fuckin' barrel was pointed at Kathy. And it went off. He crammed it up in my hand and it went off, man."

"What did the other girls do?"

"Heather went for the door—she tried to make it to the door. But Dave grabbed her and threw her back down on the bed and shot her."

"Did Danae scream?"

Vinnie's reply is inaudible.

"What about Cayle?"

"Dave went up and asked if he was down with him."

"What did Cayle say?"

"Hell, yes! He had a gun crammed up in his face."

"Then what?"

"Then we got our clothes."

"Are you telling me that trigger went off because it got crammed into your hand? I'm going to have to find the gun to check the trigger. Where is it?"

"In some woods in Southern California."

"How many hours were you on the freeway before you dropped off the gun?"

"About a half-hour."

Now Korpal asks about a small door that was found broken in the garage. Vinnie says he has no idea how the garage door got that way. Korpal asks if Vinnie knows how and why the bathroom door in the guesthouse had gotten kicked in. Again, Vinnie tells the detective he has no idea how that happened, either.

"Did you wash up afterwards?"

"No."

"Where did you go?"

"We drove down the mountain to Cayle's. And Dave said, 'Don't tell anyone or I'll be back to kill you.' Then we went to Sandie's. Then we went to the Shell station for gas."

"Did you still have the gun?"

"Yeah. It was in the backseat."

"Where'd you drop it off?"

"Somewhere around . . . I don't know. We jumped off an exit."

"Was it near Magic Mountain?"

"No. We hadn't drove that long."

"You came up the coast?"

"Straight up Five."

"Let's talk about this. Did you guys talk at all?"

"I was in a daze. We didn't say *nothing*—we didn't talk."

"Did you hear your names on the radio? See your pictures in the paper?"

Vinnie's reply is inaudible. When Korpal speaks again, his voice is softer; he sounds less like an interviewer. There is now a more personalized edge to his tone.

"Why'd this happen, Vinnie?"

And Vinnie's voice, in reply, crackles with emotion.

"I don't know. I'm telling you, honest to God, I don't know!"

"Were you drinking?"

"Yeah, a six-pack—maybe a couple of shots. But I was in a daze, man." More intense, more emotion now. "It's like a bad high, like you can't get away from it." You can hear him sucking in air. "I shot someone who didn't need to be shot! She didn't do a fuckin' thing to me!" A beat. "She got shot for no reason!"

There is another pause on the tape, then Vinnie goes on. His voice has dropped to a calmer, less impassioned delivery. "Danae didn't need to be shot. Heather didn't need to be shot. They were three innocent girls. They weren't doing nothing."

Another beat. "We were just roughhousing and Heather kicked me in the balls."

"Is that why the shooting started?"

The first half of Vinnie's reply is inaudible, but then the tape picks up what he is saying:

". . . and Kathy was talking, a long time ago, about robbing her house. And, you know, we were drunk. Stuff comes up when you're drunk."

During the time the tape has been unreeling, Vinnie has remained unmoving in his chair. He has not looked at the jury, he has not looked at Santwier. It's as if, for Vinnie, he is already in another place, another time. As if this trial and all that went before—his relationship with Dave Adkins, his precarious position in Dave and Kathy's crowd, the animosity with Heather and his strange attraction to her, even the murders—no longer have anything to do with him.

The interview continues. Korpal asks a series of questions about the jewelry that was traded for gas along the way to Oregon. Vinnie says he has no idea where the trades took place, no idea how much money was involved. He does recall that a bracelet with the initial "K" was one of the items traded. He knows it was Kathy's bracelet, but he does not remember if Dave took it from Kathy's body.

Now we hear another voice on the tape. It is Detective Tim Sweetman's. He says that Heather was shot first, Kathy second, and Danae third. Vinnie responds quickly.

"Kathy got shot first."

"I have real good knowledge *you* shot the last girl."

"I positively didn't shoot Danae!" The words are tumbling out again. "Kathy was standing right by the table and Dave shoved the gun in my hand."

"When he shoved the gun in your hand, did you plead with him not to shoot anyone?"

"I said, 'Don't shoot! *Don't shoot!*' "

Now Korpal's voice is heard again. "But you had your finger on the trigger . . . "

"It was stupid. It shouldn't've happened." A beat or two of silence. The tape hisses. "I said, 'Don't shoot' . . . "

"After Kathy was shot, how much time went by before the other girls got shot?"

There's a slight pause, then, "After he pulled the gun outta my hand and jacked it and I said, '*Don't* shoot! *Don't shoot!*' But he had no hesitation. I heard a pop. Another pop. I put my hands over my face . . . 'cause that's the worst thing."

"If your hands were over your face, how did you know he shot Heather and Danae?"

"My fingers were open. He had no hesitation. The only hesitation he had was with Cayle." Another pause. "Danae was bleeding all over the place."

"On Cayle?"

"I don't know—all over the bed." Vinnie hesitates. "Cayle didn't do nothing. All he tried to do was stay alive."

Korpal asks if Dave left a message on Cayle's answering machine. Vinnie says yes, he did. And then, unaccountably, "I couldn't walk."

"Did you guys steal anything from the house?"

"The gun. The car. And the money."

"Anything else?"

"No. No."

The tape ends. Nancy Naftel has no questions. Rickard Santwier goes to the rostrum with a sheaf of papers. Running through a number of questions in the transcript for which the answers had been inaudible, he asks Korpal what Vinnie's responses had been.

"In each instance Vinnie answered by shaking his head to indicate yes or no."

After Korpal is excused from the stand, Judge Byrne calls for a break.

When both juries are back in place, Romero makes another motion for a mistrial. It is denied.

There will be a demonstration of the pair of Levi's found in the back seat of the Mercedes. These are the jeans with the small bloodstain on one leg. Neither defendant will claim ownership. So both Dave and Vinnie will now try them on.

Vinnie goes first. He is taken into Byrne's chambers with Byrne, Santwier, and a deputy sheriff. When he steps into the courtroom again, he has on the jeans: they seem to fit at the waist and hips but they are far too long for him. He stands, turning slowly, in front of both jury panels. Dave Adkins's jury is seated in the spectator section today and several people in the back row stand up to get a better look. Other people in the spectator sections get to their feet too, craning their necks to see.

Now Dave. When he walks back into the courtroom, followed closely by Stephen Romero (and with Judge Byrne and the deputy), he presents a ludicrous picture: the jeans are so small on him they cannot be buttoned; in fact, will not slide all the way up over his hips. Clutching the tops of the jeans, Dave hobbles toward Vinnie's jury in the box, shows them. Then he moves back to turn a couple of times in front of his own jury. Romero has taken his chair at the counsel table, and during the exhibit, he swivels all the way around to look intently at Dave's jury. His hands rest easily on the arms of the chair; his head is high; the expression on his face can be best described as exultant. He continues to look at each person in turn as they rise and file out of the courtroom, along with Vinnie's jury, after Byrne excuses both panels for the day. Dave, too, is unable to suppress a grin as he turns to look at his mother in the front row.

. . . .

The following Monday, Dave Adkins's defense begins, and Nancy Naftel has a complaint: there has been no discovery* on the first witness, Mrs. Marilyn Fiedler Davies, Cayle's grandmother. Romero explains that this witness is uncooperative. Byrne asks when Romero got the notes on Mrs. Davies. December, Romero tells him; he was hoping to consolidate them into his other notes. "There was never an act to conceal these notes, your Honor."

Byrne is not happy about this. He thinks it was "a clear act to conceal."

Naftel has the notes in her hand now. She looks up at Byrne.

"Your Honor, these written notes were taken on December 14, 1991. They should have been handed in after our discovery order was entered. This witness is not on the witness list."

Romero: "These are notes, obtained by our investigators, that I made Ms. Naftel aware of. If Ms. Naftel needs a few minutes to read them now, I have no objection."

Byrne tells Naftel to "take ten minutes."

The Adkins jury is brought in and Mrs. Davies is called. Her son, Mike Fiedler, walks into the courtroom with her and takes a seat at the back of the spectator section. Mrs. Davies is frail and clearly on edge. She is sworn in and states that on March 21, 1991, she was living in South Pasadena. Romero hands her a copy of her telephone bill; she glances at it and says, yes, there are calls here from her home to Washington State.

Romero asks her about the night of March 21.

"My son, Mike, and grandson, Cayle, came to my house between twelve and twelve-forty-five. I remember I was watching Johnny Carson."

When Romero asks what Cayle was wearing, Mrs. Davies says he had on "jeans, a sweater, and a shirt."

Romero has no further questions. Naftel gets to her feet.

*Any disclosure that either party is compelled to make, as of facts or documents.

"Mrs. Davies, what was Cayle's condition on the night of March 21 when he came into your house?"

"He was white. Hysterical and very upset. He said, 'You won't believe what happened—all my friends were shot!' "

Mrs. Davies is excused.

The next witness is Claudine Ratcliffe; she is a coroner's investigator for the City of Los Angeles. She tells the court that on the morning of March 22, she responded to a location at Fairlawn Way (she gives the exact address) to investigate "what our office calls a triple homicide. I arrived at approximately zero-nine-thirty hours."

Ratcliffe answers Romero's questions about her investigation of the crime scene; many of the queries have to do with the puddle of vomit found near Kathy Macaulay's head. Ratcliffe says there was "emissis [vomit] present on [Kathy Macaulay's] mouth, face, and next to her." Under further questioning, Ratcliffe says that Kathy might have vomited before she was shot, but that there is no way to be sure; it is her opinion only.

When Nancy Naftel asks if Kathy might have been shot first and *then* vomited, Ratcliffe states that, in her opinion, there would have been no time for Kathy to vomit after being shot.

The next witness is Phil Teramoto, senior criminologist for the L.A. County Sheriff's Department.

A schematic of the guesthouse is placed against the blackboard; there are marks on it indicating the position of the bodies. Now Romero shows Teramoto two photographs, taken at Teramoto's request, at the crime scene, of blood splatter patterns on the wall behind the stereo cabinet. Teramoto tells the court that these splatters are consistent with those coming from "a large, open wound."

Romero shows him another photograph. Teramoto identifies it as "a pool of blood on the floor next to the stereo cabinet, with what appears to be vomit with a dark spot on top." Teramoto explains that the reason these photos were taken was so that "if, at some point, a blood splatter interpretation was requested, the photos would provide a scale depiction of them."

The next witness is Sandie Wells. After a brief resume of Ms. Wells's teaching relationship with Dave Adkins, Romero asks about Dave's "special needs."

Mrs. Wells states that Dave had a "short attention span and a problem with short-term verbal memory. You must repeat—he doesn't take information in like a regular student. His verbal skills are approximately four years behind those you would expect from a student of that age." (Dave Adkins was fifteen years old when this assessment was made.) Wells adds that "Dave has a problem with comprehension. You must reteach and re-explain something before it settles into his brain. After thirty minutes, he loses what he had to start with; he becomes muddled. If what you are teaching him drags on too long, it is lost. Dave Adkins cannot sustain prolonged learning periods."

"What was Dave Adkins's behavior like in the classroom?"

There is an objection from Naftel. It is sustained.

"When was Dave Adkins last in your class?"

"June of 1989."

Naftel gets to her feet.

"If you ask Dave Adkins a question, you would have to repeat it back until he got it?"

"That is one of several methods."

"What did you teach him?"

"Language, arts, math, everything. I had to use different modalities with everything, whether they were conceptual or everyday things. Dave has trouble with what he hears."

"It's better if he reads?"

"Yes. But he still has a problem."

"When he and Vinnie Hebrock stopped by your apartment on the early morning of March 22, 1991, did they have any trouble walking and talking?"

"No. No trouble."

"They gave appropriate answers to questions?"

"Yes."

"What problems did he discuss at that time?"

"He told me that some problems he had before had been cleared up. That he took care of them."

"Did these problems have to do with school?"

"No."

"Did the defendant have trouble with understanding right or wrong?"

"No."

The case for the defense is done. The next time Stephen Romero and Nancy Naftel face each other in court, it will be to deliver their final summations to the Adkins jury.

Vinnie Hebrock's case may go to the jury this Tuesday afternoon, July 28. His mother and sister are in the courtroom for the first time during the trial. Darrell Goodwin, who was not here yesterday, is also in the courtroom, as are other relatives of the dead girls.

Vinnie does not look up at his family as he is led to the counsel table. As always, his eyes are on the floor. His mother is without expression; his sister, Tiki, is near tears.

Dave Adkins is not here, but Stephen Romero is sitting in the spectator section. As the morning progresses, he will take notes.

Nancy Naftel greets the jury and runs quickly—but thoroughly—through the degrees of murder that can be applied to their finding on Vinnie Hebrock. She describes the special allegation for each count: that the defendant personally used a firearm to shoot, to hit, or in a menacing manner.

"Vinnie Hebrock shot Kathy Macaulay. He did not personally shoot Heather Goodwin or Danae Palermo, but I am going to ask you to find him responsible for all three murders, even though he did not pull the trigger.

"There are three ways to find Vinnie Hebrock guilty for the shooting deaths of Heather Goodwin and Danae Palermo, in addition to killing Kathy Macaulay: One: Conspiracy; the agreement of two or more people, with specific intent and an overt act in the furtherance of that conspiracy. Each person is responsible for the natural consequences of the act. Vinnie Hebrock is equally responsible for shooting those three girls. We do not have to prove express agreement; that can be shown through circumstantial evidence.

"Two: Aiding and Abetting: to find on this count requires that one person has knowledge of unlawful purpose of the act and agrees to aid and encourage another party in the furtherance of the act. The party who knows and assists is liable for that crime and its consequences.

"Three: Felony Murder: this applies when the murder takes place during the commission of an unlawful act. As in a robbery. Whether the murder was intentional or unintentional—even if it was accidental—the person committing the act is liable."

Each person on the Hebrock jury is listening intently; Mrs. Hebrock and Vinnie's sister are expressionless. Linda Macaulay Koss, Darrell Goodwin, and the Palermo family are, all of them, riveted by Naftel's words.

Now Naftel takes the jury through the events of March 21, 1991. The party at the guesthouse; the beer run; the fight between Vinnie, Heather, and Danae. She quotes one of Vinnie's later statements: "Heather kicked me in the balls and scratched the fuck outta me."

The jury is taken through the break-in via the kitchen window of the main house; the loading of the weapon; the return to the guesthouse and the murders.

"The defendant shoots Kathy Macaulay—Kathy, his friend. His friend who was letting him stay there—he shoots her and takes off the top of her head. Now he tries to give the gun to Dave Adkins, but Dave is busy: Heather Goodwin is trying to make a run for the door. Dave grabs her, throws her back down on the bed, and now Vinnie gives Dave the gun and Dave blows Heather's head off. Then he goes up to Danae Palermo and shoots her in the back of the head."

Naftel describes Cayle Fiedler "waking up to see Danae's brains." The gun at his head, the questions, "Are you down?

Are you coming with us?" And Cayle saying, "Let's get out of here."

"And the defendant? He wants to 'get some shit outta the house.' Cayle Fiedler is with two people who just shot three girls in cold blood."

She describes the trip downstairs to the laundry room and the drive to Cayle's house in Kathy's mother's Mercedes. The threats to Cayle.

"They drive away. And do what? *They go buy dope!* And then they go see Dave's teacher, Sandie Wells. They're 'agitated but cheerful.' Dave Adkins talks, says his problems are over, and talks about going to see his aunt and uncle. The murders are two hours old and they have already made plans!"

Now Naftel talks about the drive to Oregon, the arrest, the lies to the police.

At the lunch break, as Vinnie is led past his mother and sister, there is no exchange of looks, no eye contact whatsoever. When he is brought back in, two hours later, for the afternoon session, they are gone. This will have been his family's only appearance at his trial.

Before the jurors take their places, Santwier leans in close to Vinnie; the attorney is talking and smiling, trying, it would seem, to bring his client into the moment. Trying to get this seemingly entranced boy to participate in his own trial.

Nancy Naftel continues her summation. She takes the jury through the elements of first-degree murder. She has the shotgun in her hands now, and, as she talks about the intentional act of loading it, she pumps it two or three times, demonstrating the difficulties of loading and shooting. "You have to pump it every time you shoot; it is a very specific act."

Deliberation and premeditation.

She speaks again of the earlier conversation with Cayle Fiedler, the statements made, by both defendants, about "getting out of town." The statement, "I had to shoot his [Dave's] girlfriend." The threats made to Cayle Fiedler (even though Vinnie did not acknowledge the fact that *he* made threats; he said Dave Adkins made them). "But when Vinnie Hebrock uttered the phrase, 'Yeah, dude—we smoked 'em all,' he took full responsibility.

"Vinnie Hebrock assisted Dave Adkins with the full knowledge of what he was doing."

Aiding and abetting.

Naftel tells the jurors that the evidence shown so far is really all they need. But—if they need more: The killing occurred during a robbery. They can rely on felony/murder. She is asking for first-degree murder.

She leans forward on the rostrum. "There will be talk of other facts. Intoxication. Vinnie said, 'It was all a blur,' trying to not take responsibility. The fact is that neither Dave Adkins nor Vinnie Hebrock was so intoxicated they could not form plans."

She holds up one finger. "Down to Alvarado Street to buy dope." Another finger. "Go see Sandie." She drops her hands. "Where they were not scared. Where they were 'cheerful.' "

Now, one by one, a group of key photographs is shown again. The aerial view of the property on Fairlawn Way, showing the distance the defendants had to travel from the guesthouse to the main house and back again with the shotgun. The Polaroids of Dave and Vinnie with the gun. The terrible pictures of the girls' bodies.

"Ladies and gentlemen, I ask you to rely on the evidence and on what you have heard in court. I ask you to return a verdict finding Vinnie Hebrock guilty of first-degree murder."

Nancy Naftel takes her seat at the counsel table. Rickard Santwier rises to deliver his final argument in defense of Vinnie Hebrock. After a couple of general remarks about testimony and Vinnie's interview with Detective Korpal, Santwier goes to the heart of his statement.

"I asked Cayle Fiedler for exact words because you will be asked to come to a conclusion based on those words. If you have a doubt, we have a problem. Is exact wording *all* there is to this case? No. Absolutely not. But the words are very significant." He pauses, then goes on. "I offer, for your consideration, the fact that Cayle Fiedler was told, 'You heard a lot, saw TV, read a lot [about the case], etc.' Now, I don't know if Cayle Fiedler set out to lie to you, but one thing: he is consistent in his inconsistencies."

Santwier follows up with a list of conflicting quotes: "He said"; "They said"; "They had the gun."

" '*They*' cannot have a single gun, ladies and gentlemen. Cayle Fiedler is telling us what he *thinks* he saw: Vinnie Hebrock had scratches on him, so there must have been a fight. Cayle Fiedler didn't know about a fight; he said he heard them [Heather Goodwin and Danae Palermo] 'laughing and talking.'

"There is no one piece of evidence you can count on. Cayle Fiedler was very intoxicated on the night of March 21, 1991. He was severely impaired. They all were. Not even counting marijuana, they were well over twice the legal limit."

Santwier reminds the jurors of Peggy Shurtleff's testimony; that it was a regular occurrence for these kids to drink over two six-packs of beer a day.

Now he goes to the blackboard and writes, in large block letters: TWO REASONABLE INTERPRETATIONS.

He turns to the jury again. "If both the defense and the prosecution have reasonable interpretations of the crime, then you must go with one of them."

Now he writes the word INTENT on the blackboard.

"If the victims were shot quickly, does that show intent? Is that the only reasonable interpretation? Counsel would have you believe there was 'planning' involved here. The moves they made—the house, the gun, the shells, the shooting, the laundry room, 'stealing'—stealing what? The car. These were stupid moves. They were not planned out. This is a reasonable conclusion.

"*If* you find real, deliberate intent to kill, it must be formed on a preexisting reflection. The legal requirements for intent are that the slayer weighed and considered the question of killing, then considered the consequences of that act, and then decided to kill. Are we talking about that here?

"To get a verdict of first-degree murder it must be proven that Dave Adkins and Vinnie Hebrock deliberated to the degree required by law." He shakes his head, slowly. "They never got close to it.

"For felony/murder: When they went upstairs, they had to have a preplanned robbery in mind. There was none. They were drunk. They had access to the car, so why not just take it? They had access to the house. There was no intent to rob.

"Can you say robbery was the *only* intention if you bring felony/murder charges? Then the People don't have to prove premeditation. Without felony/murder, you have to look at degree of intoxication; it has the same bearing as 'intent to rob.' Do not confuse stealing with robbery. Stealing keys, a gun and shells is theft; robbery is taking by force."

The jurors are listening as attentively to Santwier as they did to Naftel.

"What we have here is three theories. I'm reminded of the old adage, 'If you throw enough stuff at a wall, some of it will stick.' "

Now Santwier gets into the charge of aiding and abetting. He asks if Vinnie Hebrock promoted the crime. If he advised it. If, in fact, his entry into the main house was unlawful. Vinnie had *access* to the house. What about loading the gun, he asks.

"Who's to say they weren't going outside to 'cap off' a few

rounds? There were, after all, pictures of them holding the gun. Who's to say they hadn't shot it off before?"

Santwier asks the jury if it is a reasonable interpretation that the act of loading the gun meant that Dave and Vinnie were going to shoot someone.

He tells the jury there is no evidence of *any* agreement to commit murder between Dave and Vinnie. He asks the jurors to use "compassion and prudence" when they go in to deliberate.

"Vinnie Hebrock *is* guilty. He is guilty of second-degree murder. He *did* use the gun on Kathy, and he owned up to it. He is not guilty of what happened to Heather and Danae. He has a social and moral responsibility."

Santwier tells the jurors they must be *convinced*—beyond reasonable doubt—that Vinnie Hebrock menaced Heather Goodwin and Danae Palermo.

Now Santwier takes the Hebrock jury through what he calls "holes in the evidence." These "holes" contain, for the most part, statements made by Cayle Fiedler and by Vinnie himself. The phrase, "Yeah, dude—we smoked 'em all," is focused on once more. As is Cayle's inconsistent memory for exact details.

Santwier leans forward, his hands grip both sides of the rostrum. His voice lifts.

"You must not be influenced by passion, sympathy, or public opinion. There are no winners here. You must base your decisions on evidence and the law.

"I would urge you to find Vinnie Hebrock guilty of second-degree murder."

Santwier walks back to the counsel table and takes his seat. He glances briefly at Vinnie Hebrock and smiles. Vinnie returns the look, goes for a kind of smile.

Nancy Naftel moves to the rostrum again.

"Ladies and gentlemen, you would think that Cayle Fiedler was on trial for not remembering everything." She pauses. "But Cayle Fiedler is not on trial.

"Vinnie Hebrock verified the threat on Cayle Fiedler. He verified the fight with Heather and Danae. He verified the fight in the car. And he verified that he dropped Cayle off at home and threatened him again.

"Consider that while you are considering Cayle Fiedler's testimony."

Naftel goes on to talk about the level of intoxication; the only tests were performed on the girls' bodies. It is not known what Vinnie Hebrock's level of intoxication was; all that is known is that everyone was drinking and smoking pot that night. But neither boy seemed impaired to Sandie Wells—she had no trouble letting them drive off.

Now Naftel talks about Vinnie's statement, "Dave wanted me to shoot Danae and Cayle." She puts forth the theory that maybe, somewhere along the way, plans got changed. "Maybe, Dave Adkins couldn't bring himself to shoot his girl-friend. Maybe when Heather Goodwin started her run for the door, things started to move a little bit too fast for them.

"Ladies and gentlemen, if there had been four shells in that shotgun, Cayle Fiedler would have been killed too."

She begins her windup.

"We do not have to establish exactly what the motive was. There were plenty: the fight; Vinnie's anger at the way Heather Goodwin treated him; the plan to get out of town. Neither defendant was bothered with morals and compunctions about taking lives. Their thoughts were about getting the car and getting out of town.

"Listen carefully to the tape:

" 'After we shot the girls, you couldn't hear nothing. The music stopped.'

" 'I shot somebody who didn't need to be shot.'

" 'I did the first one. I shot Kathy.'

" 'We smoked 'em all.'

" 'Dude, they got us.'

"Listen carefully, consider well, and return verdicts of first-degree murder for the murders of, one: Katherine Macaulay; two: Heather Goodwin; and, three: Danae Palermo."

Deliberations will begin the following day.

*I*t is the fourth day of the third week of trial. Stephen Romero is ready with his summation in the defense of Dave Adkins, but as before, Nancy Naftel will present the People's case first.

At 11:13 A.M. the jury is brought in. Nancy Naftel goes to the rostrum and begins to speak in much the same way she began her summation to the Hebrock jury. She describes the various degrees of murder and goes through the list of allegations. There is an extra allegation here: Multiple murders. Dave Adkins shot both Heather Goodwin and Danae Palermo.

When Naftel turns toward the photographs of the victims, Danae's sister leaves the courtroom.

"These pictures show the malice with which these murders were committed. They show how close the shotgun was held to their heads. And because of the close proximity of the bodies, the pictures show the rapid succession of shots. You can see the expended shells. You can imagine Cayle Fiedler's feelings when he heard that shotgun racked again."

Naftel holds up the enlargements of the two Polaroids of Dave and Vinnie with the shotgun. She points out the background, reminding the jurors that these pictures were taken in the master bedroom of the crime scene.

She shows a photograph of the burgled safe. "Don't make too much of this. It only shows there had been valuables in the house."

Now she begins to talk about the statement Dave Adkins made in Oregon. She reminds the jurors that Mike Korpal read Dave his rights.

"The defendant was not unaware. He knew his rights, he knew the Salem police could not arrest him 'for just anything.' Regardless of Sandie Wells's statement of a learning disability, this was not a learning situation. Detective Korpal was not trying to *teach* Dave Adkins anything.

"Dave Adkins told lie after lie in his taped interview. But certain statements made *after* those lies are very important." She refers to the transcript of the tapes. " 'If somebody was there, is that person just as guilty?' 'So, if I *was* there and I didn't do anything, I'm pretty much not guilty?' At that point Dave Adkins admitted to Detective Korpal that he had been at the guesthouse when the murders took place."

She reminds the jury of Dave's initial claim: that "they" asked him if he was down. Later he admitted it was he who said it. He talked about being in the car with Cayle and Vinnie, overhearing them say, "I got two, you got one," and, "No, *I* got two, *you* got one." But still later, on the way to Oregon, Dave said to Vinnie, "You gotta get rid of the gun. You gotta come with me to my relatives—we'll tell them what we did."

In that statement, Naftel tells the jurors, Dave Adkins acknowledged his guilt.

But, if that is not enough, Dave told Korpal, "we went in the house, got the gun, went back up and Vinnie shot Kathy and I shot Heather and Danae."

And if still more is needed, Dave also said, in his taped interview with Detective Korpal, "Cayle was lying next to Danae and I said, 'You're my friend, I don't want to kill you. Are you down with us?' "

Naftel reminds the jury of a dialogue in the car between Dave Adkins and Cayle Fiedler, after Cayle had expressed his surprise about Dave and Vinnie being "so down." Dave said, in reply, "I'm not. I just made a mistake." And Cayle said, "That's all right. Everybody makes mistakes."

Naftel removes the photographs from the board and sits

down at the counsel table. The jurors, almost as a group, shift position in their chairs.

Romero gets to his feet and Steven Sonoro hands him a large placard. When Romero places the placard up against the blackboard, we can see that it has been professionally printed. Two lists on either side of the card. The heading over the left-hand list is LAW, the other, on the right-hand side, is BURDEN OF PROOF. Under LAW, the list begins with Beyond Reasonable Doubt and moves down, through Circumstantial Evidence Felony Murder and Duty to Family—among others—to Not Guilty. Under BURDEN OF PROOF, the list begins at Guilty, travels through Guilt Highly Likely, Probably Guilty, Perhaps Guilty, down to Highly Unlikely, Proven Not Guilty, and Not Guilty.

Romero stands in front of the placard for a moment, as if reading it, then he turns and strides purposefully to the rostrum.

"Ladies and gentlemen, even as I speak there is a shroud around David Adkins. That shroud is presumption of innocence. You are the sole trier of facts. Your job is to listen, to recall the facts and the testimony of the witnesses. The evidence heard is a different version of each party; your job is to analyze and determine which version is consistent with the truth."

Romero pauses. Then he goes to the single most mystifying aspect of the case.

"The first issue here is motive. Why would Dave Adkins say, 'I took out Heather and Danae'? Did he fight with anybody? No. Was he mad at anybody? No. Did he hurt anybody? *No.* There was no factor or reason *why* Dave Adkins would shoot or discharge that weapon."

Romero turns and looks at Dave for a moment, then he turns back to face the jury.

"And there is no proof that he did so. There is only forty-five minutes of being tricked and lied to by Mr. Korpal. And finally, this sixteen-year-old boy, who had had no sleep, who was tired, who had been drinking beer and smoking marijuana, said, 'Okay, I'll tell you anything you want to hear.' "

Romero goes on to enumerate what he calls "Mr. Korpal's little tricks": the lie detector ruse; the mention of Dave's mother and Kathy's family; the urgent need for the truth about what happened.

"Dave Adkins's confession is really Mr. Korpal's confession. It was Mr. Korpal who said, 'I wasn't going to quit until I heard what I wanted to hear.' "

Romero speaks for a time about the bloodstains, hammering in the fact that the pair of jeans with the drop of blood on the leg did not fit Dave when he tried them on for the jury. "They were Vinnie Hebrock's jeans." Hammering in the fact that the bloodstain tests were made in April, a month after the murders, in spite of known deterioration of blood in that time span.

"The prosecution accuses me of making smoke screens so that you won't pay attention. Well, I *want* you to pay attention." He turns to gesture broadly toward Dave Adkins. "That young man is facing three counts of first-degree murder."

A new chart goes up on the board. This one displays the chronological order of testimony.

Beginning with Peggy Shurtleff ("She destroyed the entire credibility of Cayle Fiedler"), Romero moves painstakingly through all of the testimony. The true target is Cayle himself. Every inconsistency is reexamined. Dave Adkins's "cooperative and respectful behavior" with the Salem police is remarked upon. "Is that the behavior of guilt?" The dagger found in Officer Barnes's patrol car is spoken of, as is the tattoo of a dagger on Vinnie's arm. The photographs, taken in Salem, of the scratches and bruises on Vinnie's arms and neck are shown to the jury again.

"Look at Vinnie's neck. *Vinnie Hebrock* got in a knock-down-drag-out fight with Heather Goodwin and Danae Palermo. *Not Dave Adkins*."

Romero has returned to the drop of blood on top of the puddle of vomit near Kathy Macaulay's body. "Why wasn't someone brought in to test that vomitus and blood droplet? Think about how there could be blood on top of vomit if the person was dead. Can a dead person vomit?"

Now Romero speaks again about the interview with Mike Korpal. The "tricks" employed to gain a confession. The intimidating factor of Korpal's size and weight. "Sandie Wells's tests have proven that Dave Adkins has a learning problem, that he was approximately four years below the normal level. Four from sixteen equals twelve. Mr. Korpal was using his tricks and lies on a twelve-year-old boy."

Now he goes back to Cayle Fiedler's statements and testimony: too many inconsistencies. The police investigation: slipshod. The prosecution: tunnel-visioned. Vinnie Hebrock's fight with Heather and Danae: motive. Cayle Fiedler's "propensity to rage and violence": motive. And finally, the lack of evidence and motive in the case against Dave Adkins.

During Romero's summation, Pam Adkins has been sitting forward in her chair. She clutches a handkerchief in one hand and every once in a while she uses it to dab away a tear. Her eyes shine and her head nods, barely perceptibly, as Stephen Romero pleads for her son. As he has throughout the trial, Dave sits easily in his place at the counsel table. He is turned toward the jury, looking at each person on the panel with a calm and steady gaze.

Romero's voice lifts as he prepares to deliver his final statement.

"We do not have to prove Dave Adkins's innocence. *They* must prove, beyond reasonable doubt, that Dave Adkins shot Kathy Macaulay, Heather Goodwin, and Danae Palermo. *Beyond reasonable doubt*." Romero pauses dramatically. "You are not going to make this boy a scapegoat for lack of investigation, Cayle Fiedler's heinous acts, or Vinnie Hebrock's heinous acts." He pauses again, leaning forward on the rostrum, "And I am confident, once you review all the evidence, that a verdict of not guilty on all three counts will be brought in."

Romero removes the placards from the board and resumes his seat next to Dave Adkins. He has gone for broke.

Nancy Naftel rises and walks to the rostrum.

"At the beginning of the case there was a presumption of innocence. Now, after evidence and testimony, that presumption is shredded."

Then, going point by point, she responds to each of Stephen Romero's remarks. Detective Korpal wanted the truth; he did not put words into the defendant's mouth. Peggy Shurtleff said, in court, what she remembered hearing. Ms. Ratcliffe, in her testimony about the drop of blood on the vomit, did not talk about physics or about whether Kathy Macaulay was shot first. Ms. Ratcliffe said she could not tell.

"There is no evidence to suggest that the sequence of events was different than what Cayle Fiedler—and Dave Adkins himself—said."

Naftel touches on Sandie Wells's testimony. "Defense has ignored all of Dave Adkins's lies. If the defendant was innocent, why did he lie to Sandie Wells? Why did he lie in Salem?

"The defense attorney would have you believe the defendant is a twelve-year-old boy. Twelve-year-old boys do not shoot three people in the head, but if they do, they should be found guilty."

Naftel makes her final plea: "When you think of evidence and testimony, you can, in fact, put aside *all* of Cayle Fiedler's testimony." She pauses for a long beat. "We have the words of Dave Adkins, himself. He's the one who tells you he is guilty beyond reasonable doubt.

"To Cayle Fiedler: 'I just killed my girlfriend.'

"On tape: 'He shot Kathy and handed me the gun and I shot Heather and Danae,' and, 'Kathy got it first—we walked in and we shot 'em,' and, 'Well, obviously I'm guilty and there's not going to be a trial,' and, 'What I'm saying is, what happens in this kind of case? Do they throw me in jail for life?'

"With premeditation and malice, Dave Adkins blew the brains out of three girls who were guilty of nothing more than wanting to have a good time. Dave Adkins is guilty of the first-degree murder of Kathy Macaulay, Heather Goodwin, and Danae Palermo. He personally blew the brains out of Heather Goodwin and Danae Palermo. I ask you to convict this defendant for one very good reason: He is guilty."

. . . .

The Adkins jury arrives at their verdict on Thursday, August 6, 1992. The Hebrock panel is still in deliberation.

Word has gone out: Network news vans cluster outside the courthouse. The corridor outside Courtroom F teems with journalists and reporters. Pam Adkins is the first family member to arrive. She is surrounded by a wedge of supporters; her face is ashen, her eyes unseeing. Sandie Wells steps out of the elevator a short time later. Linda Macaulay Koss, her son and daughter, Darrell Goodwin, and the Palermo family are the last people to take their places in the spectator section.

Dave Adkins is brought into the courtroom. His jury moves into the box; not a person on the panel looks at him.

Everything is in readiness for the arrival of Judge Byrne.

When Byrne takes his place on the bench, the first thing he asks for is a sidebar with the three attorneys.

The sidebar ends; the attorneys return to the counsel tables. Rickard Santwier remains on his feet. He requests that the Dave Adkins verdict remain sealed until at least this afternoon, so that it will not interfere with the verdict on Vinnie Hebrock.

Byrne turns toward the Adkins jury. Has a verdict been reached on every count? Has a verdict been reached on every allegation? Is everything consistent? Was everything gone through again?

The foreman of the jury delivers an affirmative answer to each query.

The slip of paper with the verdict printed on it is handed to the bailiff. She, in turn, passes it to Byrne.

He unfolds it and reads. The expression on his face remains unchanged.

Now Byrne turns to the jurors, cautioning them not to discuss their decisions or any aspect of the deliberations. He reminds them there must be no contact with any member of the press or any member on the other jury. He thanks them and asks the remaining alternate juror (the other alternate had to be excused earlier) to stay on. Then he calls a lunch break.

Everyone is back at the courthouse after lunch. We are all waiting for the two short buzzes that will tell us the Hebrock jury has reached a verdict.

It does not happen.

It does not happen the next day, Friday, either.

On Monday, August 10, Dave Adkins is brought into the courtroom at 4:00 P.M. The TV people and news media have been waiting, all day, in the corridor. Pam Adkins and her supporters are in and out. The victims' families will be notified when a verdict is reached and will be given enough time to drive to the courthouse.

Dave Adkins looks more and more like a wealthy young university student. Today he sits, legs crossed rather elegantly, whispering to Stephen Romero. When the Adkins jurors are brought in, Dave watches them openly. They do not look at him. Three sheriff's deputies stand at ease against the bank of filing cabinets on one side of the courtroom; they do not take their eyes from the defendant.

Now Byrne goes on record. He thanks the Adkins jury for their patience, and cautions them once more about the importance of keeping their verdict to themselves. He reminds them that they must be here daily (although they do not have to arrive first thing in the morning) so that they can be polled when their verdict is finally read in open court.

Romero asks for the verdict to be read now. Byrne tells him that due to media coverage of the case, he cannot allow it: one verdict might impact on the other.

"I'm very aware of the torture of waiting . . . for all concerned. But my priority is for a fair trial."

The days drag on. Los Angeles is in the grip of a record-breaking heat wave and it shows no sign of letting up any time soon. People lining the walls of the corridor outside Courtroom F are grateful for the air-conditioned chill.

By Thursday, August 13, a rumor buzzes through the courthouse; a verdict is near.

When Vinnie Hebrock is brought into the courtroom, his demeanor is the same as it has been throughout the trial. He walks with downcast eyes, carrying his glasses in one hand, holding down the tip of his narrow black tie with the other. He does not look up at the jury, not even after he puts on the glasses.

The jury does not have a verdict; it has questions.

The foreman gets to his feet. Can a person be found guilty when he did not shoot the gun? Can a person be found guilty of second-degree murder if that person did not actually kill another person?

The answer is yes on both counts, but Byrne wants more detail as to what this jury wants and needs. And he wants it in writing. "You people need to make your decision based on evidence and facts; you need to be focused. And we'll work on it too."

The Hebrock jury is taken back to the deliberation room.

Santwier tells Byrne that he has mixed feelings about the deliberations. He says he got the impression, from the foreman, that the panel didn't know what the discussions were about.

Byrne is silent for a moment, thinking. Then he shakes his head. "If we can give them some kind of intelligent answers that will assist them, we can avoid going through another trial."

AUGUST 14, 1992

It has been decided that the verdict on Dave Adkins will be read today, with or without the Hebrock verdict.

The first half of the morning is given over to the Hebrock jury. Byrne spends the time answering, in detail, more jury questions about the degrees of murder and clarifying the liability theories set down by law. The jurors seem less confused when they rise to go back to deliberations.

There is a short break before the Adkins verdict will be read. The courtroom is packed. Kathy Macaulay's mother, her stepfather, her brother and sister are here. On the other side of the room, Pam Adkins is surrounded by her friends. Dave's brother Dan is not here; one of the friends says that he is too devastated to make an appearance. Sandie Wells is sitting next to Melanie Pinkney. Detectives Korpal and Sweetman are here. TV personnel crowd the back of the room; journalists and reporters fan out, around them, jostling the cameras. The hallway outside Courtroom F is awash with people from all parts of the building.

"You know this is an important case when the people come up from downstairs for the verdict." A deputy sheriff is speaking to no one in particular.

Now the bailiff escorts Dave Adkins in from the holding cell. He smiles softly at his mother, and when he spots Melanie Pinkney sitting next to Sandie Wells, his eyes widen slightly. As he takes his chair, three deputies move in to stand close to his side.

The jury is brought in; they take their seats quickly. There is a deadly hush in the courtroom.

Judge Byrne opens the sealed envelope that contains the verdict and begins to read aloud.

David Adkins has been found guilty of three counts of first-degree murder. The counts are read out one at a time, and as the name of each victim is spoken, Dave flushes a deeper shade of red. By the time Byrne declares the defendant guilty of multiple murder, Dave's right foot has begun to tap the floor spasmodically.

The families on both sides of the courtroom are crying.

There is a poll of the jury at Stephen Romero's request. Each juror speaks out the verdict now, in court.

Byrne turns his full attention to the Adkins jury, thanking them for their time and for their complex analysis of the case. He thanks the alternate jurors as well. Then he dismisses them, reminding them that they are free to talk about the case to anyone they choose, with the exception of the Hebrock jury.

After the jury has filed out of the courtroom, Romero asks Byrne for a date for motions.

Byrne tells Romero he wants the probation report on Dave Adkins first. Then he will give a date for motions. Byrne looks at the calendar on the wall behind the clerk.

"I won't be available for motions until the ninth of October." Byrne looks at Dave Adkins now. "Mr. Adkins, you do have the right to be sentenced before twenty-one court days have passed."

Dave nods his head. Then the bailiff places her hand on his shoulder, the three deputies close in, and he is led back to the holding cells. Pam Adkins, tears streaming down her face, watches her son until he disappears through the door next to the jury box.

Nancy Naftel turns from the counsel table and walks to the railing of the spectator section. She is immediately surrounded by grateful relatives. Danae Palermo's mother hugs her; Linda and Michael Koss murmur their thank-you's and leave by a side door. Darrell Goodwin waits in the background; he wants to speak with Naftel.

Outside Courtroom F the corridor is jammed with people all the way back to the elevators. A few members of the Adkins jury are being interviewed. One juror calls the case an "all-lose situation." Another admits, "We all had problems with Cayle. But the fact was that Dave's confession on the tape and Cayle's testimony were almost identical. You could hear the truth in Dave's voice, at the end, when he said he was 'obviously guilty.' " A third juror, a woman, spoke thoughtfully. "This whole thing has made me leery with my own kids. I watch them more now. Because those kids"—she gestures in the direction of the courtroom—"had way too much freedom. And look what happened."

....

By 2:45 P.M. Courtroom F has begun to fill up again. The Hebrock jury has reached a verdict. Members of the media are here, and people from other parts of the building. Darrell Goodwin is in his seat on the aisle of the spectator section, but he is the only family member in the courtroom. Korpal and Sweetman are sitting just behind the counsel table. There is still excitement in the air, but less than there was earlier, for Dave Adkins's verdict.

Byrne takes his place on the bench. Vinnie is brought in from the holding cells. His gait is the same as always: downcast eyes; small, careful steps. Now the jury moves into place. The sealed envelope containing the verdict is passed to the clerk; he hands it to the judge. Byrne opens it, scans the verdict, looks up at Vinnie Hebrock. Santwier and Vinnie get to their feet. Vinnie's hands are plunged deep in his pockets as Judge Byrne reads the verdict aloud.

Vinnie Hebrock has been found guilty of three counts of second-degree murder.

As the verdict is read, Vinnie's face does not change expression.

Byrne turns to the Hebrock jurors and thanks them, commending them for their "intelligent analysis." He tells them they are free to leave, adding, "What took place in your deliberations is private to you. You don't have to talk about it—but you are free to do so."

After the jury has left the courtroom, Byrne speaks to both attorneys.

"This case was unique, not at all the same for both defendants. Your work was thorough, tremendously so. My commendations to you both."

Motions will be heard on October 16.

Vinnie Hebrock is remanded to custody.

The Hebrock jurors have scattered. Most of them are in a hurry to leave the courthouse, but one of the younger women is willing to give a moment or two to the press. She says that the older members of the panel didn't understand the kids *as* kids; they simply couldn't get a handle on the use of drugs, or the drinking.

"The older people on the jury just wanted to hang Vinnie." Her voice seems strained; fatigue is evident on her face. There is not much more she feels like saying: the dual trial was hard on everyone. The attorneys did well. Just before she steps into the elevator, she turns back to look at the reporters.

"It's the families—on both sides—you have to feel sorry for. How do any of them get over this?"

. . . .

Immediately following his conviction Vinnie Hebrock was taken back to the Hall of Justice at County Jail, where he would begin a series of diagnostic tests. The findings of these tests and the results of interviews with a probation officer would be factors in determining the sentence handed down. Rickard Santwier will say, later, that Vinnie's probation report was the largest he had ever seen in his years of practice.

Dave Adkins was sent back to Wayside after his conviction. He remained there for a short time and then he was transferred to County Jail for diagnostic testing and probation review. Soon after his arrival at County, Dave became "deeply depressed." Depressed enough to get him transferred to the prison infirmary and the module the inmates call the "Ding Ward." He was placed on medication there, "heavy stuff," according to him. He didn't swallow the full dose every time, however. He squirreled pills until he had enough for what he figured would be a lethal amount. It might have worked too, but another inmate, looking to bum a cigarette, found Adkins unconscious in his bunk and alerted the deputy on duty.

When I asked Dave why he tried to kill himself, the answer was immediate. He said, "Look what happened to my life."

Dave survived the pills, but sentencing was pushed forward while he recuperated. All motions for a new trial were denied.

Sentencing. By eight o'clock in the morning the network news vans are lining the curb outside the Pasadena Courthouse.

The courtroom is full. Linda Macaulay Koss and her two surviving children are seated in the front row of the spectator section. The Palermo family fills the row behind them. Mimi Goodwin is here today, with her husband and their son, Heather's brother. Mrs. Goodwin is still a pretty, soft-looking woman, but she has been ravaged by the murder of her daughter. Her eyes burn with barely controlled emotion; she is dangerously thin. Detectives Korpal and Sweetman are seated just beyond the partition; the two detectives provide a physical separation between the victims' families and their daughters' murderers. On the other side of the courtroom, Pam Adkins sits with two of her friends and four other people. No one from the Hebrock family is present. Sandie Wells and I have come to the sentencing together. We take seats in the middle section, where one or the other of the juries sat during the trial.

Nancy Naftel, Stephen Romero, and Rickard Santwier are at the counsel tables. Judge Byrne takes his place at the bench.

Now Dave and Vinnie are escorted into the courtroom. Both prisoners have their arms manacled to chains around their waists. Dave is further restrained by leg shackles. (He was caught with a rigged handcuff key while he was in County Jail.) Vinnie is not wearing glasses today.

"I have read and considered the diagnostic reports and the probation reviews," Judge Byrne begins. "I have read and considered letters from family and friends. I will now hear statements."

Romero rises. First up will be witnesses for Dave Adkins. An older man seated near Pam Adkins moves to stand with his hands on the back of Dave's chair. He identifies himself as a Reverend Hurdle and states that he came to know Dave when the boy was brought, by his aunt, to Hurdle's church. Hurdle speaks about Dave's buried rage and dysfunctional background, but urges Byrne to believe that there is "a sweet side to the boy." He feels that Dave has been denied "real help" through the years, but is convinced he can change, providing he survives the "extremely angry environment" into which he is being placed.

The next person to speak on Dave Adkins's behalf is Marci Sandford. Her older sister, Michelle, used to go out with Dave; Michelle Sandford and Kathy Macaulay were only half a semester apart in school, they knew each other well. Marci is seventeen now. Her hands tremble noticeably as she moves up to stand behind Dave's chair. When she begins to speak, her voice is nearly inaudible.

"I've known Dave since the eighth grade. Dave's a nice, gentle person ... he's ... considerate. He doesn't want to hurt anyone." She is near tears and she takes a moment to gain control before she goes on. "Dave is very compassionate. He understands people, and ... " Another pause. The tears come now. "And ... I love him."

Marci goes back to her seat. Pam Adkins steps forward.

"My son ... I love my son. If he did this, it wasn't done in the same mind as now." She weeps quietly for a few long seconds. "Lots of things came out at the trial that pointed to my son's innocence. That's all I can say."

The final witness for Dave Adkins is a counselor from Chino Boys Republic, where Dave was sent in 1989. She speaks of Dave's compassion in camp, and his supportiveness of younger boys. She tells Byrne how cooperative Dave was when he was at Chino. How he assumed the role of "big brother."

There are no witnesses for Vinnie Hebrock.

It is now time for the victims' families to speak.

The first witness is Kathy Macaulay's sister. She speaks movingly of learning about Kathy's murder from a television newscast while she was away at law school. "I will never forget that gut-wrenching moment, or get over the anguish." She speaks about Kathy's kindness and gentleness of manner. About her love for children. She asks for the maximum punishment for Dave Adkins and Vinnie Hebrock.

Kathy's brother speaks next. "It is nearly impossible to describe the impact this horrible murder has had on my life and my parents' lives. My sister Katherine spent her whole life under the rule of her heart. Her good nature cost her her life; she took these two people in because they needed help. They repaid her by taking her life. I cannot recall anyone executed in this country who was guilty of any more heinous crimes than Dave Adkins and Vinnie Hebrock. If they could kill like this, they can kill again. It would be unconscionable to return these two killers to society."

Now Linda Macaulay Koss moves to the rostrum. First she reads a statement written by her husband, Michael Koss. " 'Your Honor: I don't think you can understand what it means to be the victim of a crime today. We have learned that we should expect the worst from members of the media. Apparently, in the United States today, the murder of a woman is like the crime of rape: The victim must explain *why*. But murder victims are dead.

" 'Despite everything that was written about this case, despite everything that was shown on TV, Dave Adkins and Vinnie Hebrock *were* found guilty. Katherine and her friends might have been drinking tea that night and the results would have been the same.

" 'Kathy was a good human being if not a happy one. She was going to college; she had a future.' " Here, Linda Macaulay Koss's voice fails her. She struggles for control, goes on reading. " 'If Dave Adkins had shown *some* remorse there might have been some hope. But he showed none.' "

Mrs. Koss folds the pages of her husband's statement. She pauses for a second or two, and then she begins to speak again.

"Nothing in life prepares you for the murder of your child. When Katherine was a baby, I worried about her breathing in the night. Later, I worried about her driving a car. Worried about her going out. I never worried that she would be murdered by her friends."

Mrs. Koss speaks of how she and her husband allowed Kathy to be at home alone on the weekend of the murders. She talks about the other two girls: "Heather Goodwin was a sweet child, and she considered me to be a second mother to her. We had a study plan for Heather to follow. I promised my help. Danae Palermo was a young lady who was going to make it. Now I face their families. Mimi Goodwin has lost weight, she has been made sick by this terrible event. She lies awake reliving the awful moment when she and her husband were awakened by that telephone call in the middle of the night.

"I have experienced sadness, shock, depression. I have dreams that relive the horror. But the worst dream is the one where Katherine is still alive and my world is whole again. Until I wake up.

"I envy the advanced years of my parents. I will probably live many years before I see Katherine again."

Mrs. Koss sighs deeply, then goes on. "The media has made much about Katherine's 'wealthy background.' We are not wealthy. You can only imagine the decline in value of our home. Who would want to buy a house in which three horrible murders occurred?"

Now Mrs. Koss talks about Kathy again. Her intelligence and sweetness. "She would have been a good mother. A good citizen.

"David Adkins and Vinnie Hebrock conspired to take the life of my daughter and her two friends. They are dangerous young men. They will be dangerous middle-aged men and dangerous old men. Please protect the community and other families, your Honor. Please sentence David Adkins and Vinnie Hebrock at the maximum sentence."

Heather Goodwin's brother will speak for the Goodwins. "Your Honor, these events are forever etched in my mind. The murder of my sister. The terror of my mother and father. Their worst fears confirmed. The utter senselessness of a crime can never be explained. Those three girls were no threat to their murderers. Dave Adkins and Vinnie Hebrock are cold-blooded, heartless killers. I ask that the maximum sentence be imposed upon them."

Danae Palermo's mother is next at the rostrum. She speaks briefly and movingly about Danae, whom she refers to as "the family's treasure, our youngest."

"Danae was taken away from us without a goodbye. The pain is constant; even pictures of her remind us of what we have lost. They remind us that Danae will never have a wedding day. She will never have children." Mrs. Palermo's voice is thick with tears. "I need medication now to get through the day. I tremble when I see young men on the street—I am afraid of all young men now. The life I knew no longer exists. The maximum sentence will not bring back my daughter, but it will prevent another family from suffering. Please, your Honor, impose that maximum sentence."

Mrs. Palermo turns away from the rostrum and Danae's sister takes her place. She describes how she heard the news of Danae's death while driving her car. She tells about a telephone call she received from "a girl with a trembling voice—like mine is trembling now. I denied that my sister was dead. I said that things like that just don't happen to people like us.

"I can't describe my feelings of loss. I'm twenty-five years old and I still wake up afraid. I still hear songs that remind me of my sister and what happened to her. I no longer watch television news shows with their stories of killings and murders.

"Who will make the madness end? Maybe you, as a judge, can begin by sending these two killers to prison for life."

Danae Palermo's eldest sister is the final witness. She is pregnant with her second child.

"Your Honor, I watch my mother, my sister, and my two grandmothers cry every day. How can I explain to my little son that his Auntie Danae has gone away forever? Those two killers sitting there didn't think Danae was important enough to live. They killed three times. Please, your Honor, put them away for life."

There is a complete hush in the courtroom as Judge Byrne allows a moment of silence. Tears have been flowing on both sides of the spectator sections. Both Dave Adkins and Vinnie Hebrock are motionless in their chairs; neither boy has shown emotion.

Now Judge Byrne asks for the attorneys' statements.

Nancy Naftel is requesting the maximum. For Dave Adkins, life imprisonment without the possibility of parole. For Vinnie Hebrock, fifty years to life.

"These were coldhearted crimes, and those who commit crimes must suffer the consequences. Dave Adkins and Vinnie Hebrock showed no remorse, displayed no conscience. They admitted the crimes. It is time for these defendants to stop blaming the victims, to stop blaming the drugs, to stop blaming the liquor. It is time to take responsibility for these premeditated murders. I ask for the maximum sentence, please."

SMOKED

Stephen Romero begins his statement by expressing his sympathy for the families of all concerned. He takes issue, however, with Naftel's statement about "no remorse." He cites Dave Adkins's emotional age of "eight to eleven years old." He reminds the judge that Dave was not in the guest-house at the time of the precipitating event. He talks about the dysfunctional home life, the access to drugs and alcohol, the access to the murder weapon.

"The ultimate result is not Dave Adkins as an individual but *us,* as a society to be held responsible here."

"Asshole!"

Every head in the room turns toward the spectator section. Mimi Goodwin, her face a mask of rage and grief, has leaped to her feet and is now racing out of the courtroom. Her son moves quickly to follow her.

Romero is clearly shaken by the interruption, but he continues his statement. He questions whether Dave Adkins should spend his life incarcerated for an incident that happened in "a matter of seconds." He reminds the court that whatever the sentence, "it will not bring back the three young ladies.

"Haven't we gone beyond an eye for an eye? Should a sixteen-year-old be sentenced to the maximum sentence which is, in some ways, worse than the death penalty?

"If Dave Adkins had been interviewed before Cayle Fiedler, it would, perhaps, have been a different case. Whatever sentence is imposed, I ask that it be a fair one. It should not be greater than the one imposed on the codefendant. The sentences should be equal."

Romero sits down again; he glances briefly at Dave Adkins. Dave inclines his head slightly.

Now Rickard Santwier takes the floor. He mentions the difficulties for everyone concerned here, magnified now by listening to what the families have said. "We cannot bring the victims back. The difficulties, too, are for your Honor to ig-

nore emotions." He reminds Judge Byrne that Vinnie Hebrock's diagnostic report shows him to be "a troubled individual." He refers to the maximum sentence, saying that if it
would bring back the victims, he too, would recommend it.
He points out the remorse displayed in Vinnie's statement
when the tape was heard in court.

"Another problem we have seen today, through the artic-
ulate statements of the victims' families, is the incredible
difference in background between the defendants and the
victims themselves."

Santwier urges Byrne not to impose the maximum sentence, reminding him that the Hebrock jury deliberated for
ten days.

"I ask the court to use its experience with other cases.
Remember the age of the defendants. And remember, too,
that Vinnie Hebrock probably never had a chance."

There is another moment of silence. Then Judge Byrne
begins to speak. He thanks everyone who worked on the case:
the bailiff, the clerk, the court reporter. He compliments the
attorneys on "a case with complicated legal issues, a case
well tried." He congratulates the Pasadena police and the
Sheriff's Department. He reaffirms his appreciation for the
two juries who resolved "a difficult case, spent time and did
their work well."

Now he looks out at both sides of the spectator sections.

"I listened carefully to what the families had to say, because it is important to be reminded of the damage done to
them." He pauses for a moment. "My sympathy goes out to
Mrs. Adkins as well. She, too, has been damaged.

"I studied the diagnostic reports carefully and I can find
no justification, no rationale, no common sense in these killings. The victims were taken by surprise, killed by their
friends. I can find no reason to set aside the finding of the
juries."

Byrne looks directly at Dave Adkins.

"David Adkins planned the murders of Katherine Macaulay, Heather Goodwin, and Danae Palermo. He carried out the murders systematically, and he used Mr. Hebrock to help him. He has been found guilty on all three counts of first-degree murder. He is committed to state prison for life, without the possibility of parole."

Byrne's eyes swing immediately to Vinnie Hebrock.

"The same comments apply to Vinnie Hebrock. He, too, is guilty of systematic killing, planning, and execution. He has been found guilty of three counts of second-degree murder, and he is sentenced, on each count, to serve fifteen years to life in state prison. For the direct use of a firearm, against Katherine Macaulay, there will be an additional sentence of five years on the first count, and an extra year each on the other two counts. These terms are to run consecutively, giving Mr. Hebrock a sentence of fifty-one years to life.

"In addition, there will be a fine imposed on both defendants in the amount of ten thousand dollars each.

"It is my duty to advise the defendants that there is a six-day time limit to appeal the decision of this court. These appeals must be made in this court. If the defendants cannot afford counsel, the court will appoint attorneys for them."

Both Romero and Santwier are ready with the appeals, which they hand over to the clerk.

The deputy sheriffs close in on Dave and Vinnie. As Dave gets to his feet, his mother rushes toward the partition, moving against the flow of people headed for the exit. She is sobbing out loud.

"I love you, Dave!"

But Dave is already gone. He and Vinnie Hebrock have left the courtroom for the last time.

. . . .

There is a gauntlet to be run outside Courtroom F, a funnel of video cameras, lights, and reporters. Microphones are outstretched, questions are hurled at every person who walks through.

Sandie Wells and I move as quickly as we can; we are both eager to leave the building, eager to get away. Most of the family members have gone out by way of a side door.

In front of the courthouse, the TV anchor people are preparing to make live broadcasts for their respective networks. Curious passersby have stopped to watch. Five or six teenagers walking together in a group slow their pace as they glance idly at the camera setups. One of the girls asks a technician what it is they're getting ready to film.

"A verdict just got reached in a big murder trial."

The girl shrugs, uninterested in the information. Then she and her friends walk away, heading down toward the sprawling Pasadena mall a couple of blocks away. Sandie Wells watches them for a moment, then she turns to me.

"You see? It really is true. Nobody ever thinks it could happen to them."

During a recess in the trial of Dave Adkins and Vinnie Hebrock I sat, with my daughter, Lisa, on one of the wooden benches that line the corridor outside Courtroom F. Lisa, a college student, was with me every day, taking backup notes for this book. The testimony that morning had been hard on every person in the courtroom: the Medical Examiner's reports had been graphic, the photographs of the girls' bodies were still up on the board. Lisa and I weren't talking much. We were simply sitting, each of us gathering strength to go back to the proceedings.

At some point during those few minutes' respite from the trial, I glanced over at my daughter. She wasn't aware that I was looking at her; she was busy with her notebook, going over what she had written. I watched her for a long moment, and what went through my mind was like one of those short, quick-cut history reels: my child as an infant, smiling up at me; as a toddler, burbling with triumph at her first steps; as an adolescent, maddeningly unreasonable, heartbreakingly vulnerable. I heard, in my mind, loving kisses smacked over the phone and angry doors slamming. I thought of the times I had been angrier at her than she was with me. The emotion I felt, overriding all others, was a great gratitude that she was here, on this bench, next to me. Without thinking much about what I was doing, I embraced her. Lisa was surprised, but she hugged back. I needed more, though. Reaching around her, I swept the hair away from the nape of her neck and then I put my nose there, where her own aroma is at its most recognizable. That was what I needed to do. Because I *could*. It was, thank God, an option I could take. It was the single option Kathy Macaulay's parents, Heather Goodwin's parents, Danae Palermo's parents, would never have again.

While I was working on the book, I was often asked if I thought Dave Adkins and Vinnie Hebrock were sociopaths. I didn't have an answer then and I don't have one now. When I asked Mike Korpal what he thought, he told me the conclusion he had come to after his close involvement with the crime.

"Dave and Vinnie are bad seeds. They both fall into the category of people who, no matter when we impact them, and no matter what their stage of development, do bad things. That describes Dave, for sure. And Vinnie just needed the push."

It is a compelling observation. And it is strangely comforting. It's easy to see Dave and Vinnie as bad seeds, as aberrations; they committed a monstrous crime. But another, disquieting thought, lurks in the background. What about the sixteen-year-old boy who said, two weeks after the murders, "I keep on wondering if, at the moment it happened, if killing another person was, like, the most incredible high."

Just a regular kid, sitting at a table with a bunch of other kids at an after-school hangout in South Pasadena. But he said it and, at that moment, he meant it. The question is, of course, given the same set of circumstances, could he pull the trigger of that shotgun?

American kids kill each other with horrifying regularity. A recent study at Northeastern University showed that the number of sixteen-year-olds arrested for murder climbed 158 percent between 1985 and 1991. The biggest increase was in the fifteen-year-old group: 200 percent.

It was in 1985 that I first saw the symbol for anarchy. It had been tagged onto the side of an abandoned apartment